Palgrave Studies in International Relations

Series Editors
Mai'a K. Davis Cross
Northeastern University
Boston, MA, USA

Benjamin de Carvalho
Norwegian Institute of International Affairs
Oslo, Norway

Shahar Hameiri
University of Queensland
St. Lucia, QLD, Australia

Knud Erik Jørgensen
University of Aarhus
Aarhus, Denmark

Ole Jacob Sending
Norwegian Institute of International Affairs
Oslo, Norway

Ayşe Zarakol
University of Cambridge
Cambridge, UK

Palgrave Studies in International Relations (the EISA book series), published in association with European International Studies Association, provides scholars with the best theoretically-informed scholarship on the global issues of our time. The series includes cutting-edge monographs and edited collections which bridge schools of thought and cross the boundaries of conventional fields of study. EISA members can access a 50% discount to PSIR, the EISA book series, here http://www.eisa-net. org/sitecore/content/be-bruga/mci-registrations/eisa/login/landing. aspx. Mai'a K. Davis Cross is the Edward W. Brooke Professor of Political Science at Northeastern University, USA, and Senior Researcher at the ARENA Centre for European Studies, University of Oslo, Norway. Benjamin de Carvalho is a Senior Research Fellow at the Norwegian Institute of International Affairs (NUPI), Norway. Shahar Hameiri is Associate Professor of International Politics and Associate Director of the Graduate Centre in Governance and International Affairs, School of Political Science and International Studies, University of Queensland, Australia. Knud Erik Jørgensen is Professor of International Relations at Aarhus University, Denmark, and at Yaşar University, Izmir, Turkey. Ole Jacob Sending is the Research Director at the Norwegian Institute of International Affairs (NUPI), Norway. Ayşe Zarakol is Reader in International Relations at the University of Cambridge and a fellow at Emmanuel College, UK.

More information about this series at
http://www.palgrave.com/gp/series/14619

Julie Garey

The US Role in NATO's Survival After the Cold War

palgrave
macmillan

Julie Garey
Department of Political Science
Northeastern University
Boston, MA, USA

Palgrave Studies in International Relations
ISBN 978-3-030-13674-1   ISBN 978-3-030-13675-8   (eBook)
https://doi.org/10.1007/978-3-030-13675-8

Cover Image © 501 collection / Alamy Stock Photo

This Palgrave Macmillan imprint is published by the registered company Springer Nature
Switzerland AG
The registered company address is: Gewerbestrasse 11, 6330 Cham, Switzerland

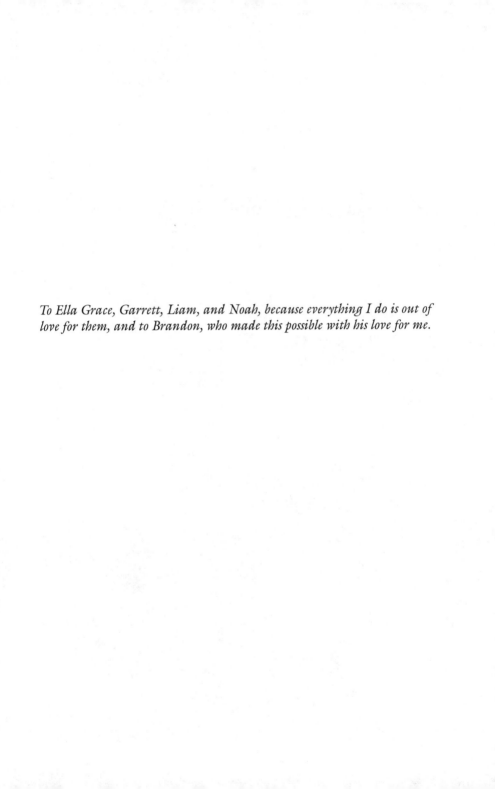

To Ella Grace, Garrett, Liam, and Noah, because everything I do is out of love for them, and to Brandon, who made this possible with his love for me.

ACKNOWLEDGMENTS

The hardest task of preparing this manuscript was without question remembering all of the incredible people who made this work possible, but the compiled list would undoubtedly fill a manuscript-length document. I have never possessed the ability to make my prose jump off the page like a melodic dance of words, or an ability to fully express the depths of my gratitude on paper, so simple thank-yous will have to suffice. None of this would be in print, let alone decipherable, if it were not for my incredible mentor, colleague, and friend Mai'a Davis Cross. David Schmitt was the second person I met as a prospective student, but the first I went to with any and every problem with the project, the discipline, and everything in between. Stephen Flynn was instrumental in guiding me toward a meaningful yet exceptionally policy-relevant project. These amazing scholars and wonderful people deserve all of the credit for what is good about this manuscript, and none of the blame for its errors. I'm not sure anyone is as lucky as I am when it comes to leadership, as my department chair Thomas Vicino has been one of my biggest supporters. John Portz took so many chances on me, and I hope he has seen at least a marginal return on investment. To my wonderful colleagues: please know I am incredibly grateful for your mentorship, guidance, support, and friendship. Thank you also to the department staff, as well as the countless graduate teaching assistants and undergraduate work study students who made both direct and indirect contributions to the project through their support of my work. No good research is possible without the continued pursuit of knowledge and truth, and the time I have spent with hundreds of students I have had the pleasure of teaching and advising consistently reminded me of why teaching, research, and mentorship must go hand-in-hand and also made this project exponentially more rewarding.

I am also tremendously appreciative of those who agreed to be interviewed for this project, including Admiral James Stavridis (U.S. Navy—Ret.), Lieutenant General Michael Barbero (U.S. Army—Ret.), and General Carter Ham (U.S. Army—Ret.), and those who provided their NATO expertise, especially Lawrence Chalmer from the Center for Transatlantic Security Studies at National Defense University.

And to my first mentors, Barry Tadlock, Michelle Frasher, and Patricia Weitsman. When I finished my doctoral work, I wrote that Patty's memory never leaves my mind, and the same is true today. The 3 × 5 index card with a joke about knowing something about alliance cohesion still hangs in my office, reminding me not only how far I've come but how much further there is to go.

While professional mentorship was absolutely pivotal to developing the manuscript, I would be nowhere without the small but fierce group of colleagues and friends. Thank you to Katharine Petrich, Saskia van Wees, Andrew Goodhart, Summer Marion, and the many others who always offered whatever they could—which was always more than I needed or deserved. Amy Mullen and Courtney Grimm are truly the most wonderful friends and I'd be lost without them. From donuts to draft feedback and everything in between, they have always been there for me.

Finally, my family, who supported and persevered not only this project but also years of my idiosyncrasies, deserve the highest honors that could be bestowed, and then some. My parents, sister, and grandparents have fully supported anything and everything I've done since day one, even when it meant countless hours in schools and libraries, hundreds of miles away, during birthdays and holidays and many more. Ella Grace, Garrett, Liam, and Noah are absolutely the best niece and nephews someone could ask for, and the centers of my universe. And my partner Brandon (and puppy Max), who redefined what love means in an immeasurably positive way and whose never-ending encouragement is the reason I'm still here.

To all of you: I'll never be able to thank you enough.

CONTENTS

CHAPTER 1

Introduction

The persistence of the North Atlantic Treaty Organization (NATO) challenges the existing frameworks for understanding the formation, evolution, cohesion, and dissolution of military alliances. Much is understood about the conditions under which states ally, and better explanations for alliance cohesion have emerged in recent decades. To date, however, explanations for the persistence of military alliances in peacetime are incomplete. International relations theory has long asserted the improbable possibility of these arrangements lasting outside of war. Only recently have scholars and policymakers developed better explanations for the reasons and conditions under which alliances persist. Still, the significance of peacetime alliances is not fully understood.

The post-Cold War period is one of the first to have a military alliance persist in the absence of an imminent threat. In many ways, NATO is inconsistent with the frameworks for understanding military alliances. It is one of the longest-standing alliances of the contemporary period, with a "high degree of institutionalization unprecedented in military pacts" (Rafferty 2003). Authorized under Article 51 of the United Nations Charter and established by the 1949 North Atlantic Treaty, the alliance embodies the fundamental principles of collective defense: NATO membership requires a commitment to support and defend other member states in the event of an attack. At best, previous explanations of NATO persistence are disconnected pieces to the larger puzzle: none of the existing theories of alliances are wholly satisfactory in explaining the alliance's

© The Author(s) 2020
J. Garey, *The US Role in NATO's Survival After the Cold War*,
Palgrave Studies in International Relations,
https://doi.org/10.1007/978-3-030-13675-8_1

continuation. Thus, the case of NATO in the post-war period merits further investigation. This book answers the question: why has the NATO alliance persisted in the post-Cold War period, and why does it matter?

NATO Persistence: The Sum of Unequal Parts

In the months leading up to his election on November 8, 2016, Donald Trump's campaign zeroed in on NATO as one of the United States' most detrimental relationships. In March 2016, candidate Trump gave an interview to *The Washington Post* editorial board in which he stated "NATO was set up at a different time. NATO was set up when we were a richer country...I think the distribution of costs has to be changed. I think NATO as a concept is good, but it is not as good as it was when it first evolved." He expanded on this point hours later in an interview with CNN anchor Wolf Blitzer, arguing "it's costing us too much money. And frankly they have to put up more money. They're going to have to put some up also. We're playing disproportionately. It's too much" (Freisleben 2017).

The theme of the Americans bearing the burden of NATO while the remaining allies sat idly by continued in the following months. Efforts to make the alliance more capable, such as increasing its counterterrorism initiatives in the wake of attacks in Paris, Brussels, and elsewhere were met with praise (for both the alliance and for his self-acclaimed ability to singlehandedly force change within the alliance) from candidate Trump. Still, the "America contributes too much and the Europeans too little" rhetoric continued, relenting only after the election. In April 2017, when President Trump met with NATO Secretary General Jens Stoltenberg, Trump said "(t)he Secretary General and I had a productive conversation about what more NATO can do in the fight against terrorism. I complained about that a long time ago, and they made a change. Now they do fight terrorism. I said it was obsolete. It's no longer obsolete" (Johnson 2017).

The perspectives of the European allies could not have been in starker contrast to those of President Trump. Though his remarks were successful in reigniting debate over member states' inability or unwillingness to meet the two percent defense spending threshold,[1] Trump's comments also

---

[1] This threshold is not expressly written in the North Atlantic Treaty; rather, it was agreed upon by alliance members in 2006 and reaffirmed in 2014.

increased worry over the United States' commitment to Article 5, the Washington Treaty's collective defense clause. Secretary General Stoltenberg reminded American policymakers of NATO's value while reasserting the need for commitment, stating "Solidarity among allies is a key value for NATO. This is good for European security and good for U.S. security. We defend one another. We have seen this in Afghanistan, where tens of thousands of European, Canadian and partner-nation troops have stood shoulder to shoulder with U.S. soldiers." British Defense Secretary Michael Fallon said "Article 5 is an absolute commitment. It doesn't come with conditions or caveats" (Chan 2016). Following a week of meetings, including the NATO Brussels Summit and a meeting of the G-7, German Chancellor Angela Merkel told the German public "The times in which we could rely fully on others – they are somewhat over…this is what I experienced in the last few days." She went on: "We have to know that we must fight for our future on our own, for our destiny as Europeans… I can only say that we Europeans must really take our fate into our own hands – of course in friendship with the United States of America, in friendship with Great Britain and as good neighbors wherever that is possible also with other countries, even with Russia" (Smale and Erlanger 2017).

Trump's perspective of the alliance was delivered to the allies and the public unconventionally, but the sentiments expressed by both the Americans and the Europeans were nothing new. The evolution of NATO has been hotly contested since the end of the Cold War. In the decades since, NATO expanded its membership from 16 to 29 members, and several other states—including former Soviet satellite states—continue striving to meet the recommendations of NATO's Membership Action Plan (MAP) in the hopes of someday obtaining NATO membership. Many of the allies, however, regularly failed to meet the alliance's collective defense spending requests, and NATO suffered from the continuing decline in contributions. Several of the allies ended military conscription and deactivated thousands of troops, shrinking the size of their deployable forces. In addition to not meeting the two percent threshold, the European allies collectively provided only one-quarter of NATO's defense expenditures, with the remaining resources provided by the United States (Stoltenberg 2014; Londoño 2014; *The Economist* 2017).

In addition to the gap between US and European defense spending and contributions to the alliance, many of the allies adopted divergent perspectives regarding European security and the role of NATO in future conflicts. Immediately following the collapse of the Soviet Union, some allies pushed for the establishment of a European-only collective defense mechanism similar to NATO, but interventions in Bosnia and Kosovo demonstrated Europe was unprepared to move forward without the United States. France, Germany, and others continued to advocate for the development of non-US-led defensive measures while stressing the importance of diplomacy and the United Nations. Some allies were reluctant or unwilling to engage in the United States and NATO's interventions without explicit authorization from the UN Security Council.

Nonmember states regularly raised concerns regarding NATO's persistence as well, despite the alliance's efforts to expand its partnerships. Russia insisted that NATO persistence was a direct threat to the possibility of long-standing peace between East and West and feared the alliance would attempt to intervene in its own disputed territories. Although Russia partnered with the alliance to address many issues pertaining to international security, Russian President Vladimir Putin's annexation of Crimea and escalating hostility in Ukraine seemingly negated these concerns while also reigniting allies' fears of Russian aggression and the threat to European stability (Flenley 2009; Goldgeier 2009; Nau 2009; Pourchot 2009; Braun 2008; Vershbow 2015). Additionally, Russia regularly attempts to prevent NATO from using force by threatening to veto UN Security Council resolutions authorizing international intervention. Russia advocated against NATO intervention in the Balkans (both in Bosnia and later Kosovo) and in Libya, as well US intervention in Iraq. Syrian President Bashar al Assad, regularly relied on Syria's relationship with Russia to prevent the United Nations, NATO, or individual states from intervening to stop ongoing humanitarian abuses stemming from both the occupation of the Islamic State of Iraq and Syria (ISIS) and its civil war.

Despite continuing disagreements between member states, changes to the geopolitical and strategic environment, opposition from allies and adversaries to the actions of the alliance, the United States and the European allies have remained committed to NATO. Thus, the question of NATO's persistence becomes pivotal. To answer this question, I examine another important piece of the NATO puzzle: the role of the United States and its relationship to the alliance.

An Argument in Support of US-Centric Analyses

Whereas NATO scholars are inclined to attribute the alliance's persistence to institutional factors or a changing international order, scholars of the US-NATO relationship largely frame NATO's survival and evolution as an unintended consequence of American actions, at best. However, in very few of these works is NATO's persistence treated as an intentional or predictable consequence of the post-war era, nor is it acknowledged as favorable for US power projection, the transatlantic relationship, or international peace and stability. Unlike the existing scholarship on NATO persistence, I posit that the relationship between the United States and NATO is the key explanatory variable to understanding the alliance's persistence after the Cold War.

In many ways, the United States has struggled in its relationship with NATO and the rest of the international community. In the immediate aftermath of the Cold War, the United States' political, economic, and military power was unrivaled. This, coupled with the web of international institutions emerging out of World War II, created an unprecedented opportunity. The George H.W. Bush administration developed plans for a "New World Order" and pursued the proliferation of liberal-democratic values, economic expansion, and increased multilateral cooperation via international organizations. Though war between the major powers seemed unlikely in the post-Cold War era, struggles between ethnic and nationalist groups challenged the international community's ability to mitigate conflict.

At the same time, the United States regularly pursued multilateralism even when its success on the battlefield did not depend on the support of allied or coalition forces. Though it has rarely attempted to act unilaterally, US policymakers altered their approach to engaging allies. To understand the US-NATO relationship and its evolution, I examine US-NATO relations in four conflicts: Kosovo, Afghanistan, Iraq, and Libya. These four conflicts represent major challenges the United States and NATO faced in the post-Cold War period. Each of these conflicts posed a different level of threat to the alliance and its individual members, and each conflict was met with a different response from the alliance. These engagements demonstrated the strengths and weaknesses of the alliance. Each conflict also made demonstrable impacts on the institution: during and after each engagement, the alliance altered its political agenda, military agenda, operational capacity, or some combination of these. Examining these events chronologically demonstrates the evolution of the alliance, as well as its capacity to adapt to the contemporary threat environment. These conflict engagements elucidated the alliance was important to the United States and led it to exercise US political and military power to ensure the alliance's survival.

Evidence from each of the four cases illustrates why the United States continued to pursue the alliance relationship and ensure its survival. Although NATO is an alliance comprised of 29 member states and structured on the principles of decision-making by consensus, the United States' status as a global hegemon made it the de facto leader of the alliance. NATO evolved to serve a very specific role in conflict closely aligning with US interests. Due in large part to this evolution, the alliance persisted despite projections that either the United States or Western European states would abandon the alliance in favor of alternative arrangements. Thus, NATO persistence is explained, at least in part, by the US-NATO relationship and the United States' leadership within the alliance.

However, this explanation raises other critically important questions: in what ways is the alliance beneficial or detrimental to the United States' military or political objectives? How do the aforementioned conflicts illustrate the importance of the alliance to the United States? And, more broadly, *why* does the United States have a vested interest in ensuring NATO's persistence?

HYPOTHESES ON NATO'S PERSISTENCE: VALUE MAXIMIZATION

In the proceeding chapters, I demonstrate how the alliance's persistence allows the United States to pursue some conflicts multilaterally, and why the pursuit of multilateral conflict with NATO engagement is important to the United States. With an exceptionally well-funded defense apparatus that includes the most well-equipped, technologically advanced military in the world, the United States has demonstrated that it rarely needs the resources of its allies to prevail in war (Kreps 2011; Weitsman 2014). At times, it also demonstrates its willingness and capacity for unilateral action or to operate multilaterally but outside of the NATO alliance. However, it pursues NATO political support at all stages of conflict, and military or operational support as necessary to the United States' goals. For example, in the 2001 war in Afghanistan, the United States pursued few individual allies at the outset of Operation Enduring Freedom (OEF), despite having overwhelming multilateral support and pledges of resources from several international organizations and individual states. Decisions about the participation of allies were based almost entirely on the state's military ability to contribute to the mission. Concerns regarding NATO's capacities and ability to act quickly led US policymakers to operate with limited NATO participation during OEF. As the war transitioned to stabilization and reconstruction efforts, US officials then worked to engage more allies, including the NATO alliance. In the 2003 Iraq War, the United States pursued NATO support before the intervention but was unsuccessful in convincing the allies to act. After failing to secure an agreement for NATO participation, the United States undertook Operation Iraqi Freedom (OIF) with an ad hoc coalition of the willing. However, policymakers continued to pursue support for from the alliance as well as individual member states, with some limited success.

These examples broadly demonstrate how the United States pursues multilateralism through NATO, while indicating how the European allies retain the ability to prevent the United States from using the alliance as an unrestrained extension of its foreign policy objectives. NATO political support is sought at all stages of conflict engagement, while the United States pursues military resources on a case-by-case basis. To answer more specifically the second question regarding the importance of the US-NATO relationship, I propose four explanations for why NATO persistence is important to the United States. These hypotheses fall into two categories. The first category addresses the *legitimizing effects* of NATO engagement, while the second category explains the *utility* of NATO engagement.

At its most fundamental level, legitimacy concerns the relationship between the state and the citizen. Political scientists and social philosophers explore this concept, resulting in a vast literature on the definition, manifestation, and consequences of legitimacy. In this analysis, I adopt Ian Hurd's definition of legitimacy: "*Legitimacy*...refers to the normative belief by an actor that a rule or institution ought to be obeyed. It is a subjective quality, relational between actor and institution, and defined by the actor's *perception* of the institution" (Hurd 1999). Though the primary focus of the scholarship on legitimacy focuses on the relationship between the state and its citizens, more recent analyses examine the relationship between states and international organizations (Hurd 1999; Ku and Jacobsen 2002; Coicaud and Heiskanen 2001; Hancock 2007; Buchanan 2010; Bjola 2009; Armstrong and Farrell 2005). States explicitly consent to the rules established by international organizations. They accept the organization has the right to enforce compliance with the rules, either by creating incentives for cooperation or disincentives for defection (Buchanan

2010). From this perspective, organizations are legitimate because they serve the interests of the states comprising their membership. Because states are the source of legitimacy for the authority of the organization, they preserve their sovereignty and the right to circumvent the organization when deemed appropriate (Coicaud and Heiskanen 2001). International organizations are also believed to have the right to rule (sociological legitimacy) when they are perceived to enforce moral or legal norms outside of states' self-interests. Thus, international organizations have the right to rule (authorized by states to govern), as well as being *perceived* as having the right to rule (based on the moral and legal standards of the international community) (Buchanan 2010).

When a state intends to use force against another state, or transnational nonstate actors, it will often appeal to the international community to legitimize its actions. Military alliances, regional organizations, and the United Nations are able to confer legitimacy on the state's actions because participants recognize the authority of the organization. A state motivated to use force, even for arguably altruistic purposes (e.g. to prevent crimes against humanity or other severe violations of international law), faces a great deal of suspicion from other states (Attanasio and Norton 2004). However, the decision to engage international organizations in a multilateral intervention may signal to others the state is not acting purely out of self-interest.

The relationship between international organizations, legitimacy, and the use of force is well understood (Bjola 2009; Attanasio and Norton 2004; Reisman and Shuchart 2004; Armstrong and Farrell 2005; Civic and Miklaucic 2011; Buchanan 2010). Just war theory provides a set of moral criteria for judging the legitimacy of the use of force (Bjola 2009). The United Nations Security Council is integral in legitimizing intervention, particularly in cases in which intervention occurs without the consent of the offending government. Other organizations, including regional organizations like NATO, can also enhance the legitimacy of the intervention and coerce states into compliance (Attanasio and Norton 2004). This enhancement is unique to international organizations: as noted by scholars, coalition and other warfighting arrangements do not confer legitimacy as organizations do (Weitsman 2010). Rather, it is only through a UN Security Council resolution (UNSCR) or other authorizing mechanism that legitimacy is conferred on a multilateral operation, though not to the same degree as operations led or supported by international organizations.

Hypothesis: The United States values NATO as a vehicle for legitimacy enhancement.

Hypothesis: The United States wants its conflict engagement to conform (or appear to conform) to international norms and expectations about war; thus, it seeks to act through multilateral organizations such as NATO.

The existing scholarship largely overlooks the importance of the connections between international organizations, legitimacy, and the use of force in explaining US-NATO relations and NATO persistence. In each of the four cases, I demonstrate how the United States sought an endorsement from the international community for its actions and pursued NATO support even when it intended to act without direct NATO participation. I present the domestic and international factors leading the United States to adopt policies that encourage some kind of multilateralism in the pursuit of legitimization, even when fighting capacity or efficiency was sacrificed. Additionally, the pursuit of legitimacy enhancement is driven by both practical (operational) and ethical considerations. I demonstrate the unique pressures for legitimacy in each case and examine whether the United States' behavior indicates a deeply entrenched need to legitimize its actions.

HYPOTHESES ON NATO's PERSISTENCE: ALLIANCE UTILITY

The United States has sought power projection via a global web of institutions, and alliance arrangements such as NATO are integral to interstate conflict engagement (Weitsman 2014). In the cases presented here, I expand on Weitsman's analysis to further explanations for NATO persistence. Because the United States has a number of other resources—unparalleled military capabilities and the global combatant command structure, for example—the ability of willing allies to provide substantial contributions at the outset of conflict is limited. However, as Kreps (2011) demonstrates, policymakers adopted a "hybrid approach" to multilateralism in the 1990s that has continued through today. This approach employs a few strong allies in the initial phases of conflict and incorporates more multilateral efforts during the later reconstruction phases (Kreps 2011). In other words, while it is politically advantageous to seek NATO support during the planning stages (because of legitimacy enhancement), the operational advantage is optimized during the later stages of the conflict, not the initial outset.

*Hypothesis: The alliance's persistence allows the United States to improve its
ability to engage in conflict.*

*Hypothesis: The historical legacy of US-NATO relations, US primacy after the
Cold War, and US leadership within the alliance allowed the United States
to exert a high level of influence over the post-war development of the
alliance.*

The concept of measuring the ways in which NATO supplemented
American conflict engagement is relatively straightforward and not unprecedented; as the next chapter reveals, a number of utilitarian-based
approaches to NATO are presented by the existing scholarship. The historical legacy and US leadership within the alliance, however, requires a more
nuanced assessment as it presents measurement difficulties. Despite this, a
solid foundation for assessing the role these factors played on NATO's persistence is established within identity-based approaches to alliance formation and cohesion as presented in the following chapter.

CASE SELECTION AND RESEARCH CONTRIBUTIONS

This book relies on a qualitative design to test each of the preceding
hypotheses. I use two primary sources of data, archival research and con-
tent analysis, to observe US attitudes and actions toward NATO during
each conflict. I supplement these sources with both elite interviews and
polling data. I compare the four cases to determine patterns of behavior
over time. Lastly, I measure the effect of US-NATO relations on US legitimacy (domestic and international), the balance of power, and interstate
relations. This project focuses on three conflicts in which there was a substantial multilateral intervention including both US and NATO participation: Kosovo, Afghanistan, and Libya. The fourth conflict, Iraq,
demonstrates the effect of non-NATO participation on the legitimacy,
fighting effectiveness, and perceived success of the US-led multilateral
intervention, as well as the impact of non-NATO participation on the alliance relationship.

Whereas previous analyses overlook the importance of the United
States to NATO persistence, in the proceeding chapters I demonstrate
how much of NATO's evolution and contemporary relevance is due to the
United States' continued leadership within the alliance. Despite the divergent perspectives of the United States and European allies, American officials have consistently pursued innovation and reform within the alliance,

and the European allies have complied—though to varying degrees—while remaining committed to NATO. The ability of the United States to have such a dominant influence within the alliance is due not only to its sustained political and military contributions, but also to its hegemonic status. As previous analyses demonstrate, there are substantial political, military, and economic incentives for the European allies to remain connected to the United States through NATO. However, these analyses do not adequately explain why the United States remained committed to NATO because they do not fully consider two factors: the United States' role as the de facto leader of the alliance, and the incentives for continued US participation and leadership. By answering the question of NATO's persistence, the United States' motivations for maintaining the alliance are clearer.

This research has significant implications for US foreign policy. I demonstrate the legitimizing effects of NATO participation or nonparticipation, as well as the consequences of pursuing NATO support during the four conflict periods. The evolution of the US-NATO relationship in each of these conflicts indicates the United States remains the central power of the alliance in the immediate future. The United States will continue its participation in the alliance for as long as it derives some utility from the alliance, and pursuit of this relationship will lead foreign policymakers to look for opportunities beyond legitimacy enhancement. Currently, the alliance's utility is derived from its ability to contribute to stabilization and reconstruction efforts in conflict areas (both inside and outside NATO's areas of interest). The refinement of its capacity to provide support in these areas through previous operations has demonstrated its utility and relevance in the post-Cold War period. Despite declining contributions from some members, all 29 NATO allies recognize the utility of NATO's integrated command structure and collective resources. Though the United States has at times found NATO negotiations to be time-consuming and arduous, policymakers recognize some benefits to the institutionalized decision-making process.

This research also furthers explanations as to the persistence of NATO in the post-Cold War period that are currently lacking in the theoretical literature on alliance behavior. As presented in Chap. 2, the literature on alliance persistence is incomplete: none of the posited theories fully explain NATO's continuation and expansion in the absence of a Soviet threat. These cost-benefit explanations give heavier weight to other considerations such as capability aggregation, fighting effectiveness, proliferation of liberal-democratic values, and shared security interests, without a thorough examination of the value of legitimization for both the United States and Europe. The existing explanations for NATO persistence also underestimate the importance of US leadership. European states re-evaluated their security interests after the Cold War, and some called for an "Europeanization" of the alliance. As a result of changes to security policies, many states reduced monetary and material contributions to NATO. Yet there is no wholly satisfactory explanation as to why Western European states did not successfully developed an alliance to replace NATO and end the United States' role in European security. There is also great debate over the burden-sharing problems of the alliance. As my research concludes, there is little incentive for the United States to abandon NATO despite the European members' shrinking contributions to the alliance. The likelihood of the United States being drawn into a conflict in which it had little or no interest simply because of its NATO membership, or withdrawing from the alliance entirely, is small. So long as US primacy is maintained, the United States will still be able to selectively engage in unilateral and multilateral operations vital to its interests, without threatening the longevity of the alliance.

Largely because of demographic changes and a shifting security environment, as well as US leadership in the international system, the utility and role of NATO in combat have changed. Lower monetary and material contributions from European members have resulted in decreased fighting effectiveness, but not in opportunity for the alliance to contribute to the global use of force. Engagements in Kosovo, Afghanistan, Iraq, and Libya caused the alliance to realize the needs of the new security environment, and the opportunity to adapt to US and international demands. This research analyzes the new obligations the alliance has undertaken, as well as how this evolution has impacted the alliance's legitimizing effects.

WHAT'S AT STAKE FOR THE UNITED STATES AND NATO

The case studies and other analyses contained in the remaining chapters focus primarily on the recent past, and how they inform the present in terms of NATO's evolution and US-NATO relations. How the future relationship transpires as a result of these findings, however, is not resolved. It is not a principal objective of this book to postulate how the world might look if NATO had not persisted or had the United States not attained its current status in the international system, nor is the intent to predict the future threat environment, the forms NATO's ongoing evolution might take, or the long-term consequences of US-NATO relations on American foreign policy. It is vitally imperative, however, to situate the book's findings in the contemporary threat environment to demonstrate the importance of answering these questions.

Although the United States played a formative role in shaping the post-Cold War environment, threats to national security, as well as international peace and security, persist. A resurgent Russia remains high on both the US and NATO security agenda, alongside threats from Iran, cyberattacks, terrorism, human trafficking, hybrid warfare, Islamic State of Iraq and Syria (ISIS), weapons of mass destruction, and ongoing instability in Libya, Afghanistan, and elsewhere (*NATO* 2018). Further, American policymakers and their European counterparts are grappling with how to address the very real security challenges of climate change; the melting Arctic circle presents a territorial threat to the North American allies, while increasingly unpredictable and more intense weather patterns have been recognized by NATO as a threat multiplier (*NATO Parliamentary Assembly* 2015; Shea 2018; Nuccitelli 2017). The findings presented in this analysis suggest many of the ways in which the United States and NATO are better off addressing these threats in unison. Yet the transatlantic rift between the United States and European members is a hindrance to collaboration and the benefits derived from the United States' membership in the alliance.

Resource deficiencies, whether real or perceived, challenge NATO's capacity across several dimensions. As the 2018 NATO summit communique reiterates, the contemporary alliance sees itself as pursuing a "360-degree approach to security" through "collective defense, crisis management, and cooperative security" (*NATO* 2018). All of these dimensions are threatened by the inability or unwillingness of allies to meet the military spending threshold, despite having a consensus among members regarding how much was needed to execute NATO's agenda. Further, although allies recently reaffirmed their commitment to both spending minimums and allocation minimums (including at least a 20 percent apportionment of military expenditures to equipment needs), many states will not meet these targets until 2024. At a time where NATO has arguably retracted from "out of area" combat and is now dealing with more imminent threats in the alliance's own backyard, not having the capacity to adequately address threats not only endangers the alliance but could arguably make it more of a threat and less of a deterrent to Russia.

Because the alliance's decision-making mechanisms rely so heavily on consensus, a deepening political or ideological rift between the allies could effectively paralyze most of NATO's functions, rendering it little more than a paper tiger or collection of undeployable resources. Disunity within the alliance, even if it is eventually able to build consensus, could undermine its ability to legitimize intervention as well as its ability to coerce. Further, a willingness or active pursuit of European collective defense without the United States would arguably restructure the geopolitical landscape, potentially altering the balance of power and reshaping international politics.

The effects of transatlantic division on US foreign policy are multidimensional and significant. Absent renegotiated bilateral or multilateral agreements, the United States would lose access to resources previously utilized by the US military, such as the Strategic Airlift Capability, the first multinational heavy airlift unit in the world, the NATO Response Force (NRF), and NATO's Airborne Warning and Control Systems (AWACS), which were deployed over US territory after the 9/11 terrorist attacks and invocation of Article 5, as well as in Syria, Iraq, and Turkey in the years since to combat the Islamic State of Iraq and Syria (ISIS) (*NATO* 2019; Strategic Airlift Capability Program, n.d.). The United States would also lose its position as the lead on all NATO military missions,[2] sacrificing its ability to inform, influence, and direct NATO operations. Sacrificing US leadership in this area creates other opportunities for the European allies to proceed separately from the United States. It also allows the United States to proceed independent of the alliance, though this does not always result in an optimized outcome as demonstrated by the 2003 Iraq invasion and the "coalition of the willing." US military installations would likely require renegotiation, and base/airfield access as well as flyover rights could be diminished or eliminated, thereby posing significant threat to the United States' forward presence and global power projection. Though the Trump administration has been at times one of the alliance's fiercest critics, the agenda described in the 2017 National Security Strategy—including combatting terrorism, trafficking, chemical, biological, radiological,

---

[2] The U.S.'s combatant commander for the European Command (USEUCOM) is a dual role: in addition to overseeing American resources in the region, the USEUCOM Commander is also the Supreme Allied Commander, Europe (SACEUR), chief military officer for the alliance.

and nuclear weapons, and cyberterrorism—parallel many of NATO's major initiatives (Trump 2017). As evidenced in the proceeding chapters, this is less the result of coincidence or appeasement and more the intentional outcome of decades of alliance engagement. Pursuing unilateral solutions to transnational problems is not a promising course of action.

There is some precedent for leaving part of or all of the alliance, namely, France's decision to leave all alliance military operations in the 1950s. But the post-Cold War environment bears little resemblance to Western Europe—and international politics more broadly—in the 1950s, and the United States' hegemonic status vis-à-vis other states is markedly different from France's post-World War II position. A worst-case scenario in the transatlantic relationship would be dissolution, which could result in concerns spanning far beyond military and utilitarian concerns. Not only would bilateral political and economic relationships likely suffer, but US legitimacy could be at risk. Even short of separation, a persistent US-NATO rift poses an obstacle to UN Security Council authorization for the use of force, as well as global perceptions of American legitimacy in conflict engagement.

BOOK OUTLINE

In the next chapter, I present the relevant theoretical approaches to alliance behavior and participation to further develop the analytical framework. The third, fourth, fifth, and sixth chapters trace the engagements in Kosovo, Afghanistan, Iraq, and Libya. These four cases are a diverse representation of major US operations in the post-Cold War period wherein NATO was an important actor (even if it did not directly participate, as in the case of Iraq). I confirm each of the hypotheses on US-NATO relations for each case. The seventh chapter is a comprehensive assessment of the US-NATO relationship and its evolution during and after the four cases. It includes an analysis of the United States' responses to the post-Cold War period and shifts in the balance of power. The evidence presented in the seventh chapter and the collective case evidence confirms the first hypothesis regarding NATO's persistence after the Cold War as resulting from the United States' role in the alliance. The eighth chapter further explores the implications of these findings.

REFERENCES

Armstrong, David, and Theo Farrell. 2005. Force and Legitimacy in World Politics: Introduction. *Review of International Studies* 31 (S1): 3–13. https://www.jstor.org/stable/40072145.

Attanasio, J.B., and J.J. Norton. 2004. *Multilateralism V Unilateralism: Policy Choices in a Global Society*. London: The British Institute of International and Comparative Law.

Bjola, Corneliu. 2009. *Legitimising the Use of Force in International Politics*, Contemporary Security Studies. London: Routledge.

Braun, Aurel. 2008. *NATO-Russia Relations in the Twenty-First Century*. New York: Routledge.

Buchanan, Allen. 2010. *Human Rights, Legitimacy, and the Use of Force*. New York: Oxford University Press.

Chan, Sewell. 2016. Donald Trump's Remarks Rattle NATO Allies and Stoke Debate on Cost Sharing. *The New York Times*, July 21. https://www.nytimes.com/2016/07/22/world/europe/donald-trumps-remarks-rattlenato-allies-and-stoke-debate-on-cost-sharing.html

Civic, Melanne A., and Michael Miklaucic. 2011. *Monopoly of Force: The Nexus of DDR and SSR*. Washington, DC: National Defense University Press.

Coicaud, Jean-Marc, and Veijo Heiskanen. 2001. *The Legitimacy of International Organizations*. New York: The United Nations University Press.

Flenley, Paul. 2009. Russia and NATO: The Need for a New Security Relationship. *The Magazine of International Affairs Forum: NATO at Sixty*, Spring.

Freisleben, Shanya. A Guide to Trump's Past Comments About NATO. *CBS News*, Last Modified April 12. http://www.cbsnews.com/news/trump-nato-past-comments/. Accessed 30 Aug 2017.

Goldgeier, James. 2009. NATO Enlargement and Russia. *The Magazine of International Affairs Forum: NATO at Sixty*, Spring.

Hancock, Jan. 2007. *Human Rights and US Foreign Policy*. New York: Routledge.

Hurd, Ian. 1999. Legitimacy and Authority in International Politics. *International Organization* 53 (2): 379–408.

Johnson, Jenna. 2017. Trump on NATO: 'I Said It Was Obsolete. It's No Longer Obsolete. *The Washington Post*, April 12. https://www.washingtonpost.com/news/post-politics/wp/2017/04/12/trump-on-nato-i-said-itwas-obsolete-its-no-longer-obsolete/?utm_term=.f16650f98609

Kreps, Sarah E. 2011. *Coalitions of Convenience: United States Military Interventions After the Cold War*. New York: Oxford University Press.

Ku, Charlotte, and Harold K. Jacobsen. 2002. *Democratic Accountability and the Use of Force in International Law*. New York: Cambridge University Press.

Londoño, Ernesto. 2014. The U.S. Wants Its Allies to Spend More on Defense. *The Washington Post*, March 26. www.washingtonpost.com/blogs/worldviews/wp/2014/03/26/the-u-s-wants-its-allies-to-spend-more-on-defense-heres-how-much-theyre-shelling-out/?print=1

NATO. Brussels Summit Declaration. Last Modified Aug 30, 2018. https://www.nato.int/cps/en/natohq/official_texts_156624.htm. Accessed 9 Mar 2019.

———. 2019. NATO Airborne Warning and Control System (AWACS). https://shape.nato.int/about/aco-capabilities2/nato-awacs. Accessed 8 Mar 2019.

NATO Parliamentary Assembly. 2015. Policy Recommendations Adopted by the NATO Parliamentary Assembly in 2015. https://www.nato-pa.int/document/2015-236-sesa-15-e-nato-pa-policy-recommendations. Accessed 8 Mar 2019.

Nau, Henry. 2009. Whither NATO: Alliance, Democracy, or U.N.? *The Magazine of International Affairs Forum: NATO at Sixty*, Spring.

Nuccitelli, Dana. 2017. NATO Joins the Pentagon in Deeming Climate Change a Threat Multiplier. *Bulletin of the Atomic Scientists*. https://thebulletin.org/2017/05/nato-joins-the-pentagon-in-deeming-climate-change-a-threat-multiplier/

Pourchot, Georgeta. 2009. Collision Course: NATO, Russian, and the Former Communist Block in the 21st Century. *The Magazine of International Affairs Forum: NATO at Sixty*, Spring.

Rafferty, Kirsten. 2003. An Institutionalist Reinterpretation of Cold War Alliance Systems: Insights for Alliance Theory. *Canadian Journal of Political Science* 36 (2): 341–362.

Reisman, W. Michael, and Scott Shuchart. 2004. Unilateral Action in an Imperfect World Order. In *Multilateralism V Unilateralism: Policy Choices in a Global Society*, ed. J.B. Attanasio and J.J. Norton. London: The British Institute of International and Comparative Law.

Shea, Neil. 2018. Scenes from the New Cold War Unfolding at the Top of the World. *National Geographic*. https://www.nationalgeographic.com/environment/2018/10/new-cold-war-brews-as-arctic-ice-melts/

Smale, Alison, and Steven Erlanger. 2017. Merkel, After Discordant G7 Meeting, Is Looking Past Trump. *The New York Times*, May 28. https://www.nytimes.com/2017/05/28/world/europe/angela-merkel-trumpalliances-g7-leaders.html

Stoltenberg, Jens. 2014. Keynote Address by NATO Secretary General Jens Stoltenberg. Last Modified Nov 24, 2014. http://www.nato.int/cps/en/natohq/opinions_115098.htm. Accessed 5 July 2017.

Strategic Airlift Capability Program, n.d. The Strategic Airlift Capability (SAC). https://www.sacprogram.org/en/Pages/The%20Strategic%20Airlift%20Capability.aspx. Accessed 9 Mar 2019.

The Economist. 2017. Military Spending by NATO Members. February 16. https://www.economist.com/blogs/graphicdetail/2017/02/daily-chart-11

Trump, Donald. 2017. National Security Strategy. https://www.whitehouse.gov/wp-content/uploads/2017/12/NSS-Final-12-18-2017-0905.pdf

Vershbow, Alexander. 2015. Deputy Secretary General: Russia's Aggression Is a Game-Changer in European Security. http://www.nato.int/cps/en/natohq/news_117068.htm. Accessed 5 July 2017.

Weitsman, Patricia. 2010. Wartime Alliances Versus Coalition Warfare. *Strategic Studies Quarterly* 4 (2): 113–136.

———. 2014. *Waging War: Alliances, Coalitions, and Institutions of Interstate Violence*. Stanford: Stanford University Press.

CHAPTER 2

Alliances, NATO, and the Post-Cold War Era

The existing analytical frameworks on the North Atlantic Treaty Organization (NATO) created a foundation upon which to build explanations for the alliance's formation as well as provide insight into how and why NATO functions as it does. As NATO evolved so too did these analyses, as scholars sought explanations for the *how* and *why* of this evolution. However, the need for further inquiry to understand the alliance's *persistence* is evident, especially in light of the end of the Cold War and the dozens of proceeding claims that in the absence of imminent threat, the allies would cease to formulate cohesive, alliance-supported foreign policy. A more systematic framework for assessing the United States' role in this process, such as the one contained in this book, fills some of these gaps.

This chapter proceeds in two parts. First, it provides an examination of the existing NATO scholarship, in pursuit of situating the contributions of this book in advancing explanations for how and why the alliance persists with inclusion of a US-specific approach. I survey two somewhat disparate strands of literature: the first strand addressing the alliance's persistence, and the second strand centering on interpreting US-NATO relations. From this, I establish a basis for the framework upon which this book's analysis builds. Disaggregation of the American influence on NATO's persistence reveals in role in ensuring the alliance's survival, as well as its *interests* in doing so.

© The Author(s) 2020
J. Garey, *The US Role in NATO's Survival After the Cold War*,
Palgrave Studies in International Relations,
https://doi.org/10.1007/978-3-030-13675-8_2

In regard to alliance persistence, I identify several important trends in previous analyses. Contemporary alliance scholars relied on the suppositions of both structural realism and liberal institutionalism to extrapolate theories for NATO's peacetime persistence. Utilitarian explanations focused on answering three questions: first, what threat, if any to allied members remained; second, whether the benefits of capability aggregation in NATO outweighed the perceived costs of commitment; and third, whether there were characteristics unique to the NATO alliance that would indicate its post-Cold War tenure. Identity-based analyses postulated the uniqueness of the allies themselves as an explanation as to why the alliance remained. The answers to these questions led to the conclusion that NATO's persistence is attributed to institutional factors, all-encompassing changes to the global world order, an unintended consequence of the allies' actions, or some combination of these variables. Individually, these analyses are informative but incomplete. Collectively, they establish a clearer explanation of persistence but with some important oversights addressed here. For example, from where did the unprecedentedly distinctive alliance characteristics emerge? And why did the alliance evolve to address new threats and new types of threats, incorporate new members and accept new commitments, and accept the constraining conditions of a receding pool of resources—particularly from the European allies?

In regard to US-NATO relations, a substantial body of literature on the US-NATO relationship emerged in the post-Cold War era focusing on a number of domestic (for the United States) and international issues. This literature centered on a number of themes, including: the (domestic) political and economic consequences of sustained US involvement as a primary "defender" of Europe; the possibility of increasing burden-sharing disparities between larger and smaller states, particularly in light of membership expansion; the changing nature of conflicts that could result in NATO intervention, and how the success or failure of intervention could damage the alliance; and the need for both the United States and NATO to adapt its institutionalized leadership and decision-making capacities in the new security environment. However, this literature focused less on the role of the United States in ensuring the alliance's persistence to date and more on the role of the United States in sustaining the alliance against, in some cases, the will of American policymakers. Instead of treating NATO's survival as an unintended consequence, I use the aforementioned framework to establish a basis for evaluating whether US involvement was a deliberate force in maintaining the alliance, thus making it the key explanatory variable in NATO's persistence. From this, I conclude with the hypotheses as to *how* and *why* the United States played this integral role.

EXPLAINING NATO'S PERSISTENCE

Earlier scholarship on the causes of alliance persistence is primarily rooted in structural realist and liberal institutional explanations of alliance cohesion. Structural realists first posited alliances as a response to the distribution of power in the international system (Morgenthau 1954). As the end of World War II brought about a call for a more systematic approach to understanding state behavior, more robust conceptualizations emerged, positing alliances as an external balancing mechanism to counter the relative power of other states (Waltz 1986; Keohane 1989). Balance-of-power theories addressed alliances from the Waltzian tradition, focusing on the aggregation of capabilities to counter threat as the primary motivation for alliance formation (Walt 1987; Morrow 1991). Balance-of-threat theories looked more to the conditions in the international system to explain the formation of alliances, addressing the calculations of trade-offs between internal security enhancement and alliance engagement by states (Holsti et al. 1973; Morrow 1991; Duffield 2001).

In the post-Cold War era, scholars employed both balance-of-power and balance-of-threat theories to explain the conditions under which alliances may exist outside of conflict. Patricia Weitsman's analysis in *Dangerous Alliances* (2004) creates a multidimensional model to examine the relationship between the level of internal threat, external threat, and a state's willingness to remain committed to the alliance. Robert McCalla (1996) addresses the ways in which fluctuations in the level of threat strengthen or weaken states' alliance commitment. James Morrow (1991) examines the impact of alliance participation on state reputation. If states engage in alliances, Morrow argues, they enjoy more than just capability enhancement; states that ally are given the opportunity to articulate their national interests and engage in a meaningful and prosperous relationship with states sharing their interests. This exchange may lead to a more cohesive and enduring alliance. Conversely, a state's failure to engage in alliances is damaging to its credibility and poses risks extending beyond being outmatched in its capabilities (Morrow 1991).

Conversely, liberal institutional approaches to alliances rejected previous assumptions concerning the self-help system and the structure of international politics as constraints on state behavior, subsequently limiting states' desire for cooperation (Waltz 1986). Additionally, liberal institutionalism diverged with its classical counterpart in several areas; namely, scholars asserted institutions do not *cause* states to behave peacefully or cooperate but instead *encourages* them to do so (Keohane 1989). The primary mechanism by which institutions facilitate this behavior is through information sharing. For liberal institutionalism, information becomes embedded in institutions out of utility and the desire of states to reduce transaction costs and improve the information environment (Keohane 2002). Because international agreements are difficult to keep, Keohane (1989) argues, the desire of states to uphold their commitments suggests how institutions shape behavior.

The idea of a peacetime military alliance was not difficult for liberal institutional scholars to conceptualize, and a vast literature on alliance persistence emerged from this tradition. Scholars linked alliance cohesion to a more cooperative international environment. Additionally, they sought new understandings of how alliances affected the likelihood of war, lessening the emphasis on security enhancement and centering the debate on the promotion of cooperation (Leeds 2003). For example, the work of Christopher Gelpi (1999) analyzes the ways in which alliance participation enhances the ability of states to reduce the likelihood of aggression between members. Deudney and Ikenberry (1999) developed a framework congruent with Gelpi's assertions to understand how states engage in "co-binding," or creating institutions to effectively constrain the behavior of member states and reduce the level of threat. Thus, according to liberal institutionalism, the ability of alliances to stabilize relations, increase transparency, and reduce transaction costs cement their value to member states, ensuring long-term viability (Keohane 1990).

Structural realist and liberal institutional analyses of alliance cohesion established a foundation for the literature on alliance persistence. While the two approaches have been portrayed as antithetical to one another, in tandem they facilitate the creation of a more robust explanatory model for NATO's continuation and American participation. In regards to this book, the scholarship of Weitsman, McCalla, Morrow, and other structural realists informs hypotheses on the utility of American alliance engagement by identifying the causal relationships between threat mitigation and alliance cohesion on several dimensions. Weitsman's analysis also establishes the basis for disaggregating American participation: while all allies faced threats from other states both inside and outside of the alliance, the United States suffered the additional consequences of its status as global hegemon in the new unipolar world order. Thus, the threats it faced differed from that of its allies, yet its commitment to the alliance did not waver—in fact, American policymakers continued to embrace its role as the largest contributor and de facto leader of alliance from which the value derived had changed. Further, the works of Keohane, Leeds, Gelpi, and Deudney and Ikenberry inform this book's hypotheses concerning the role of legitimacy enhancement and norm conformity in guiding US actions toward NATO.

At the end of the Cold War, NATO suffered from what Wallace Thies (2009) aptly describes as "alliance crisis syndrome," a perpetual debate between scholars and policymakers regarding the practicality of maintaining the alliance in peacetime and a concern its demise was imminent. Although the longevity of the alliance was continually challenged, scholars presented multiple competing explanations as to the causes of its persistence. Building on the previous literature concerning alliance cohesion during conflict, scholars established both utilitarian and identity-based explanations for understanding the same phenomenon in peacetime. Still, no clear consensus emerged. In the following section, I explore each of these types of explanations and demonstrate how these bodies of research inform the remaining hypotheses of this book.

Utilitarian Explanations for NATO's Persistence

Utilitarian explanations for NATO's persistence primarily focused on the remaining threats to allies' national security interests, cost-benefit analyses of NATO participation, and NATO's "uniqueness" as an alliance. As Ronald Asmus, Richard Kugler, and Stephen Larrabee (1993) argue, the traditional threats NATO was intended to combat still existed, but instead of coming from the Soviet Union, they emerged from two new arcs of crisis: the Eastern arc (northern Europe between Russia and Germany, Turkey, the Caucuses, and middle Asia) and the Southern arc (northern Africa and the Mediterranean, the Middle East and southwest Asia). Furthermore, according to John Duffield (1994), NATO's enduring nature was enhanced by its role in neutralizing threats in Central and Eastern Europe. NATO's institutional structure fostered transparency and prevented a renationalization of militaries in Western Europe, Duffield argued, and maintaining the United States as a pivotal player kept the global balance of power in a favorable position.

Threat-centric explanations for NATO's persistence support both the hypothesis concerning the utility of the alliance for the United States and the case selection of the proceeding chapters. Asmus et al.'s characterization of possible threats emerging from the Eastern and Southern arcs was realized in NATO's role in the former Yugoslavia. Afghanistan, Iraq, and Libya also fit these characterizations, and although NATO did not directly engage in conflict in Central Europe, both Ukraine and Georgia emerged as flashpoints between Russia and the allies in the final years of the twentieth century.

Answering the question regarding threat was made more difficult by NATO's membership expansion (from 16 to 29 states) and it adoption of new, "non-traditional" missions such as securing the cyber technologies of alliance members and combating terrorism. Each consideration for conflict engagement was met with resistance from different member states arguing these were "out-of-area" conflicts that did not directly challenge alliance members (Gordon 1997). Thus, utilitarian scholars further explored the costs and benefits of capability aggregation through NATO.

Celeste Wallander (2000) identifies the cost-benefit calculation of states in explaining prevailing institutions, explaining that if the cost of maintaining the existing organization is lower than the cost of creating a whole new institution, states will support the existing establishment. When alliances such as NATO are successful, they become "security institutions" and persist so long as there is some perceived utility to member states, while the rules, norms, and operating procedures resulting from decades of alliance interaction are not only institutionalized but can also be adapted for use in other types of conflicts. Michael Howard (1999) equates post-war NATO to an unhappy marriage, declaring that even if member states were dissatisfied with the benefits they received from alliance participation, the alliance remained in place because they were both familiar with one another and because the consequences of disbanding (even to create a new organization) extended to states both inside and outside of the alliance. Strobe Talbott (2002) expands the utilitarian approach to NATO by looking at it as part of a greater international network of institutions, arguing the institution's longevity is explained by a combination of US leadership and a strategic expansion of its primary objectives.

Inquiries as to whether NATO possesses some unique characteristic allowing it to persist in the absence of conflict produced mixed answers. Though scholars often debated how unequal burden-sharing within the alliance would lead to its demise (Sprecher and Krause 2006;

Sandler and Murdoch 2000; Cahen 1989; Sloan 1985), these assumptions were challenged by the works of Ivo Daalder and James Goldgeier, Philip Jones, and Martin van Heuven, among others. Daalder and Goldgeier (2006) advance the discussion of the utility of NATO for democracy promotion. They suggest that NATO's future success is embedded in the ability of the alliance to serve as a peace-spreading mechanism, and the best way to do so is to incentivize states into adopting democratic practices by extending membership offers to any state seeking to join NATO. Jones (2007) utilizes a public goods model to understand the relationships between NATO members, establishing a framework for understanding the individual incentives of policymakers within the alliance. He finds individual policymakers are inclined to support NATO policies when there is a significant benefit for doing so—for example, policymakers who represent the interests of defense good manufacturers are prone to support NATO because of the trade relationships that exist as a result of the alliance. van Heuven (2001) argues that there is equality in many aspects of the alliance, including in enlargement goals, risk sharing, organization and leadership, and influence on NATO-Russia relations. He acknowledges an unequal distribution of capabilities and the debates over burden-sharing, but explains that the inequality has always been present and subsequently, does not impact the likelihood of persistence. Jack Vincent, Ira Straus, and Richard Biondi (2001) utilize capability theory to understand member states attitudes toward decision-making in NATO. As a result of the changes NATO underwent in the 1990s, Vincent et al. argue that different member states have different preferences for the future of the alliance based on their ability to contribute to the alliance and their outside influence on the international system. Based on survey data and information about the capabilities of states, they find that states with the highest capacity are also more likely to support changes to the NATO decision-making structures, but all allies remain vested in the alliance's persistence.

The answers to each of the utilitarian approaches—but particularly the second and third questions—are essentially variations on the same theme: path dependence (Levi 1997). According to Margaret Levi (1997) "when organization develops, the path is even more firmly established, for organization tends to bring with it vested interests who will choose to maintain a path even when it is not optimal." The historical legacy hypothesis presented here is supported by claims of path dependency within NATO, under which all of Paul Pierson's "features" of political life are present:

multiple equilibria, contingency, a critical role for timing and sequencing, and inertia (Pierson 2000). The concept of NATO as a path-dependent organization also supports the selection of case studies. In each case, a number of courses of action (what Pierson characterizes as "outcomes" or multiple equilibria points) are available from which policymakers may choose. Further, small events can and do have enduring consequence for the alliance and the timing of engagement is especially important, which is particularly evident in examination of the inter-conflict periods of NATO's post-Cold War development. Finally, the effects of inertia identified by Wallander and others are supported by the substantial evolution and adaptation facilitated by the US in lieu of abandonment.

Identity-Based Explanations for NATO's Persistence

Deudney and Ikenberry (1999) note how the post-war environment was characterized by Western idealist philosophy: "co-binding security institutions, penetrated American hegemony, semi-sovereign great powers, economic openness, and civic identity." Even before the end of the war, institutionalists argued that NATO's mission had developed from an instrument intended to enhance security to a vehicle for conducting transatlantic relations (Duffield 1994). Because of this, some scholars departed from traditional utilitarian explanations of NATO's persistence and instead reexamined the relationship between alliance participation and identity politics.

Helene Sjursen (2004) suggests NATO members, even in the absence of the Soviet Union as a primary threat, have been bound for such a long period and with such intensity of purpose that the shared history of its members will allow the alliance to persist. Sjursen builds on the analysis of Thomas Risse-Kappen (1995), who suggests the shared histories of the United States, the United Kingdom, and France in particular resulted in the North Atlantic Treaty. By understanding its characteristics as an institution and its role in institutionalizing cooperation among states, Sjursen argues that the continued existence of NATO is unsurprising. Bradley Klein (1990) posits NATO's persistence is likely because of its shift from the traditional threat of the Soviet Union to an emphasis on preserving and spreading traditionally Western ideas. "NATO's success resides in having provided a network of intertextual representations for the articulation of global political space" writes Klein, suggesting that NATO cultivated the Soviet threat into a broader set of social practices. This led member states to develop a set of ideologies that they then ascribed to— "the Western way of life."

Robert Jervis (2002) writes of the likelihood of a sustained security community between the United States and Western Europe. He argues that the post-Cold War era presented an unprecedented opportunity for a security community to endure, as "the states that constitute this (community) are the leading members of the international system and so are natural rivals who in the past were central to the violent struggle for security, power, and contested values." He posits "no one state can move away from the reliance on war itself lest it become a victim, they can collectively do so if each forsakes the resort to force." Robbin Laird (1991) suggests that there is a necessity for organizations like NATO to persist in order to nurture a "Western European identity" and ensure the stability of Europe. Additionally, NATO needs to look to its institutional partners to work effectively instead of becoming the only organization for promoting collective defense. He highlights three issues for post-Cold War Europe that signify the importance of a Western collective defense effort spanning far beyond NATO: the residual threat of Russia, the range of threats that exist outside of Europe, and the continued dynamics between European states.

The identity-based literature on NATO's persistence informs the first, second, and fourth hypotheses in important ways. Legitimization of conflict engagement and conformity to norms are central features of Western liberal philosophy on war, as evidenced by the emphasis on the concept of just war (Brown 2015). The proliferation of historical and Western norms as described by Deudney and Ikenberry, Sjursen, Klein, Jervis, and Laird further support this. Finally, the idea of the United States wielding its hegemonic influence as the purveyor of not only these Western values but also *how* to best preserve these values while pursuing a more efficient and effective NATO is a natural progression from the tradition of understanding the alliance as an identity enhancer.

CREATING A NEW FRAMEWORK FOR NATO PERSISTENCE: THE US-NATO RELATIONSHIP

A second strand of literature on the evolution of the US-NATO relationship emerged as a departure from organization-centric analyses. A number of scholars focused on the prevailing burden-sharing disparities and foreign policy consequences of the American defense of Western Europe after the communist threat was neutralized. Very few treated NATO's persistence as the result of deliberate, strategic efforts by the United States, instead analyzing how policymakers sustained the United States' relationship with the alliance against (in some cases) their perceived better judgment.

Stanley Sloan (1985) analyzes the relationship between supports of NATO and Congress, arguing that is unlikely that Congress will ever feel as though there is an equal distribution of burden-sharing between the United States and other NATO members. Even in the period leading up to the end of the Cold War, Congress was reluctant to accept policymakers' calls for large troop commitments in Europe despite their acceptance of the United States' obligations to NATO. Michael Brown (1999) adds to this debate, suggesting that as NATO expands its membership, the cost of US commitments in Western Europe could become too high. If NATO's purpose is to promote security, and this is still the greatest benefit in terms of US participation, membership expansion is counterproductive to both the alliance as incoming member states have already achieved a high level of stability and may further tax NATO's resources. Additionally, membership growth only further promotes free-riding problems for the United States.

Matthew Rhodes analyzes how the 2008 global economic crisis led to a renewal of the debate in the United States regarding the utility of the NATO relationship. In addition to challenging the global power status of the US and Western European states, the economic crisis also highlighted the disparity in defense spending between the United States and Europe and renewed debates over the capability of NATO allies to contribute to future missions and the possibility European partners would free ride. These conditions, in combination with domestic constraints and socioeconomic changes, could result in the United States finding that both its capacity and desire to lead have decreased. Additionally, the changed global environment may leave European NATO allies unwilling or unable to participate. Rhodes asserts that it is NATO's relationship with the United States that has fueled its reputation as a legitimate and useful actor and has allowed for the alliance to persist. American attitudes regarding the utility of military force have maintained the alliance, writes Rhodes, but even the high value given to NATO by the United States is not enough to ensure its long-term durability (Rhodes 2012).

Philip Gordon (2002) assesses the US-NATO relationship in the context of the United States' more recent military engagements: Afghanistan and Iraq. Gordon looks at the initial decision-making process of the United States in Afghanistan and the decision to not engage NATO at the outset, despite the invocation of Article V by NATO members. He argues that this decision reflected the alliance's perceived inability to properly deal with the new threat of terrorism and the concern European allies were not generally supportive of the idea that terrorism posed a global threat (as opposed to a domestic problem) and therefore needed to be handled through international channels. Ellen Hallams (2009) takes a similar position in her discussion of the 2003 Iraq invasion, suggesting that the crisis not only reflected American attitudes about NATO's capacity but also revealed weaknesses in NATO's adaptability.

While these analyses are valuable in framing the US-NATO debate, the case studies presented here challenge some of the most fundamental assumptions regarding this relationship. Most notably, despite evidence of concerns regarding how alliance expansion may increase the propensity for free riding, and the political consequences members of the executive and legislature could face as a result of supporting the relationship, the United States has not left the alliance. Instead, the US was a vocal proponent for the two major membership expansions in 2004 and 2009, as well as Montenegro's accession in 2017. Policymakers knew these states possessed limited military capacity and instead capitalized on the political support of these allies. Further, the new members included in the two major expansion waves—Albania, Bulgaria, Croatia, Estonia, Latvia, Lithuania, Slovakia, Slovenia, and Romania—were either relatively well-established democracies, or progressing toward such political systems, thus disproving identity-based explanations centered on the alliance's role of promoting democracy. Closer analysis of US engagement in Afghanistan and Iraq, presented in the fourth and fifth chapters, reveals how claims of American unilateralism oversimplified analyses of US-NATO relations.

Only a small portion of the literature on US-NATO relations addresses the United States' role in the alliance's persistence. Gale Mattox (1999) explores the impact of NATO membership expansion on US attitudes regarding the alliance, highlighting the rigorous debate that US policymakers undertook in considering how to engage with the alliance on issues of expansion. When Russia supported German reunification, the United States abandoned its strategy of distancing itself from Europe's security, and the United States (and other NATO allies) saw that NATO may serve a future purpose. The debates over enlargement led not only to consensus between the United States and NATO, but also led to a renewed sense of purpose for the alliance and for the US-NATO relationship.

Jason Davidson (2011) identifies how states were incentivized to contribute to US alliances because they sought to maintain or improve their standing in the international system, as well as their relationships with the United States. Even when states could free ride, they engage in allied efforts because participation and a more equal burden-sharing enhances states' prestige, which according to Davidson outweighs both the value from and cost of participation in the alliance. Charles Barry (2012) addresses the manifestation of US-NATO relations in operational terms, focusing primarily on issues of interoperability. Advocating for sustained participation in the alliance, Barry asserts NATO is beneficial to the US military because it provides an overwhelming advantage in overseas engagements, ranging from cultural knowledge and language skills, to number of troops deployed, to political and diplomatic benefits as well as financial incentives. Additionally, the United States devoted a number of resources for standardizing operations within NATO—the "NATO way"—and ideas about interoperability establish the foundation on which contemporary US doctrine is based. Barry asserts that it is these military advantages that not only prove the NATO relationship beneficial for the United States, but also show the opportunity for the alliance to adapt to the contemporary threat environment and persist (with US leadership).

The conceptual framework used to analyze each of the cases presented in the proceeding chapters, as well as the inter-conflict periods, is informed by each body of literature while also contributing new insights in and bridging the gap between utilitarian explanations for NATO persistence, institutional explanations for NATO persistence, and US-NATO relations. Both utilitarian and identity-based explanations for NATO's persistence expressly address the role of legitimacy and legitimation of action at both the state and organizational level. As described by utilitarian analyses, the information sharing, transparency, familiarity, and relationship-building that occurs within the alliance are valuable in their own right, for the alliance as a whole and its individual members. However, collectively these processes build additional foundations for the proliferation of identities, values, norms, and expectations for conformity to each, as described by identity-based explanations for NATO's persistence.

In realizing its conception of the new world order, the United States went to great lengths to shape the world in a manner consistent with its interests and values, including norm proliferation and conformity. Further, it actively sought relationships to cement these values into the foundation of the new world order, as well as to encourage transparency and openness. NATO was a vehicle for all of these, which fostered American interest in sustaining the alliance. Thus, in analyzing how the United States engaged the alliance, the United States' desire to adhere (or appear to adhere) to international norms, as well as whether and how the alliance supported these efforts, is identified and isolated.

The benefits of norm proliferation to US policymakers are multifold: as the utilitarian literature suggests, the alliance's ability to foster transparency between allies contributed in part to preventing the renationalization of Western European militaries, while also attracting new members (including former adversaries). As predicted, NATO fostered observable political and military cooperation between allies despite the altered threat environment. In spite of disagreements over contributions to the alliance and whether or how to engage in conflict, the allies remained committed to both the norms of conflict engagement and the alliance as a whole. When actualized, Western idealism, the dominant paradigm of the post-Cold War era, was predicated primarily on US-centric conceptions of the world. The central tenants of policies consistent with these values were centered on expectations for norm conformity, particularly legitimacy.

Each post-Cold War conflict engagement presents compelling evidence of American concerns for the legitimacy of its actions, both domestically and internationally via the United Nations, NATO, and other regional or multilateral institutions. Utilitarian explanations for NATO's persistence expressly identify legitimation as a feature of international organizations, while identity-based explanations create the connection between legitimacy and other ideas about American hegemony, institutionalization, and transatlantic relations more broadly. Thus, and especially in light of existing US-NATO relations scholarship deriding how the alliance enables practices contrary to US interests (chief among these free riding and unequal burden-sharing), NATO's post-Cold War conflict engagements create an opportunity in the conceptual framework to identify how the US values legitimation, how NATO legitimizes behavior, and whether legitimation via NATO sustains US support of the alliance.

The relationship between the United States and NATO's post-Cold War survival is most linearly illustrated in the ways in which NATO enhanced the United States' ability to fight wars. However, utilitarian and identity-based explanations for NATO's persistence, as well as US-NATO analyses, set explicit precedents for a multidimensional conception of enhanced ability to engage in conflict. In addition to identifying tactical, operational, and strategic advantages facilitated by NATO engagement, NATO's utility in combat is expanded in the conceptual framework along political, economic, and social dimensions, domestically and internationally. Confirmation of these nontraditional contributions challenges some of the existing scholarship on US-NATO relations by demonstrating the ways in which value is derived in combat.

Through examination of the political, military, and economic influence of its most powerful allies, a telling narrative emerges: in lieu of applying its significant influence to pressure the European allies into establishing their own security mechanism to replace NATO, the United States perceived military and political value in sustaining both the alliance and its relationship to it. In the remaining chapters, I examine the balance of political influence, economic resources, and military capabilities within the alliance. In doing so, the American role in NATO's persistence is revealed. Further, the utilitarian and identity-based explanations for NATO's persistent establish the foundation from which the reasons *why* the United States engaged in pursuit of a sustained NATO. In reality, NATO's persistence is best explained by the current balance of power, nature of contemporary security threats, and the importance of multilateralism to NATO's most powerful member, the United States.

CASE SELECTION

The proceeding chapters present four cases to demonstrate the ways in which the United States facilitated NATO's persistence.

Kosovo

In the 1990s, NATO undertook two missions in the Balkans. The first, Operation Deliberate Force (ODF), was a 12-day, very limited air campaign conducted during the 1992–1995 Bosnian War. ODF was a key factor in convincing Serbian President Slobodan Milosevic to negotiate a settlement at the 1995 Dayton Peace Accords. Despite ongoing human rights abuses across the former Yugoslavia, it was not until 1998 that NATO and the United States undertook a second, far more aggressive, and sustained air war against Milosevic. When the Serbian police cracked down on the Kosovo Liberation Army (KLA) and attempted to capture a

KLA member in early March 1998, their efforts resulted in the killing of over 80 ethnic Albanians and the injuring of many more. As a result, the international community increased diplomatic sanctions against Milosevic, pushed to open access to UN and international observers, including the envoy led by US diplomats Richard Holbrooke and Christopher Hill, and amped up negotiations between the KLA and Serbian leaders. Even in the wake of continued violence, the UN Security Council refused to authorize international intervention.

At the failed Rambouillet negotiations in February and March 1999, the need for intervention became obvious to many allies, even in the absence of UN authorization. On March 24, 1999, NATO launched air-strikes against the Serbian military forces under Operation Allied Force (OAF). The airstrikes would last nearly three months and resulted in the NATO-led, post-war reconstruction operation Kosovo Force, or KFOR (Bjola 2009). Today, KFOR forces have been dramatically transformed but are still in place. Retrospective evaluations of NATO's actions deemed OAF an "illegal but legitimate" intervention.

Many have argued about both the value and utility of NATO during the 1999 Kosovo intervention. Interest in the alliance had been declining since the end of the Cold War. It was predicted a European-Atlantic partnership would be unnecessary, and states would become more and more reliant on loose arrangements, rather than formal alliances (Crotty 1995). In addition, some argued that NATO lost credibility because the nature of threats to member states had changed dramatically, and there would not be an overriding threat that could be used to unite NATO members (Hallams 2009). The mission in Kosovo also seemed to signify a shift in strategic goals for NATO; the world was a less threatening place to the member states and therefore the alliance could expand its goals and work in conjunction with organizations such as the UN in nonstability securing operations.

OAF exposed some of the United States' concerns with NATO and its European allies, primarily in terms of military capabilities and efficient, united decision-making (Williams 2008). Although President Clinton was extremely reluctant to intervene in the Balkans, the intervention in Bosnia led the United States to believe that if it wanted quick and decisive action in Kosovo, it would have to take a lead role in deciding the extent of NATO involvement (Mowle and Sacko 2007). President Clinton's reluctance reflected in his refusal to commit ground troops, which greatly influenced the alliance's decision to pursue an air-only campaign. Operation

Allied Force exposed NATO's operational weaknesses and left the United States leery of employing NATO for future multilateral action.

Nonetheless, the United States would continue its participation and investment in the alliance. It would use its experiences in Kosovo and its political strength in the alliance to improve NATO's decision-making structure, operational capacity, and utility in conflict. As the case of Kosovo demonstrates, the Clinton administration engaged NATO for both legitimacy and utility, confirming the hypotheses on the importance of NATO persistence to the United States. Legitimacy was important to many of the allies because of the absence of a UN Security Council resolution authorizing the intervention. Adherence to international norms was also important to US policymakers, particularly in regard to the use of force for humanitarian intervention. Although the Kosovo operation exposed the operational weaknesses of the alliance, NATO's utility was also a deciding factor for the administration. During both the Bosnian and Kosovo interventions, the United States used its influence in the alliance to encourage political and operational changes that would allow the European allies to act without US support if necessary.

Afghanistan

In the days following the 9/11 attacks on the United States, the Bush administration received overwhelming support from its international partners. Of the 2977 people killed in the 4 assaults (excluding the 19 terrorists), 372 were foreign nationals, many from states such as Great Britain, India, South Korea, Canada, and Japan. In addition, over 7000 people (including foreign nationals) were wounded (Lansford 2012). The United States quickly identified al Qaeda, led by Osama bin Laden, as the perpetrators of the attacks and moved to present evidence of al Qaeda's close ties to the Taliban, the governing party of Afghanistan. On September 12, 2001, NATO invoked Article V for the first time in its history, thus calling the allies to come to the United States' defense. The United Nations, the European Union, the Organization of American States, and other multilateral organizations also expressed support for the US retaliatory strikes in the interest of self-defense.

Though the United States enjoyed significant international support, its initial combat plans for Afghanistan, Operation Enduring Freedom, did not include NATO. US policymakers, including Secretary of Defense Donald Rumsfeld, instead devised a strategy that relied heavily on special operations forces for the groundwork in country, and utilized international support in other areas—such as patrolling US airspace with Airborne Warning and Control Systems (AWACs) airplanes under NATO command. NATO would continue to provide auxiliary support for US operations in Afghanistan until August 2003, when it assumed leadership of International Security Assistance Force Afghanistan (ISAF). In October 2006, the ISAF mandate was transferred from the UN to NATO, and in conjunction with the United States, NATO assumed a leadership role in the stabilization and reconstruction effort.

The evolution of NATO's role in Afghanistan added to the ongoing story of US-NATO relations and the post-Cold War persistence of the alliance. Because less than two years had elapsed since the 1999 Kosovo intervention, the alliance had not rectified many of the operational and technical difficulties experienced during OAF. The United States' plans for the Afghanistan war were completely different from its strategy in Kosovo, and the alliance's ability to contribute to an operation that relied heavily on special operations forces was untested. Additionally, whereas the United States was reluctant to engage in Kosovo, it led the charge for intervention in Afghanistan. These factors greatly influenced the United States' decision to forego operational support from NATO during OEF.

Despite the decision to act outside of NATO's command structure during Operation Enduring Freedom, US policymakers recognized the importance of adhering to international norms regarding the use of force and multilateralism, thus assembling a large coalition and looking for opportunities to engage the alliance. The United States wanted to maintain the high levels of support from its international partners, as well as the perception of legitimacy for its actions. Policymakers also recognized the utility of NATO participation in the stabilization and reconstruction efforts under the UN-mandated ISAF. NATO's leadership alleviated the necessity of having individual states lead ISAF on a rotating basis, opened new access to the alliance's resources and leadership, and created opportunities for partnership between ISAF and the Afghan National Security Forces (ANSF). NATO's participation in Afghanistan also resulted in several changes within the alliance aimed at improving its ability to respond to terrorism, out-of-area missions, and the changing dynamic of the post-Cold War era. As demonstrated in later chapters, many of these changes were driven by the United States. Thus, the Afghanistan case confirms all four hypotheses regarding the United States' interests in maintaining the alliance.

Iraq

While some policymakers urged President Bush to pursue an aggressive agenda toward Iraq in the aftermath of 9/11, planning for an offensive was delayed until early 2002 when in his State of the Union address, Bush identified Iraq as one of the three members of the "Axis of Evil." The National Security Strategy (NSS) released later in the year made it clear the administration intended to vigorously pursue these states as part of its war on terror campaign. In late 2002, the United States repeatedly appealed to the international community for multilateral support. However, many states were suspicious of the United States' intentions, leading to a very public, vociferous debate in both the United Nations and NATO. When the United States finally invaded Iraq in March 2003, it did so with a "coalition of the willing" comprised of over 40 states, but without the backing of both of the major organizations. Though major combat operations would be declared complete in May 2003, Operation Iraqi Freedom (OIF) would continue until September 2010. A new operation, Operation New Dawn (OND), would replace OIF as the United States transitioned forces out of Iraq, and US combat operations ceased in December 2011 (although the US forces would return to combat operations in 2014 as a response to the rise of the Islamic State of Iraq and Syria, or ISIS).

In the months following the 2003 invasion, the debate between the United States and allies opposed to the United States' actions (namely France and Germany) continued in the Atlantic Council. The United States appealed to the alliance for support in training new Iraqi security forces, and NATO complied in establishing the NATO Training Mission-Iraq (NTM-I), circumventing the objections of France. But, as Philip Gordon and Jeremy Shapiro argue, the short-term damage to the US-NATO relationship was immediately evident. "By the time the war actually began in March 2003, the Iraq crisis was no longer just a result of transatlantic differences, but a significant cause of them. The crisis reinforced many of the worst transatlantic stereotypes – depicting the United States as unilateralist and militaristic in European eyes, and Europeans as unreliable and ungrateful allies in American eyes" (Gordon and Shapiro 2004).

The Iraq case provides valuable information about the effects of NATO's nonparticipation on legitimacy. While the US mission's likelihood of success for finding weapons of mass destruction (WMDs) was uncertain at best, disputes between the allies and NATO's absence in Operation Iraqi Freedom further damaged both the legitimacy of the operation and the perception of US adherence to international norms.

When the Bush administration acted without the alliance, it was seen as aggressive and unilateral despite having assembled a coalition for the Iraq effort and continued to pursue NATO's support throughout the operation. Policymakers also recognized the utility of the alliance and benefitted from the allies' participation through the NTM-I. Thus, while the Iraq War did not result in a US-NATO partnership or a major NATO undertaking, the hypotheses on the importance of the alliance to the United States are confirmed. Both legitimacy and utility led the United States to pursue the alliance.

Libya

Speculation of both US and NATO intervention in Libya began with the protests in Benghazi in February 2011. Shortly after protestors stormed the city, the United Nations Security Council (UNSC) passed Resolution 1970 condemning the government's actions and applying sanctions. In the following weeks, the Security Council also passed UNSC Resolution 1973 authorizing international intervention (NATO 2012). On March 19, 2011, one day after the UNSC Resolution 1973, the United States launched Operation Odyssey Dawn (OOD) to further enforce the no-fly zone. In the days following the initiation of OOD, NATO placed ships and aircraft in the Central Mediterranean to prevent the shipment of arms to Colonel Qaddafi's army. They also instituted a search and seizure order of all incoming ships. One week after the passage of UNSCR 1973, NATO agreed to take control of the multinational effort at the behest of several organizations, including the Arab League and other non-NATO partners. Beginning March 31, 2011, NATO air and sea assets deployed as NATO launched Operation Unified Protector (OUP) (NATO 2011). The mandate of OUP was threefold: to enforce an arms embargo, to maintain a no-fly zone over Libya, and to ensure the protection of Libyan civilians.

Through the two overlapping operations, the United States participated in the air campaign over Libya for eight months, first as the leader of the coalition effort (under OOD), and then as a vital component of the NATO-led OUP. Not only was the United States successful in enforcing these sanctions, but NATO also counted the operation as a "win." The Libyan operation confirms all four of the hypotheses on the importance of US-NATO relations. Although many states and international organizations—including the Arab League and other regional partners—agreed on the necessity of some kind of intervention, and the UN Security Council essentially authorized the allies' actions, the United States pursued NATO partnership to enhance its legitimacy as a multinational effort and adhere to international norms. Furthermore, the Obama administration insisted on NATO leadership because of the heightened utility of the alliance vis-à-vis other multilateral arrangements. Policymakers recognized the alliance's capacities to coordinate the multinational coalition were unmatched by any other organization, and they wanted to ensure the successful handoff of responsibility for the mission. The United States also exerted its influence within the alliance to highlight NATO's shortcomings in intelligence, surveillance, and reconnaissance (ISR) capabilities, and pushed the alliance to acquire the necessary resources for future ISR missions.

Conclusion

While both utilitarian and identity-based approaches to understanding NATO's post-Cold War development furthered the discussion of its persistence, both fall short of establishing a wholly satisfactory explanation as to why the alliance did not dissolve at the end of the war. Utilitarian explanations emphasized the potential of the alliance to enhance member states' responses to threats and the institutionalization of decision-making mechanisms. Identity-based approaches noted the shared values and histories of member states, attributing the persistence of NATO to a shared interest in the perpetuation of Western values and the rising importance of multilateralism to its members. Analyses of the internal dynamics of NATO resulted in a better understanding of alliance politics after the Cold War, but no cohesive explanation for NATO persistence emerged. Furthermore, questions about unequal burden-sharing within the alliance, as well as explanations as to why some states were willing to bear a higher cost within the alliance (and, conversely, when they are not willing to do so), remain unresolved. Whereas the existing scholarship emphasizes the global balance of power and external conditions as explanatory variables, subsequent examine the balance of political influence, economic resources, and military capabilities *within* the alliance.

To better articulate the connection between US foreign policy objectives and NATO's persistence, the following section dissects the alliance's development in interventions in Bosnia and Kosovo, Afghanistan, and Libya, as well as its minor role in the US war in Iraq. The United States' role in facilitating the resulting initiatives within the alliance become integral in explaining and evaluating the alliance's persistence. I demonstrate that in addition to exercising a substantial influence during the four conflicts, the United States significantly impacted the inter-conflict development of the alliance. This allows for a more complete understanding of NATO's evolution and fills important gaps in the existing perspectives on alliance persistence.

REFERENCES

Asmus, Ronald D., Richard L. Kluger, and F. Stephen Larrabee. 1993. Building a New NATO. *Foreign Affairs* 72 (4): 27–40.

Barry, Charles. 2012. Building Future Transatlantic Interoperability Around a Robust NATO Response Force. *Transatlantic Current* 7: 1–14.

Bjola, Corneliu. 2009. *Legitimising the Use of Force in International Politics*, Contemporary Security Studies. London: Routledge Ltd.

Brown, Michael E. 1999. Minimalist NATO: A Wise Alliance Knows When to Retrench. *Foreign Affairs* 78 (3): 204–218.

Brown, Seyom. 2015. The Just War Tradition. In *The Use of Force: Military Power and International Politics*, ed. Robert J. Art and Kelly M. Greenhill, 8th ed. Lanham: Rowman & Littlefield Publishing Group, Inc.

Cahen, Alfred. 1989. *The Western European Union and NATO*. McLean: Brassey's Ltd.

Crotty, William J. 1995. *Post-Cold War Policy*. Chicago: Nelson-Hall.

Daalder, Ivo H., and James Goldgeier. 2006. Global NATO. *Foreign Affairs* 85 (5): 105–113.

Davidson, Jason. 2011. *America's Allies and War*. New York: Palgrave Macmillan.

Deudney, Daniel, and G. John Ikenberry. 1999. The Nature and Sources of Liberal International Order. *Review of International Studies* 25 (2): 179–196.

Duffield, John S. 1994. NATO's Functions After the Cold War. *Political Science Quarterly* 109 (5): 763–787.

———. 2001. Transatlantic Relations After the Cold War: Theory, Evidence, and the Future. *International Studies Perspectives* 2 (1): 93–115.

Gelpi, Christopher. 1999. Alliances as Instruments of Intra-Allied Control. In *Imperfect Unions: Security Institutions over Time and Space*, ed. Helga Haftendorn, Robert Keohane, and Celeste Wallander. Oxford: Oxford University Press.

Gordon, Philip H. 1997. *NATO's Transformation: The Changing Shape of the Alliance*. Lanham: Rowman & Littlefield Publishers.

Gordon, Phillip H. 2002. NATO and the War on Terrorism a Changing Alliance. *The Brookings Review* 20 (3): 36–38.

Gordon, Philip, and Jeremy Shapiro. 2004. *Allies at War: America, Europe, and the Crisis over Iraq*. New York: McGraw Hill.

Hallams, Ellen. 2009. The Transatlantic Alliance Renewed: The United States and NATO Since 9/11. *Journal of Transatlantic Studies* 7 (1): 38–60.

Holsti, Ole R., Philip Terrence Hopmann, and John D. Sullivan. 1973. *Unity and Disintegration in International Alliances.* New York: Wiley.

Howard, Michael. 1999. An Unhappy Successful Marriage: Security Means Knowing What to Expect. *Foreign Affairs* 78 (3): 164–175.

Jervis, Robert. 2002. Theories of War in an Era of Leading-Power Peace Presidential Address, American Political Science Association, 2001. *American Political Science Review* 96 (1): 1–14.

Jones, Philip. 2007. Colluding Victims: A Public Choice Analysis of International Alliances. *Public Choice* 132 (3/4): 319–332.

Keohane, Robert O. 1989. *International Institutions and State Power.* Boulder: Westview Press.

———. 1990. Multilateralism: An Agenda for Research. *International Journal* 45 (4): 731–764.

———. 2002. Institutional Theory in International Relations. In *Realism and Institutionalism in International Studies,* ed. Michael Brecher and Frank P. Harvey. Ann Arbor: University of Michigan Press.

Klein, Bradley S. 1990. How the West Was One: Representational Politics of NATO. *International Studies Quarterly* 34 (3): 311–325.

Laird, Robbin F. 1991. *The Europeanization of the Alliance.* Boulder: Westview Press.

Lansford, Tom. 2012. *9/11 and the Wars in Afghanistan and Iraq.* Santa Barbara: ABC-CLIO.

Leeds, B.A. 2003. Do Alliances Deter Aggression? The Influence of Military Alliances on the Initiation of Militarized Interstate Disputes. *American Journal of Political Science* 47 (3): 427–439.

Levi, Margaret. 1997. A Model, a Method, and a Map: Rational Choice in Comparative and Historical Analysis. In *Comparative Politics: Rationality, Culture, and Structure,* ed. Mark Lichbach and Alan Zuckerman. Cambridge: Cambridge University Press.

Mattox, Gale. 1999. NATO Enlargement and the United States: A Deliberate and Necessary Division? In *The Future of NATO: Enlargement, Russia, and European Security,* ed. Charles-Philippe David and Jack Lévesque. Ithaca: McGill-Queen's University Press.

McCalla, Robert B. 1996. NATO's Persistence After the Cold War. *International Organization* 50 (3): 445–475.

Morgenthau, Hans J. 1954. *Politics Among Nations: The Struggle for Power and Peace.* New York: Knopf.

Morrow, James D. 1991. Alliances and Asymmetry: An Alternative to the Capability Aggregation Model of Alliances. *American Journal of Political Science* 35 (4): 285–306.

Mowle, Thomas S., and David H. Sacko. 2007. Global NATO: Bandwagoning in a Unipolar World. *Contemporary Security Policy* 28 (3): 597–618.

NATO. Operational Media Update: NATO and Libya. Last Modified Oct 31, 2011. http://www.nato.int/cps/en/natohq/news_71994.htm. Accessed 9 Apr 2015.

———. NATO and Libya: Operation Unified Protector. Last Modified Mar 27, 2012. http://www.nato.int/cps/en/natolive/71679.htm. Accessed 6 Sept 2017.

Pierson, Paul. 2000. Increasing Returns, Path Dependence, and the Study of Politics. *The American Political Science Review* 94 (2): 251–267.

Rhodes, Matthew. 2012. US Perspectives on NATO. In *Understanding NATO in the 21st Century*, ed. Graeme P. Herd and John Kriendler. New York: Routledge.

Risse-Kappen, Thomas. 1995. *Cooperation Among Democracies: The European Influence on US Foreign Policy*. Princeton: Princeton University Press.

Sandler, Todd, and James C. Murdoch. 2000. On Sharing NATO Defence Burdens in the 1990s and Beyond. *Fiscal Studies* 21 (3): 297–328.

Sjursen, Helene. 2004. On the Identity of NATO. *International Affairs (Royal Institute of International Affairs)* 80 (4): 687–704.

Sloan, Stanley R. 1985. Managing the NATO Alliance: Congress and Burdensharing. *Journal of Policy Analysis and Management* 4 (3): 396–406.

Sprecher, Christopher, and Volker Krause. 2006. Alliances, Armed Conflict, and Cooperation: Theoretical Approaches and Empirical Evidence. *Journal of Peace Research* 43 (4): 363–369.

Talbott, Strobe. 2002. From Prague to Baghdad: NATO at Risk. *Foreign Affairs* 81: 46–57.

Thies, Wallace J. 2009. *Why NATO Endures*. New York: Cambridge University Press.

Van Heuven, Marten. 2001. *NATO and Europe: Equality or a More Balanced Partnership?* Arlington: RAND Corporation.

Vincent, Jack E., Ira L. Straus, and Richard R. Biondi. 2001. Capability Theory and the Future of NATO's Decisionmaking Rules. *Journal of Peace Research* 38 (1): 67–86.

Wallander, Celeste A. 2000. Institutional Assets and Adaptability: NATO After the Cold War. *International Organization* 54 (4): 705–735.

Walt, Stephen. 1987. *The Origins of Alliances*. Ithaca: Cornell University Press.

Waltz, Kenneth N. 1986. Anarchic Orders and the Balances of Power. In *Neorealism and Its Critics*, ed. Robert Keohane, 98–130. New York: Columbia University Press.

Weitsman, Patricia A. 2004. *Dangerous Alliances: Proponents of Peace, Weapons of War*. Stanford: Stanford University Press.

Williams, Ellen. 2008. Out of Area and Very Much in Business? NATO, the U.S., and the Post-9/11 International Security Environment. *Comparative Strategy* 27 (1): 65–78.

CHAPTER 3

The 1999 Kosovo Intervention

At the end of the Cold War, the North Atlantic Treaty Organization (NATO) lacked an explicit purpose for keeping the allies together: while threats to European security persisted, the collapse of the Soviet Union meant there was no major power for the alliance to balance against. As demonstrated in the previous chapter, some scholars and policymakers believed the alliance would dissolve in the Soviet Union's absence. Alliance leaders also struggled to understand what role NATO would play in this new environment. Conflict in the Balkans posed serious challenges for American foreign policymakers, but provided an opportunity to strengthen the United States' relationship with the NATO alliance and pursue its goals in the post-Cold War environment. The 1999 Kosovo operation, Operation Allied Force (OAF), allowed the allies to realize the utility of maintaining the alliance, as well as the challenges associated with changing perceptions of European security at the end of the Cold War.

The following chapter details the circumstances leading up to and developments during the 1999 intervention in Kosovo. Although OAF was the first major NATO operation in the post-Cold War period, it was not the alliance's first foray in the Balkans region: in the 1992–1995 war in Bosnia, the United States and NATO coordinated a two-week aerial campaign known as Operation Deliberate Force (ODF). ODF was a key force in bringing the conflicting parties, including Serbian leader Slobodan Milosevic, to the table to negotiate a peaceful settlement of the disputed Bosnian state. The military and political outcomes of ODF, briefly revisited

© The Author(s) 2020   43
J. Garey, *The US Role in NATO's Survival After the Cold War*,
Palgrave Studies in International Relations,
https://doi.org/10.1007/978-3-030-13675-8_3

in the following background section, set a precedent for the 1999 Kosovo intervention, which is divided into three phases in this chapter. The prewar phase began with the Drenica massacres in February and March 1998. The conflict phase addresses the period from March 24, 1999, to June 10, 1999, which were the dates of the NATO Operation Allied Force (OAF). Finally, I address the post-conflict phase, including the stabilization and reconstruction effort known as Kosovo Force (KFOR).

Examination of each of these three phases illustrates several key components of US-NATO relations during the Kosovo conflict, as well as the impacts of the conflict on the NATO alliance. As the case of Kosovo demonstrates, the United States pursued NATO participation for political, military, and legal reasons. These motivations are consistent with hypotheses regarding the importance of NATO to the United States. Despite the Clinton administration's reluctance to engage in the Balkans conflicts—both the war in Bosnia and the Kosovo conflict—the United States exerted a tremendous amount of influence on the alliance's strategy for OAF, confirming the United States' belief in the utility of NATO. As OAF operations progressed, policymakers used America's leadership in Kosovo to pressure the allies to improve their military capabilities and alliance contributions. This is consistent with the hypothesis that US policymakers use the United States' status in the alliance to its advantage—in this case study, the motivation for exerting pressure on the other allies came from both operational needs in Kosovo and for future engagements. Because the UN Security Council (UNSC) failed to pass a resolution authorizing a direct intervention, the United States and its European allies sought legitimization through alternative channels, including NATO. Many allies hoped the Kosovo operation would force a change to the international norms regarding intervention in ethnic conflicts. Executing the operation through the NATO alliance conferred retrospective legitimacy on the intervention—in the years following, Kosovo operations were deemed by much of the international community to be "illegal but legitimate."

BACKGROUND: OPERATION DELIBERATE FORCE AND PREPARING FOR INTERVENTION IN KOSOVO

The history of conflict in Kosovo spans centuries and results from religious, cultural, and ethnic divisions endemic to the entire Balkan region. The historical legacy of Kosovo underlined what happened leading up to the 1999 NATO intervention, but it was the death of authoritarian leader Josip Tito that opened the door for war in the Balkans. When Tito died in 1980, authority in the Social Federalist Republic of Yugoslavia (SFRY) was dispersed to regional leaders in each of Yugoslavia's eight provinces, as per the 1974 constitution, precipitating the rise of Slobodan Milosevic. In 1989, Milosevic was elected president and quickly moved to strip Kosovo of its autonomy, decree it subject to the authority of the Serbian government in Belgrade, and institute discriminatory measures against Albanian Kosovars. These efforts allowed Milosevic to fulfill his campaign promises and consolidate power in Belgrade (U.S. Department of State 2015b).

In 1991, the SFRY disintegrated when amidst political, economic, and ethnic conflict both Croatia and Slovenia declared independence, followed soon thereafter by Serbia. These declarations resulted in violence and conflict throughout the region, but inspired the remaining provinces to follow suit. In early 1992, Bosnia declared its independence, and the violence escalated between Serbians, Croats, and Bosnian Muslims. War broke out as the Croats pushed to integrate Bosnia into Croatia, Bosnian Muslims fought for an independent Bosnian state, and Serbians fought to retain Bosnia as part of a greater Yugoslav regime. Milosevic supported the Serbian effort by instituting policies aimed at ethnic cleansing, forcing thousands of Muslims from their homes and sparking the Bosnian War (BBC 2006; Lambeth 2001; PBS 2018; U.S. Department of State 2015b).

The American response to the dissolution of the SFRY, the war in Bosnia, the oppressive regime of Slobodan Milosevic, and increasing violence in Kosovo was inconsistent throughout two different presidential administrations. Under the George H.W. Bush administration, the United States' foreign policy objectives centered on the dissolution of the Soviet Union, the reunification of Germany, and the establishment of a new world order. The United States' military operations were aimed primarily toward the Middle East, where Iraq's 1990 invasion of Kuwait sparked the Persian Gulf War. Because of this, the United States' focus on the independence movements in the SFRY was minimal. When the violence erupted in Bosnia in 1992, the United States hoped its Western European allies would demonstrate their ability to act without the leadership or participation of the United States. The allies, however, saw the Balkans conflict as a civil war and believed the most effective solution was to act as neutral parties in support of the UN's humanitarian missions. Thus, France, Great Britain, Germany, and others refrained from intervention even as the violence escalated (Kaplan 2004).

When President Clinton took office in 1993, the issues of the Balkans—including Kosovo's autonomy—posed significant challenges for the new administration. During the presidential campaign, Clinton was vocal of his support for the Muslim population in Bosnia (Kaplan 2004; PBS 2018). In the post-Cold War era, the United States was more willing to consider using force abroad, and President H.W. Bush's deployments of troops to Panama and the Persian Gulf set a precedent for US intervention. As violence in the Balkans escalated, the American and European presses inundated the public with images of ethnic cleansing in Bosnia (Allin 2002). Members of the Clinton administration were divided on the appropriate response—while US Ambassador to the United Nations Madeleine Albright vehemently advocated for some kind of humanitarian intervention, military advisors in the Department of Defense were concerned about the possibility of a long-term commitment (U.S. Department of State 2013).

President Clinton himself was reticent to intervene militarily, and his administration looked for nonintervention strategies to maximize the likelihood of peace in Bosnia while minimizing the threat to American forces. The administration also continued to advocate a "lift and strike" policy to remove the arms embargo against the SFRY and allow separatist fighters access to weapons, then support the newly armed fighters with aerial strikes. However, this plan was not well received by the United States' allies—particularly France and Great Britain—who did not want to lift the UN Security Council's arms embargo or commit troops for any kind of engagement outside of supporting the UN's mission (Allin 2002; Kaplan 2004; Wallack 2006).

The escalating violence in Bosnia in late 1994 forced the Clinton administration to reconsider its willingness to engage in the Balkans and cooperate with its allies. The US assisted NATO's no-fly and safe zone missions over Bosnia, as well as its limited airstrikes against Bosnian Serbs in November 1994. The Serbs retaliated against the NATO airstrikes by attacking UN forces on several occasions and continued its campaign against Bosnian Muslims (U.S. Department of State 2013). In December, the United States pledged to deploy up to 25,000 ground troops in support of the UN mission. The violence in Bosnia continued, however, and in July 1995 the Serbs attempted to capture the city of Srebrenica. When met with resistance from locals, the Serbian forces massacred thousands of Muslims. This was a turning point for the United States and its allies, and after a conference of the NATO ministers in London, the allies agreed to conduct airstrikes in order to stymie the Serbs' advances and protect the UN-designated safe zone cities (Owen 2001; Wallack 2006). On August 25, 1995, NATO launched Operation Deliberate Force (ODF), led by the United States. The operation consisted of 12 days of intensive aerial strikes against the Serbs and finally brought all of the parties to the negotiating table for peace talks (Owen 2001; Wallack 2006; U.S. Department of State 2013; Kaplan 2004).

In addition to its participation in the military operation, the United States led the diplomatic efforts in 1994 and 1995. In 1994, the United States spearheaded the creation of the Contact Group, bringing together the major Western allies and Russia to address the violence. Richard Holbrooke, US Assistant Secretary of State for European and Eurasian Affairs, became the point person in the peace process during Operation Deliberate Force. By the time the major parties in the war—representatives from Bosnia and Herzegovina, Croatia, Serbia, members of the Contact Group nations (the United States, Britain, France, Germany, and Russia), and European Union (EU) officials—convened, the situation in the Balkans was so dire that negotiators did not believe the Kosovo issue could be resolved. In order to get the necessary concessions from Milosevic, American negotiator Richard Holbrooke was forced to abandon any real discussion on Kosovo for the sake of reaching a settlement (Daalder and O'Hanlon 2000; Weller 1999). Holbrooke was largely credited for the success of the negotiations leading to the November 1995 signing of the Dayton Peace Accords (Kaplan 2004).

Though the Dayton Accords effectively ended the Bosnian War, it did little to end Milosevic's reign in Kosovo. Changes to the international landscape, the dissolution of the SFRY, and the war in Bosnia affected Kosovo in a number of ways. Motivated by the independence votes in Croatia and Slovenia, ethnic Albanians in Kosovo staged a secret ballot for independence in 1991. The international community, however, was reticent to recognize Kosovo as more than an autonomous region with the right for self-governance conferred by the 1974 constitution. International actors such as the UN and the Organization for Security and Cooperation in Europe (OSCE) pushed Milosevic to reinstate Kosovo's autonomy and hoped it would lead to a recognition of the 1991 vote for sovereignty. As the war waged on in Bosnia and Milosevic continued his ethnic cleansing campaign throughout the region, Kosovo's claim to self-governance and independence was pushed aside on the international political agenda. When the war in Bosnia ended, the Milosevic regime refocused its attention on Kosovo, where Rugova and the Democratic League of Kosovo (LDK) were establishing an independent Kosovo government. When Serbian authorities became more aggressive toward the ethnic Albanian population, the LDK's policies of nonviolence could not successfully address the continued attacks and the Albanian population grew increasingly unsupportive of the LDK. This gave rise to a number of separatist groups willing to engage in violent counterattacks against the authorities (Wintz 2010). As the separatist movement grew, several of these groups united under the flag of the Kosovo Liberation Army (KLA) began carrying out guerilla attacks.

The Contact Group was successful in negotiating a peace settlement for Bosnia at the Dayton conference, but the conflict between the Belgrade government and ethnic Albanians in Kosovo continued unabated. The previous H.W. Bush administration had done very little to stop the campaign against ethnic Albanians in Kosovo and, as previously demonstrated, Holbrooke and other key members of the Clinton administration felt peaceful settlement of the Bosnian War was more imperative and too dependent on Milosevic's cooperation to broach the issue of Kosovo. After the Dayton agreement, instead of looking toward Kosovo Clinton turned his attention away from the Balkans and back to domestic issues as Republicans gained control of both houses of Congress.

In 1996, Clinton selected UN Ambassador Madeleine Albright to replace Warren Christopher as Secretary of State. Secretary Albright, who had vehemently supported Bosnian intervention as UN Ambassador, began pushing for US leadership in addressing the violence in Kosovo (Wallack 2006). Other political leaders posited the Kosovo conflict as outside the United States' vital interests, and they hoped the European allies would take responsibility for stability in the former Yugoslavia. President Clinton maintained the United States was only prepared to use airpower—not ground forces—should it intervene in the Balkans again, and despite domestic discontent with his leadership on other foreign policy issues (e.g. inaction in Rwanda), held his position even as hostility in Kosovo escalated (Kupchan 2000; Weitsman 2014).

In February 1998, Serbian attacks on two towns—one in Prekaz, which left 58 people dead, and the other in Qirez and Likosane, in which over two dozen people were killed—drastically escalated hostilities between the Serbians and the LDK and KLA (Independent International Commission on Kosovo 2000; Daalder and O'Hanlon 2000). The Serbian authorities justified the attacks as a response to "a terrorist organization," but the high numbers of women and children killed mobilized the Kosovar population to throw even more support behind the KLA (Ibid.; Bjola 2009). The attacks also prompted the international community to once again begin preparing for a possible war in the Balkans.

International and NATO Response to Conflict in the Balkans

The United States' role in Bosnia is well understood; the international community, less so. Often dismissed as negligent inaction and characterized by its post hoc legitimation of American and European actions, a more nuanced analysis reveals how division between the United Nations and NATO hindered a timely and effective response. Instability in the SFRY posed a direct threat to European stability, but the United Nations was undecided on the appropriate response to Milosevic's increasing aggressiveness.

The UN Protection Force (UNPROFOR) peacekeeping mission in Yugoslavia, established in 1992 under UN Security Council resolution (UNSCR) 721, was comprised of nearly 39,000 military personnel, as well as civilian police, international civilian staff, and local staff, and was the largest peacekeeping operation in the UN's history. Of the 37 participating states, 11 were NATO members. However, the UN Security Council's membership led to disagreement over the appropriateness of further intervention in Bosnia and later Kosovo. UNSC members quickly recognized Croatia and Slovenia as independent states in early 1992, four months before the United States and five months before the United Nations (UNSCR 753 1992). They also recognized Bosnia and Herzegovina's independence in April 1992 (Reuters 2008). Despite their eagerness to recognize the newly independent states, the United Kingdom was reluctant to send troops for the UN missions. France was one of the most active contributors to the UN relief mission, but French President François Mitterrand was adamant that French troops would not be used for anything other than the provision of humanitarian aid. Neither the French nor the British supported the United States' call to lift the arms embargo against Bosnia or its "lift and strike" strategy (Allin 2002; Karadis 2000; Riding 1992).

When the Bosnian Serbs began attacking the UN-designated "safe zones," UNPROFOR troops were targeted. Though they were authorized to use force in self-defense, fighting back against the Bosnian Serbs threatened their credibility as a neutral peacekeeper. The United States urged the UN to strike back, but the European allies—especially those who had contributed ground troops to the UNPROFOR mission—did not support the United States' insistence on the use of force (Daalder 1998; United Nations Department of Public Information 1996).

Thus, the UN's ability to respond to the conflict in Yugoslavia, first in Bosnia and later in Kosovo, was further hampered by divergent perspectives among Security Council members. Though they mostly agreed the UN had some responsibility to the citizens of the SFRY, there was widespread disagreement as to the nature of UN intervention and unwillingness by some to contribute the resources necessary for a full-scale military or peacekeeping operation. Russia was a principal member of the Contact Group and President Boris Yeltsin continually reiterated Russia's support of UN peacekeeping and humanitarian operations in Bosnia (U.S. Department of State 2015c). But he struggled to reconcile Russia's commitments to the international community with concerns over the possibility that a Bosnian intervention could set a precedent for UN intervention in its own conflicts, such as the ongoing tensions in Chechnya. Russia continually clashed with both the United States and European states over their policies toward the Balkans, arguing the West was displaying favoritism for the Muslim population. Its shared history with the Orthodox Christians in the region led it to side with the Serbians (Cohen 1994).

In addition to the UN's efforts, NATO also enacted measures to stem the conflict in the SFRY. NATO's involvement in the former Yugoslavia—both in the Bosnian conflict and Kosovo in 1999—was slow to take shape and caused friction between the allies. Ultimately, its execution of Operation Deliberate Force was integral to ending the war in Bosnia and setting a precedent for Operation Allied Force (OAF) in Kosovo. NATO began very limited operations in June 1992, focusing solely on supporting the UN's peacekeeping mission under UNSCRs 713, 757, and 781. In 1993, NATO enforced a no-fly zone over Bosnia and Herzegovina, and in February 1994, it engaged four warplanes violating the no-fly zone (NATO 2014). Though the alliance was tasked with providing the necessary protection for UNPROFOR troops, the allies could not reach a consensus over how to respond to attacks on the UN-designated safe zones. The United States pushed its unpopular "lift and strike" strategy while allies Canada, France, and the United Kingdom worried about the potential backlash of a NATO operation on its deployed UNPROFOR troops. NATO's indecisiveness sent a message to Milosevic that the United States, the UN, and NATO were not united in their decision-making, which only further encouraged attacks against the safe zones (Hendrickson 2000, 2005).

Though it executed limited airstrikes against the Serbs in November 1994 and May 1995, the Srebrenica massacre forced the alliance to take a more active role in conducting airstrikes. On August 30, 1995, two days after an attack on Saravejo that killed 38 civilians, NATO launched Operation Deliberate Force. France, Germany, Great Britain, Italy, the Netherlands, Spain, Turkey, and the United States all contributed combat support and aircraft for the two-week Operation Deliberate Force (Owen 2001). The operation bolstered Holbrooke's negotiations at Dayton, and once the peace settlement was reached, the UNSC passed Resolution 1031, establishing the framework for the NATO-led Implementation Force (IFOR). IFOR oversaw the transfer of territories and other military aspects of the peace agreement until UNSCR 1088, which created its successor the Stabilization Force (SFOR) (NATO 2014).

The events that occurred in the early- to mid-1990s in the Balkans—and, in particular, the Bosnian intervention—set a number of precedents for intervention in Kosovo. Disagreement between the European allies led to the European Union's inability to manage threats to European stability and security (Deighton 2000). NATO intervention also signaled to the EU that a European security mechanism without US participation and leadership, which some member states advocated for in the post-Cold War period, was unfeasible (Ibid.). Some argued that the Bosnian operation breathed life into the alliance: after the collapse of the Soviet Union, NATO had to either reinvent itself or become irrelevant (Allin 2002). However, NATO's future role in the Balkans was uncertain, as the Clinton administration only reluctantly intervened in Bosnia when the possibility of a sustained ethnic cleansing campaign became evident. Clinton's reluctance to commit to a ground war in Bosnia also indicated to Milosevic that the United States would likely be reluctant to intervene in Kosovo or elsewhere in the Balkans (Norris 2005). Last, the Clinton administration believed another humanitarian intervention in the Balkans that was limited to airstrikes would be just as successful as Operation Deliberate Force (Dunn 2009).

RETURN TO THE BALKANS: PRE-WAR PLANNING

Unlike the interventions in Afghanistan and Iraq, the United States did not spearhead the initial campaign for intervention in Kosovo in 1998–1999. In its recognition of Slovenia, Croatia, and Bosnia and Herzegovina sovereignty, the United States did not acknowledge the status of Kosovo or recognize its 1991 secret ballot, much like the rest of the international community. However, in late 1992, President Bush addressed the issue of Kosovo in a private letter to Milosevic. "In the event of conflict in Kosovo caused by Serbian action, the United States will be prepared to employ military force against the Serbians in Kosovo and in Serbia proper" (The New York Times 1999). President Bush's threat of US intervention became known as the Christmas Warning and was reiterated by both President Clinton and officials in his administration in the years leading up to the 1999 intervention.

The Clinton administration was willing to use force for a humanitarian mission in Kosovo as it had in the earlier Balkans campaign, but was adamant in its unwillingness to commit ground forces. Clinton and his advisors believed that airstrikes would be sufficient and less costly politically (Dunn 2009). Writes John Norris, "The Clinton administration's faith in air power reflected the American public's ambivalence toward the war. While most Americans found Milosevic despicable, they were less certain dealing with him should fall to the United States. Clinton's approach was measured, incremental, and fundamentally cautious (Norris 2005)." Members from both political parties insisted Kosovo was not a "vital interest" of the United States and thus Europe should be tasked with taking control of any operation to end the conflict (Kupchan 2000).

The United States and its NATO allies also faced another major obstacle in formulating a Kosovo intervention: there was no UN Security Council resolution authorizing an intervention. Though there were several resolutions condemning the actions of Milosevic, none of the resolutions expressly authorized the use of force due in large part to Russia and China's threat of veto for any authorization of international intervention. After the Bosnian peace settlement, Russia's relationships with the Western allies deteriorated further as it faced domestic political turmoil, economic crises, and continued ethnic conflict. As NATO pushed eastward, extending membership to three former Soviet satellite states—Poland, Hungary, and the Czech Republic—in 1997, Russia struggled to regain its international political capital in the United Nations. President Yeltsin saw the Kosovo debate as an opportunity to improve its international reputation and ensure its influence on global politics (Norris 2005; U.S. Department of State 2015a). Though Clinton and Yeltsin's working relationship was much improved from US-Soviet relations during the Cold War, NATO's intervention in Bosnia increased tension between the two states. As demonstrated earlier, Russia struggled with how to address the Balkans conflicts: while it was a principal member of the Contact Group and held discussions with Milosevic on behalf of the international community, its shared history with the Orthodox Christian population and concern over a possible precedent for intervention in its own disputed territories led Yeltsin to oppose NATO airstrikes.

Additionally, NATO's earlier intervention in Bosnia demonstrated to the United States a growing capabilities gap between the United States and its allies, and an inability by the European Union (or any other non-US involved organization) to act effectively. The United States provided more than 50 percent of the aircraft used in NATO's Bosnia operation, Operation Deliberate Force, and only three other allies—Great Britain, France, and Spain—deployed precision munitions. Additionally, ODF sparked tension between the allies regarding US leadership of the operation and decision-making at the operational and tactical level (Owen 2001; Cimbala and Forster 2005). Despite a declaration of ODF's success, it was the diplomatic efforts that had a greater impact on the outcome of the Dayton Peace Accords—the mission only bolstered Holbrooke's ability to negotiate (Daalder 1998).

However, a number of factors influenced the United States to lead the negotiations in the pre-war phase and eventually make a substantial contribution to Operation Allied Force. As Michael Wallack writes,

Clinton did not come into office with a policy of using force against Serbia. After Dayton, however, the enthusiasm of Secretary of State Albright and NATO's Supreme Allied Commander Wesley Clark for using compellence against Milosevic, as well as the willingness of the new Secretary of Defense William Perry, and the new Chair of the JCS [Joint Chiefs of Staff] John Shalikashvili to use force in the Balkans – particularly air power and precision weapons – together with the distraction of Congress in the midst of the Clinton impeachment, combined to make a new policy possible. (Wallack 2006)

The success of Holbrooke and the Dayton negotiations also led Clinton to believe that if NATO and the United States made a credible threat, Milosevic would be deterred in continuing to attack Kosovar Albanians (Weller 1999). However, to appease his political opposition, Clinton refused to commit ground troops, authorizing only an air campaign and repeatedly refusing to engage in a ground war (Kupchan 2000).

Conflict in Kosovo began before the breakup of the SFRY, but an escalation of violence in February and March 1998 by the Serbian authorities marked a turning point. After the Bosnian peace settlement, Milosevic was concerned about additional threats from other groups seeking autonomy and ordered a crackdown on Kosovo. Milosevic sought to reignite nationalist sentiment among the Serbians while the Belgrade government continued to enact discriminatory policies directed toward ethnic Albanians. President Clinton received intelligence regarding the crackdown and the buildup of Serb forces around Kosovo in January and February 1998. For many, the February 1998 attack in the Drenica region in which 80 civilian Albanians were killed denoted the beginning of the full-scale conflict necessitating international attention and possibly intervention. In late February, the administration sent Robert Gelbard, senior envoy for the region, to Belgrade to warn both sides against escalating violence. When word of the Drenica massacre reached the United States, Secretary Albright traveled to Europe to initiate action by the Contact Group. Albright emphasized the necessity of a unified response, and the other Contact Group members largely agreed (Daalder and O'Hanlon 2000).

On March 9, the Contact Group issued a condemnation of Milosevic's strikes in Drenica. The Contact Group's statement formed the foundation for UNSCR 1160 (Bjola 2009). Resolution 1160, adopted on March 31, urged the SFRY with the Kosovar Albanians to reach a political solution, expressed support for "an enhanced status for Kosovo which would include a substantially greater degree of autonomy and meaningful self-administration," and established the arms embargo suggested by the earlier Contact Group statement (UNSCR 1160 1998a). In late April, the United States and its European allies agreed to implement new measures against the Serbian government, including a freeze on Serb funds and a ban on new investments (Daalder and O'Hanlon 2000).

In the summer of 1998, the United States and its allies began contingency planning in the event that the situation in Kosovo worsened. In May, the NATO foreign ministers met in Luxembourg, and shortly thereafter announced that the alliance was commissioning military advice on how to support the UN and OSCE monitoring of Albania and Macedonia— two states that, in addition to their own domestic issues and ethnic tensions, could be destabilized by a heavy flow of Kosovar refugees if fighting escalated. Negotiations between two US officials, US ambassador Christopher Hill and special envoy leader Richard Holbrooke, and the Belgrade government led to the first-ever meeting between President Milosevic and the unofficial president of Kosovo, Ibrahim Rugova, on May 15, 1998. But the talks broke down quickly, as no settlement could be reached regarding the political solution for Kosovo (Daalder and O'Hanlon 2000; Bjola 2009, PBS 2018).

As a result of the continued violence, the United States developed several plans for air operations over Serbia in June and July 1998. The first operation, Operation Nimble Lion, targeted some 250 sites with the United States and allied aircraft. Two more operations, Operation Flexible Anvil and Operation Sky Anvil, were developed as joint task force (JTF) efforts. These plans were placed on temporary hold in the fall of 1998 when Holbrooke successfully negotiated a ceasefire, but later became the basis for NATO's Kosovo operations planning (Lambeth 2001). Publicly, US defense officials continued to refute claims that an intervention was imminent (Daalder and O'Hanlon 2000).

In June, while US and NATO officials continued to explore their options, Russian President Boris Yeltsin met with President Milosevic and convinced him to allow international observers and humanitarian organizations to monitor human rights conditions in Kosovo (Bjola 2009). A lull in strikes initiated by the Serbian authorities was perceived as an opportunity for the KLA, who intensified its attacks and raised concerns for the rest of the international community about how an intervention could strengthen the KLA and actually escalate the conflict. In response to the increased KLA attacks, Belgrade ordered a major offensive in late July that, when completed, destroyed thousands of homes, and displaced nearly 250,000 Kosovar civilians (Daalder and O'Hanlon 2000).

Talks between Ambassador Hill, Holbrooke, President Milosevic, and Kosovo leader Rugova continued into the fall. In early September, Ambassador Hill announced that Milosevic and Rugova agreed to negotiate a temporary settlement for Kosovo. However, the KLA, perceiving Rugova to be too pacifistic to effectively counter the brutal attacks against Kosovars, was dissatisfied with the temporary arrangement. It wanted a final decision regarding Kosovo to be made as soon as possible, much sooner than the 3–5 years allowed under the agreement (Ibid.). Thus, violence between the Serbian authorities and the KLA continued.

On September 23, 1998, the Security Council passed another resolution regarding Kosovo. Sparked by humanitarian concerns regarding the growing number of civilian casualties and the flow of refugees into Albania, Bosnia, and other European nations, UNSCR 1199 demanded a ceasefire, called all parties back to the negotiating table, and insisted on the safe return of the refugees. The resolution also urged states to "make available personnel to fulfill the responsibility of carrying out effective and continuous international monitoring in Kosovo until all of this resolution and those of resolution 1160 (1998) are achieved" and asked them to continue providing humanitarian resources, but did not explicitly authorize an intervention or the use of force (UNSCR 1199 1998b). Nonetheless, the United States and its European allies continued planning for a possible NATO mission. The day after the Security Council approved UNSCR 1199 the North Atlantic Council (NAC) issued an activation warning (ACTWARN), allowing NATO's military commanders to prepare both a limited air option and a phased air campaign, and identify what resources would be necessary for either operation. The statement issued by NATO Secretary General Javier Solana also expressed NATO's explicit support UNSCR 1199 (NATO 1998). US Secretary of Defense William Cohen reaffirmed Secretary General Solana's statements regarding the importance of NATO action to protect innocent Kosovars and uphold NATO's credibility if the use of force became necessary (Daalder and O'Hanlon 2000).

Within days of UNSCR 1199 and the NATO ACTWARN, reports of another massacre by Serb forces surfaced. Twenty-one women, children, and elderly civilians were killed in a September 29 attack on Gornji Obrinje, while another 13 from a neighboring village were also killed (Ibid.). This attack, paired with concerns about returning the refugees to their homes before the harsh winter, prompted the Balkans envoy led by Holbrooke to travel to Belgrade for further negotiations with Milosevic. In support of the envoy, the NAC issued an activation order (ACTORD), giving the Secretary General the authority to launch airstrikes. Holbrooke's negotiations led to the "October Agreement," under which President Milosevic agreed to allow 2000 unarmed OSCE observers to monitor a ceasefire and a noncombatant, NATO-led aerial observation operation (Hendrickson 2000). Though NATO upheld its ACTORD, it agreed to allow Milosevic more time to meet the terms of the agreement, with a firm deadline of October 27, 1998.

On October 24, the Security Council passed another resolution, UNSCR 1203, which endorsed the October Agreement and demanded Milosevic's compliance with the agreement and the earlier Security Council resolutions. Out of concern that the resolution would be seen as an endorsement for the use of force, and per the objections of Russia and China, the resolution was vague and included no mention of what would happen if Milosevic did not comply. France, the United Kingdom, and the

United States asserted that the resolution did not explicitly address the use of force but it did allow for the enforcement of the ceasefire and the protection of civilians in and around Kosovo. In addition to the dispute over intervention, the resolution was problematic in that it did not address the possibility that if the Serbian authorities obeyed the ceasefire, the KLA might try to take advantage (Ibid.; Bjola 2009).

Despite the actions of the United Nations, the special envoy led by Holbrooke, and NATO, the violence in Kosovo persisted through the end of 1998 and into 1999. On January 15, 1999, Serb security forces attacked the Albanians in Račak in retaliation for an earlier attack that killed four policemen. Journalists in the area later discovered the bodies of 45 civilians executed at close range by the Serbian forces. The authorities defended its actions as necessary to defeat the "terrorist" KLA, but the attacks were carried out against civilian areas, not KLA strongholds (Weller 1999).

The Račak massacre marked another turning point for the Kosovo conflict. Milosevic quickly ordered the OSCE monitors to leave the country after the director of the mission, American Ambassador William Walker, publicly blamed Serbia for the attack. Milosevic also refused a visit from International Criminal Tribunal for the former Yugoslavia (ICTY) prosecutor Judge Louise Arbour to investigate possible war crimes (PBS 2018). In response to Račak, US officials urged NATO to respond, prompting a meeting between NATO Supreme Allied Commander Europe (SACEUR) General Wesley Clark, NATO military council chairman Klaus Naumann, and President Milosevic. In late January 1999, NATO issued a "solemn warning" to the leadership of both sides warning that continued hostilities would result in NATO action and demanding that both the KLA and the Belgrade government work with the Contact Group to reach a political settlement. The Contact Group also met and issued a statement and summoning the groups to meet in Rambouillet, France, by February 6. Following the Contact Group's statement, NATO issued a second statement that Secretary General Solana was authorized to initiate airstrikes if the parties did not agree to meet at the Rambouillet Conference and the violence continued (Weller 1999).

On February 6, 1999, the Rambouillet Conference began under rules established by the Contact Group. After several extensions and weeks of negotiations, the Kosovo delegation accepted the final draft of the peace settlement and confirmed it would sign the document. However, the Serbian delegation did not agree that the negotiations were complete and would not agree to the settlement in its entirety. They did, however, agree to reconvene in Paris on March 15 to discuss the settlement further (Ibid.). During the break in negotiations, the Belgrade government deployed additional troops in and around Kosovo. When the talks resumed in Paris on March 15, the Kosovo delegation indicated its willingness to sign the agreement, but the Serb delegation continued to refuse and instead offered a counterproposal. On March 18, Serbian forces began conducting "winter live fire" exercises in Kosovo using the previously deployed troops. This prompted Holbrooke and other negotiators to return to Belgrade in the hopes they could convince Milosevic to stop the exercises and accept the Rambouillet agreement. Several Western states closed their embassies in Serbia, and the OSCE Kosovo Verification Mission personnel left as Holbrooke warned Milosevic NATO attacks were imminent. Undeterred, Milosevic refused to sign the agreement. On March 24, 1999, NATO commenced Operation Allied Force (OAF), a 78-day air campaign against Serbian military forces (Weller 1999; PBS 2018).

International and NATO Support in Phase 1: Pre-War Planning

Unlike the United States' major interventions in the early 2000s, the international community and NATO were an integral part of the pre-war planning phase in Kosovo and, at times, it was only through the actions of these bodies that the United States was prompted to act. The war in Bosnia threatened the European allies not only because of its geographical proximity but also because continued humanitarian abuses challenged the alliance's values—values that were particularly important in the post-Cold War era when member states were looking to reimagine NATO's purpose (Allin 2002). The reluctance of the Clinton administration to respond to the Bosnian War frustrated its European allies, and these frustrations directly impacted the 1999 Kosovo intervention. Writes Dana Allin,

> Increasingly bitter recriminations about where and how to draw the line against wartime atrocities underscored NATO's fragility. The divergence in views – especially between the United States on the one hand and Britain and France on the other – provoked a crisis of alliance relations reminiscent of the 1956 Suez debacle. The Bosnian war's corrosive effect on transatlantic unity was one important factor that led to a more effective American and NATO intervention in late 1995. Thereafter, in the second phase of the crisis, a determined effort was made to preserve alliance unity on Balkan matters. (Ibid.)

NATO's European allies had another good reason to want a quick resolution to the Kosovo crisis: most of the thousands of peacekeeping troops still on the ground in Bosnia in 1998 and 1999 were European, and there was the possibility that the Serbs would retaliate against them if NATO intervened (Kaplan 2004).

The violence in February and March 1998 in Kosovo prompted the allies to recognize the importance of a unified response to the escalating violence. They also agreed American participation would be paramount to stopping Milosevic (Daalder and O'Hanlon 2000). This was troublesome to some allies who hoped Europe would develop its own security mechanisms without US participation. Some states also insisted NATO needed explicit authorization for any operation in Serbia. The decision to intervene in March 1999 made France uncomfortable because it required the alliance to bypass the United Nations (Macleod 2000). The British, conversely, did not oppose an intervention without UN authorization and were supportive of US participation. Though Great Britain too supported the establishment of European security mechanisms that did not rely on the United States, British officials hoped to act as a bridge between Europe and the United States. They strongly disagreed with Clinton's refusal to commit ground troops, however, having been disappointed by the United States' response to Bosnia in 1995 (Kupchan 2000).

While the American public seemed relatively indifferent to the possibility of an aerial war in Kosovo, European publics were divided about whether and how to intervene. Greece shared its history with the Orthodox Christians (similar to Russia), and the Greek public was overwhelmingly opposed to intervention. The Italian and German publics also opposed intervention, though the newly elected German Chancellor Gerhard Schroeder felt Germany should intervene. The British were steadfast in supporting an intervention, while other allies believed an intervention was necessary but worried whether it would benefit the right side of the conflict, especially as the KLA took advantage of lulls in Serbian aggression to attack police and military authorities (Norris 2005).

Just as the United States began developing its war plans in the summer of 1998, so too did NATO. The United States' Concept of Operations Plan (CONOPLAN) 10601, which called for a phased attack against Serbian targets, served as the basis for NATO's Operation Allied Force. The NATO alliance ruled out using ground forces, due in large part to the unwillingness of the United States to commit to ground operations. NATO also authorized an operation over the Macedonia and Albania borders in June 1998 to prevent the conflict from spreading further. Operation Determined Falcon involved 80 warplanes from 13 NATO countries, and was seen as an attempt by the alliance to demonstrate its unity and power to the Belgrade government (Lambeth 2001; Daalder and O'Hanlon 2000).

While the Security Council continued to avoid authorizing a NATO intervention because of Russia and China's threat to veto, much of NATO's actions in the pre-war period paralleled those of the UN. NATO faced substantial challenges gaining the consensus of all 19 members for the September 1998 ACTORD (Hendrickson 2000). In a meeting of the defense ministers in Portugal on September 23–24, 1998, Secretary General Solana repeatedly referred to the potential damage to NATO's credibility if it threatened to attack but did not follow through. Still, even after the September 29 massacre at Gornji Obrinje, the allies would not agree on the use of force for anything other than self-defense. In October, Secretary General Solana announced that there was legal justification for NATO to threaten and execute airstrikes, which opened the door for the ACTORD on October 13, 1998 (Daalder and O'Hanlon 2000).

Planning for a possible intervention continued through the end of 1998, but indecisiveness plagued the alliance. Ivo Daalder, the former US permanent representative to NATO, characterized both the United States and NATO's response to Kosovo as "haphazard and marked by a tendency to avoid making difficult decisions" (Ibid). Daalder characterized the plans that emerged as fitting one of two categories: preventative deployments and intrusive measures. The different preventative measures included troop deployments in Albania and Macedonia for monitoring and protective missions (to prevent spillover), while the more intrusive options considered both aerial strikes and the deployment of ground troops. Additionally, plans for the use of ground forces included options for consensual deployments (agreements from all parties to allow troops for enforcement of ceasefire and peace settlement) and forced entry (into both Kosovo and the greater Yugoslav territory) (Ibid.). By the time Operation Allied Force was launched in March 1999, the United States and NATO had considered more than 40 air campaigns (Weitsman 2014). Despite having developed plans for ground forces, the allies were greatly influenced by the United States' refusal to commit troops and thus plans for a ground offensive were tabled.

Legitimacy and Multilateralism in Phase 1

The need to legitimize any operation in Kosovo was enhanced by the absence of a UN Security Council resolution authorizing an intervention. Because the United Nations Security Council did not authorize international intervention in any of the resolutions, it passed on Kosovo, Russia repeatedly insisted that NATO's actions were illegal, and China expressed concerns over the alliance using humanitarian grounds to intervene. However, both states' objections likely resulted from the potential precedent for future intervention in their own territories, not the legality of action.

Clinton administration officials did not believe the missing UN's endorsement to be a sufficient reason to forego the intervention, but they recognized the difficulties of obtaining the international community's blessing for a unilateral effort and the need to engage the allies. President Clinton believed the United States had to act: the earlier Bosnian War demonstrated that the Europeans were not equipped to act on their own, but the Balkans instability threatened their security interests and the stability of other areas in Central and Eastern Europe. The administration was also concerned about its inaction in places like Rwanda, where an extensive ethnic cleansing campaign in 1994 resulted in nearly one million civilian deaths, and slowness to act in Bosnia threatened the legitimacy of the Kosovo operation, particularly because the intervention was justified by similar concerns of humanitarian abuses. Still, there was no guarantee the alliance would act. Defense Secretary William Cohen and others thought the allies could be too reluctant to mount an intervention without the UN endorsement. Although UN Secretary General Annan refused to interfere in the dispute between the Security Council members, he expressed concern that if the United States mounted an allied operation and staged the intervention, the values of the United Nations and the Security Council would be undermined (Weitsman 2014; Hendrickson 2000).

Although US military officials developed plans to act that did not rely on widespread multilateral participation, there is little evidence that the United States intended to act unilaterally in Kosovo. President Bush's Christmas Warning threatened US action if the violence in Kosovo continued but made no mention of unilateral action. As Benjamin Lambeth asserts, most of the United States' proposals during the Clinton administration used overwhelming air power at the beginning and then tapered off, but the Europeans wanted a much more gradual approach. The resulting OAF strategy reflected the Europeans' interests much more than the United States'. However, as demonstrated earlier, NATO's decision to conduct an air-only campaign was driven by the United States' unwillingness to contribute ground troops (Lambeth 2001). Although some allies, such as Great Britain, thought the United States was too quick to rule out the use of ground forces, most allies recognized an air campaign was likely to gain much more domestic support from their respective constituencies, as well as the consensus of the alliance as a whole. The Clinton administration was able to maintain political support for Kosovo operations not only because of the air-only strategy, but also because it was ultimately endorsed by the allies and employed as part of a multilateral campaign.

The international political climate and the United States' relationship with its NATO allies in the post-Cold War period was a contributing factor to the decision to act multilaterally. The Clinton administration repeatedly expressed its disinterest in the intervention in Bosnia: officials hoped the European allies would develop their military power enough to be able to combat Milosevic. Several European states hoped to develop the appropriate security mechanisms for addressing the crisis as well: in 1991, 12 European nations signed the Maastricht Treaty, effectively creating the European Union (EU). The treaty established a common foreign and security policy and gave the EU an unprecedented role in security affairs, but it did not directly address EU military capability; instead, it allowed the European Council to request military assistance from the Western European Union (WEU). Though both the French and the Germans were eager to create a military structure similar to NATO's, Great Britain was reluctant to do so on the basis that it would undermine NATO. As a result, the EU's ability to engage in Bosnia in 1995 was limited. In late 1992, the Commission on Security and Cooperation in Europe (CSCE)/Organization for Security and Cooperation in Europe (OSCE) coordinated an observer mission in Kosovo, Sandjak, and Vojvodina, but the SFRY only allowed its mission to continue until mid-1993 (Menon 2006; Deighton 2000; Allin 2002; Kaplan 2004).

The EU's inability to act in a more substantial role in Kosovo made it evident to the Clinton administration, the European allies, and to some extent, foreign policy elites and the American public, that US leadership in the alliance was paramount to success in Kosovo. Additionally, NATO allies—as well as decision-makers within the UN—realized there was no alternative alliance or organization that could act in a way NATO could and ensure a successful operation. NATO had a substantial arsenal of pooled resources, the necessary funding, and an integrated command and control structure that could facilitate a multilateral response to Milosevic's actions.

OPERATION ALLIED FORCE

NATO launched Operation Allied Force at 7 p.m. GMT (8 p.m. local time) on March 24, 1999. Of the 19 NATO allies, 13 states—Belgium, Canada, Denmark, France, Germany, Italy, the Netherlands, Norway, Portugal, Spain, Turkey, the United Kingdom, and the United States—committed aircraft for the operation. The first night of the operation, NATO targeted 53 different sites, mostly air defenses and radar sites, using planes from eight states (Human Rights Watch 2014). Writes Michael Williams, "the alliance started the bombing with one objective – to get the Serbs back to the negotiating table – and then added countless other objectives, including stopping ethnic cleansing, the withdrawal of Serb forces and return of refugees, as well as the insertion of NATO forces in the country and a political settlement" (Williams 2008). In the first month of the operation, NATO was flying roughly 130 attack sorties and 350 total sorties per day (Human Rights Watch 2014). Because of the consensus decision-making process in NATO, it took a substantial length of time to approve targets—at the beginning of OAF operations only 51 targets had been approved. This resulted in some targets being bombed repeatedly (Weitsman 2014).

President Clinton addressed the US public the first evening of the bombing, calling the intervention "a moral imperative" and declaring that stability in Kosovo was "important to America's national interest." He went on, saying

Do our interests in Kosovo justify the dangers to our Armed Forces? I've thought long and hard about that question. I am convinced that the dangers of acting are far outweighed by the dangers of not acting—dangers to the defenseless people and to our national interests. If we and our allies were to allow this war to continue with no response, President Milosevic would read our hesitation as a license to kill. There would be many more massacres, tens of thousands more refugees, more victims crying out for revenge…Imagine what would happen if we and our allies instead decided just to look the other way, as these people were massacred on NATO's doorstep. That would discredit NATO, the cornerstone on which our security has rested for 50 years now. (Clinton 1999)

However, Clinton also made his commitment to an air-only effort clear: "I do not intend to put our troops in Kosovo to fight a war" (Ibid). The American public responded to Clinton's statements, largely supporting the United States' participation in the opening days of the campaign. A Pew poll conducted on March 24–28, 1999, indicated that 60 percent of those polled approved of the NATO airstrikes. However, only 47 percent agreed that the United States should be responsible for ending the conflict, and only 38 percent thought Kosovo was of serious importance to US interests (Pew Research 1999a). Congress was less supportive: while the Senate voted on March 23 to authorize the president to use force, the concurrent measure stalled in the House before failing in April (S. Con. Res. 21, 106th Cong. 1999).

When the OAF campaign began on March 24, many Kosovars had already fled the area, but NATO's airstrikes resulted in 30,000 refugees fleeing to Albania and Macedonia within the first two days of the operation. By April 4, there was an estimated 48,000 refugees in Montenegro, 104,000 in Albania, and 30,500 in Macedonia. An additional 31,000 fled to Bosnia in the beginning weeks. By April, nearly 600,000 civilians had fled Kosovo (PBS 2018). Writes Benjamin Lambeth, "By the third week (of OAF), NATO's strategic goals had shifted from seeking to erode Milosevic's ability to force an exodus of Kosovar Albanian civilians to enforcing a withdrawal of Serb forces from Kosovo and a return of the refugees home…Up to that point, President Clinton had merely insisted that the operation's goal was to ensure that Milosevic's military capability would be 'seriously diminished'" (Lambeth 2001).

NATO continued to execute hundreds of sorties each day and expanded its targets list. On April 6, the Belgrade government announced that it would implement a ceasefire in Kosovo and was open to negotiations with Rugova but NATO rejected the offer. The NATO strikes continued unabated through April. On April 20, Secretary General Solana ordered NATO military advisors to begin updating plans for a potential ground force following an OSCE report of gunfire exchange between Serbian forces (PBS 2018).

On April 22, 1999, the NATO summit in Washington commenced. Though the original focus of the summit was to celebrate the alliance's 50th anniversary, the agenda was dominated by discussions of Kosovo. Up to that point, Milosevic was betting on attrition—he did not believe the alliance was capable of maintaining its unity to continue operations. However, when they came together in Washington, the allies agreed an intensification of the air campaign was necessary to achieve NATO's objectives. Despite growing pressure to commit to a ground campaign, the allies agreed before the summit to leave any discussion of ground troops off of the agenda (Smith 2009). During the three days of the meeting, officials elected to expand the target list, deploy more aircraft and weapons, and move from an eight-hour day to a twenty-four-hour campaign (Human Rights Watch 2014). This intensification marked a shift in the execution of the campaign and sent a signal to Milosevic that the allies were committed to ending the violence in Kosovo.

The American public generally remained supportive of the United States' efforts. A Pew poll conducted in April 1999 showed that 62 percent of those polled approved of the airstrikes. The poll did, however, indicate a growing concern about the possibility of casualties, the financial costs of a sustained operation, and the likelihood of successfully defeating Milosevic. Although 65 percent of those polled thought a ground force would be necessary, only half of the respondents approved of sending troops into Kosovo (Pew Research 1999b). A report issued by the Program on International Policy Attitudes (PIPA) in late May indicated a slight decline in support for the airstrikes as more of the public began to doubt the success of the mission. Whereas earlier polls indicated more than 60 percent of people supported the airstrikes at the beginning of the operation, later polls conducted by ABC/Washington Post, Gallup, CBS, and PIPA found that support dropped to 48–59 percent. This coincided with a decline in the belief that Milosevic would concede, from 53 percent at the beginning of operations to 25–30 percent in April. Only 33 percent of those polled by PIPA supported the use of ground troops in May, though almost 60 percent agreed to support a ground force if conditions in Serbia continued to deteriorate and the airstrikes proved ineffective (Program on International Policy Attitudes 1999).

Though military officials believed OAF would only last a few days, the campaign continued into May. As it became evident that Milosevic would not capitulate, officials in both the United States and NATO began to reconsider the use of ground troops. The British were adamant in their support for a ground operation, and pressured the United States to advocate for a NATO ground force (PBS 2018). On May 18, President Clinton subtly indicated a possible shift in his refusal to deploy ground troops, stating "NATO will not take any option off the table (Smith 2009)." On March 25, NATO announced it would increase the size of its peacekeeping force in Macedonia to 48,000 troops. Because of the increased discussion of a ground force in Kosovo, the peacekeeping force's increase was seen as strategic: some of the 48,000 troops could be quickly dispatched into Kosovo if the NATO Secretary General later approved a ground force order and the allies agreed. NATO SACEUR General Wesley Clark and others warned that if NATO was going to approve a ground force, it should do so quickly so that the mission could be executed before the long, harsh winter (Independent International Commission on Kosovo 2000). On May 27, Secretary Cohen met with NATO defense ministers in a secret meeting in Bonn to discuss a possible invasion, the same day the International War Crimes Tribunal indicted Milosevic and four other Serbian leaders (PBS 2018). It was later reported that by early June, President Clinton was ready to deploy ground troops unless the war ended (Ibid.).

Parallel to the discussions in the NATO alliance, the Group of Eight (G8) worked to forge a political settlement to end the air campaign. In April, the North Atlantic Council laid out five points for Milosevic to meet in order to end the bombing campaign. These included: verification of the end of military action and minority oppression in Kosovo, the withdrawal of Serb forces from Kosovo, the allowance of international observers, the safe and unhindered return of the hundreds of thousands of displaced refugees, and an agreement to work toward a political solution for Kosovo. Building on these, the G8 convened in Bonn, Germany, in early May to forge a peace plan (CNN 1999; Latawski and Smith 2003).

Immediately following the commencement of OAF, Russia pressured the UN Security Council to stop the NATO airstrikes, but UN Secretary General Kofi Annan insisted that responsibility for peace negotiations would fall to the Contact Group (Norris 2005). Russia also cut its ties with NATO. It condemned the NATO operation and on April 9, President Yeltsin publicly warned that Russia could be led into a European or even global war. A week later, Viktor Chernomyrdin was appointed as a special envoy to the region. In late April, following NATO's Washington Summit, President Yeltsin initiated contact with President Clinton to reopen negotiations on Kosovo, ordering Chernomyrdin to represent Russia in talks with Vice President Al Gore. In early May, Chernomyrdin traveled to Washington, and in the following days, Russia began cooperating with the allies at the G8 meeting in Germany (PBS 2018).

The intensification of the aerial campaign in late May followed by the continued planning efforts of the G8 and Russia's growing participation marked a second turning point in Operation Allied Freedom: by late May, the weather conditions had improved, NATO had increased its air assets, the KLA was becoming more effective on the ground, and Serbia was suffering from damage to its electric grids and water supply, as well as damages to businesses. Additionally, the risk to Serb soldiers was high, and the amount of damaged equipment continued to increase as operations intensified (Daalder and O'Hanlon 2000).

With Russia acting as a go-between for the G8 and Milosevic, President Yeltsin pressured Milosevic to accept the G8's peace plan. The evidence of his efforts became clear on June 1, when Belgrade informed Germany that it was ready to accept the terms of the G8 peace plan if the NATO bombing is brought to an end (PBS 2018). On June 2, both Chernomyrdin and the Finnish president Martti Ahtisaari (who had been appointed by the EU as a neutral delegate for the Kosovo conflict) traveled to Belgrade and met with Milosevic. Both Milosevic and the Serbian Parliament agreed to the conditions of the G8 and the NATO peacekeeping force (Norris 2005). However, a failure of the Yugoslav commanders in the following days to pullout from Kosovo led NATO to temporarily intensify the campaign. After several more days of negotiations, NATO reached a Military Technical Agreement with the Serb forces on June 9. On June 10, Secretary General Solana suspended Operation Allied Force (PBS 2018).

International and NATO Support for OAF

Though the participation of the NATO is well-documented in the preceding pages, there are several other important factors to consider regarding international support during Operation Allied Force. Broadly speaking, before OAF there was widespread agreement among the allies that Milosevic was violating the basic human rights of Kosovar Albanians by violent oppression, segregation, and a campaign to expel as many Albanians as possible from Serbia. There was also general agreement that the Kosovo conflict could spill over into other European states. In addition to the potential for spillover, the mass exodus of thousands of refugees threatened the stability of neighboring states. Still, there was widespread disagreement regarding the appropriateness of a NATO intervention as well as the type of intervention that would most likely result in success.

These disagreements stemmed from two factors. First, the alliance lacked an authorization for intervention from the United Nations Security Council. Former US Permanent Representative to NATO, Ivo Daalder, characterized the organization of the allies as fitting one of three categories. The "Catholics" (such as France and Italy) demanded that every attempt must be made to obtain authorization and argued the alliance could only act without the support of the UNSC in the most extreme circumstances. The French, in particular, were concerned about the possibility that NATO's actions, absent the authorization, would set a dangerous precedent for both NATO and the United States. The second group of states, the "Lutherans" (states such as Great Britain and Germany), looked for justification to bypass the UN Security Council in other areas of international law, such as UN conventions. They too pressed the urgency of the situation and the potential effects of nonintervention. The last group, which included the United States, were the "Agnostics." For the third group, a UN authorization would enhance the legitimacy of the operation and provide additional resources for the alliance but was not imperative for NATO to act (Daalder and O'Hanlon 2000).

Second, although the European allies recognized the necessity of the United States' participation, some states were unnerved by the Clinton administration's repeated refusal to engage in a ground effort in Kosovo. As demonstrated earlier, the British, in particular, stressed the importance of maintaining the possibility of ground forces, and were frustrated by the United States' vocal unwillingness to contribute to a contingent in Kosovo (Dunn 2009). Then-British Defense Secretary George Robertson repeatedly stated the British's position that NATO should retain the option to send ground troops in the event the airstrikes were unsuccessful (Donfried 1999). Though the United States was the most vocal opponent of a ground force, it was not the only ally to refuse participation. Greece also opposed participation because of its historical ties to the Orthodox Christian population in the former SFRY, and others expressed disinterest in committing ground troops. Thus, as David Dunn asserts, an air campaign was likely the only strategy that would have received consensus from all of the allies (Dunn 2009).

Political and public support for NATO operations also varied widely among the allies. Polls conducted at the beginning of the OAF campaign demonstrated high levels of support in Great Britain and France. In Great Britain, polls indicated that 55 percent of the public supported Britain's participation in the NATO operation, while nearly 60 percent of the public supported France's decision to participate. Support in France remained high throughout the operation, as a poll conducted in late May showed that 67 percent still supported France's actions. Chancellor Schroeder also enjoyed high levels of support for Germany's participation—60 percent of those polled in early April supported Germany's participation. Conversely, polls in Italy showed that the public did not support Italian participation: only 25 percent believed the operation was justified (Davidson 2011). Polling conducted in mid-April in Greece showed that 96 percent of the population opposed the airstrikes (Donfried 1999).

However, the statements of public and military officials from several states—including states whose publics did not support the NATO airstrikes—indicate their relationship to both the United States and the NATO alliance made them maintain their commitment to OAF even as public support started to decline and domestic opposition became more vocal. Many of the allies saw it to be in their national interests to ensure a settlement of the Kosovo conflict, either because of the potential for spillover or because of the possible humanitarian crisis, which would be politically, economically, and militarily expensive. Importantly, the allies also agreed with Secretary General Solana and US Defense Secretary William Cohen's repeated assertions regarding NATO's reputation: if NATO threatened the use of force (as it did in the pre-war period), its failure to follow through would destroy the credibility of the alliance and jeopardize any future NATO deployment (Davidson 2011).

A major source of tension arose between the United States and the Europeans participating in the airstrikes in the early days of OAF. When Milosevic persisted despite the United States' belief he would capitulate after only a few days of an aerial campaign, it became obvious NATO had not established a proper approval mechanism for target selection. US commanders struggled to expand the target list, and even when they did, the alliance's approval process was slow and burdensome (Lambeth 2001). Despite this, the NATO allies remained committed to OAF and became more unified as the operation continued, which severely weakened Milosevic's ability to counter the airstrikes. Writes Jason Davidson, "Milosevic knew that NATO had him outgunned by a massive margin. If the leading NATO member countries committed their capabilities and kept them engaged, Serbia would have to accept NATO's terms or be destroyed (Davidson 2011)." The Washington Summit provided political and military leaders an opportunity to reassess its actions in Kosovo and reaffirm its commitment to unity throughout the operation, which proved key to the alliance's success. In a statement on the After Action Report (AAR) on Kosovo, US Defense Secretary William Cohen and Chairman of the Joint Chiefs of Staff Henry Shelton said, "(authors' emphasis) *the solidarity of the alliance* was central in compelling Belgrade to accept NATO's conditions. Because Milosevic could not defeat NATO militarily, his best hope lay in splitting the alliance politically. Thus, it was not enough for NATO simply to concentrate on winning a military victory; at the heart of allied strategy was building and sustaining the unity of the alliance (Cohen and Shelton 1999)."

Legitimacy and Multilateralism in Phase 2

Prior to the commencement of Operation Allied Freedom, NATO leaders searched the precedents of international law to legitimize NATO's intervention. They referred to the obligations of 1948 UN Declaration of Human Rights and the 1949 Geneva Convention, and the two Security Council resolutions, UNSCR 1160 and 1199, claiming military intervention in the event Milosevic did not adhere to the UN guidelines was in the "sense and logic" of the resolutions. At the same time, some allies tried to minimize the importance of an authorizing Security Council resolution, especially given the necessity of immediate response to the urgent humanitarian crisis (Hendrickson 2000). There was also some indication that US and other Western European officials hoped the NATO intervention would set a precedent for future humanitarian crisis wherein the Security Council could not reach a consensus on the necessity of international participation. They believed the NATO intervention in Kosovo could be deemed an illegal action after the engagement ended, but hoped the operation's success would lead to important improvements in the legal system for humanitarian concerns and thus supersede any violation of international law (Buchanan 2010).

The execution of Operation Allied Force highlighted weaknesses in both the alliance's ability to act effectively and the US-NATO relationship. Following the end of operations, the US Senate passed a resolution "bemoaning the 'glaring shortcomings' in European defense capabilities, and urging the European Union to rectify the 'overall imbalance' within the alliance" (Kupchan 2000). The Defense Department's After Action Review of Kosovo identified several areas for the United States to improve in its relationship with the NATO alliance, including: better planning for non-Article 5 operations, better command and control policies, and strengthening the relationships between the political and military sides of NATO. The OAF operation identified a technological gap between the United States, which sustained a 3–4 percent defense spending rate (as a proportion of GDP), and the European allies, many of whom dramatically shrank their defense budgets after the end of the Cold War and regularly failed to meet the 2 percent threshold set by the Washington Treaty. The United States was the only state able to deploy strategic bombers and stealth aircraft (including unmanned aerial vehicles), in addition to being one of only a few with laser-guided bombs, resources for nighttime strikes, and cruise missiles. Additionally, the United States' ability to conduct intelligence, surveillance, and reconnaissance (ISR) was unparalleled by the European allies (Weitsman 2014).

During OAF, the United States maintained control over its troops by establishing a parallel command structure to NATO's command and control structure, resulting in tensions between allies as well as "unsuitable organizational structures and insufficient staff integration" (Ibid). US resources using "special sensitivities," such as the B-2, F-117, and cruise missiles, remained under the control of the US European Command (USEUCOM) and the Air Operations Center co-operated by the United States and NATO maintained separate targeting teams for operations based on USEUCOM's commands. Because the United States anticipated the airstrikes would only last a few days, it did not have an effective method for selecting and approving targets, which led to tension between the air component commander, Lieutenant General Michael Short (US Air Force), and General Wesley Clark (US Army), who was serving in a dual capacity as both commander of USEUCOM and NATO Supreme Allied Commander (Lambeth 2001).

Although the United States was required to take a leading role in the Kosovo intervention, Clinton administration officials recognized the benefits of a NATO operation. While some allies lacked the necessary technology and resources needed to mount an effective air campaign, access to bases, airfields, and airspace were critical to Operation Allied Force's success (Weitsman 2014). In a statement on the After Action Review (AAR) of Kosovo, US Defense Secretary William Cohen and Chairman of the Joint Chiefs of Staff Henry Shelton said, "*Operation Allied Force could not have been conducted without the NATO alliance* and without the infrastructure, transit and basing access, host-nation force contributions, and more importantly, political and diplomatic support provided by the allies and other members of the coalition…If NATO as an institution had not responded to this crisis, it would have meant that the world's most powerful alliance was unwilling to act when confronted with serious threats to common interests on its own doorstep" (Cohen and Shelton 1999).

THE KFOR MISSION

Over the entire OAF operation, which lasted 11 weeks, the United States and NATO flew a combined total of 38,000 sorties (Weitsman 2014). The United States flew the highest number of both strike and nonstrike sorties, with a total of 29,000 sorties flown using 700 aircraft. Of these, the United States conducted nearly 80 percent of the air raids. Of the non-US allies, France, the United Kingdom, the Netherlands, and Italy flew the highest totals of sorties. The United Kingdom also flew a higher number strike sorties (62 percent of all sorties flown by the United Kingdom) than any other non-US ally (who averaged 28 percent of total sorties flown). No friendly fire incidents were reported throughout the entirety of the operation. During the operation, two alliance jets were shot down but the pilots survived. The alliance suffered just two casualties as a result of a training exercise accident in Albania. Fourteen of the 19 NATO allies participated in Operation Allied Force (Weitsman 2014; Daalder and O'Hanlon 2000; Davidson 2011; Deighton 2000).

The air campaign revealed the tremendous capabilities gap between the United States and the European allies—not only was the United States better equipped with weapons and aircraft; it was also superior at intelligence gathering and research and development (Kaplan 2004; Weitsman 2014). Disparities in communication systems were also problematic, particularly in regard to precision strikes. Because of this, the United States executed the highest number of strike (precision) sorties because many of its allies were incapable of doing so, especially in the early stages of OAF. Only 10 percent of the European aircraft were capable of precision bombing, and 70 percent of the total firepower was American. Only a few could contribute laser-guided munitions, and France was the only non-US ally capable of bombing raids at night (Weitsman 2014).

In addition to the absence of a UN authorization for the intervention and the technical and operation difficulties of executing the air campaign, OAF became increasingly problematic because of a number of nonhostile targets being struck and the deaths of over 500 civilians by NATO munitions (Independent International Commission on Kosovo 2000). An early mishap at the beginning of April 1999 in which three missiles struck a residential neighborhood in Alksinac, killing five civilians, prompted Milosevic to declare a ceasefire and request NATO to do the same. However, NATO officials refused, citing the lack of political settlement for Kosovo. On April 12, NATO bombs hit a passenger train south of

Belgrade, killing 30 civilians. Two days later, NATO struck a civilian convoy of Kosovar Albanians, killing another 60 people. One of the most publicized, controversial accidental strikes occurred on May 7, when NATO planes mistakenly targeted the Chinese embassy in Belgrade. Three people were killed and another 20 were wounded. The Security Council convened in an emergency session the next day, while NATO and the United States combatted rumors that the targeting was intentional (PBS 2018).

Because 2500 civilians were killed by Serb authorities before NATO intervened, some argued that OAF encouraged Milosevic to escalate the violence and implement more oppressive policies. The Independent International Commission determined that 10,000 civilians were killed during Operation Allied Force; however, an investigation conducted by Human Rights Watch determined that only 489 to 528 were killed by the NATO operation. The majority of those killed were ethnic Albanians deliberately targeted by Serbian authorities. Civilians were subjected to rape and torture as well. Over 860,000 Kosovars left Kosovo as refugees, and another 590,000 were "internally displaced." These two groups constituted over 90 percent of the total population (Independent International Commission on Kosovo 2000; PBS 2015; Williams 2008). Still, Hungary, Germany, and France were among those who asserted that Kosovo was not better off than it was before the strikes (Weitsman 2014).

On June 10, 1999, the UN Security Council passed UNSCR 1244. The resolution detailed all of the terms of the G8/NATO peace agreement with Milosevic. As a condition of the agreement, the UN Security Council established the mandate for an immediate peacekeeping force consisting of both military and civilian personnel in Kosovo to ensure adherence to the peace principles (UNSCR 1244 1999). Operating under Chapter VII of the UN Charter, a NATO-led Kosovo Force (KFOR) entered Kosovo on June 12, as Serb forces moved out of the region. Nearly 50,000 troops were deployed at the beginning of the KFOR mission. Although the European allies contributed significantly less than the United States to Operation Allied Force, it took the lead on the KFOR mission, contributing thousands of troops and billions of dollars to stabilization and reconstruction efforts. Additionally, thousands of civilians joined the KFOR mission to help rebuild various programs (Weitsman 2014). The UN also established the UN Mission in Kosovo (UNMIK), a civilian mission to assist the Kosovars and the KFOR operation. By June 20, 1999, all of the Serb forces had moved out of Kosovo, and Operation

Allied Force was officially ended. Within a few months of the end of military operations, nearly all of the refugees—810,000 of the estimated 863,000 total displaced—returned to Kosovo (NATO 2015a, b; PBS 2018). Today, the KFOR mission continues, with 4651 NATO forces currently deployed. Of these, the United States is the second largest contributor with 712 troops deployed (NATO 2015b).

Legitimacy and Multilateralism in Phase 3

In post-war assessments, the operation in Kosovo was deemed by the Independent International Commission on Kosovo to be illegal but legitimate. In its report, the Commission wrote, "It was illegal because it did not receive prior approval from the United Nations Security Council. However, the Commission considers that the intervention was justified because all diplomatic avenues had been exhausted and because the intervention had the effect the liberating the majority population of Kosovo from a long period of oppression under Serbian rule" (Independent International Commission on Kosovo 2000). Although OAF violated Serbia's sovereignty and lacked a Security Council resolution authorizing the intervention, the operation was conducted to prevent a humanitarian crisis. As Susan Rice and Andrew Loomis posit, this was in "the spirit of the UN Charter" (Rice and Loomis 2007). Some believed the dispute between the Security Council members reflected that it was ill equipped to be the sole arbiter of conflict and the only body able to determine the legitimacy of international intervention (Bjola 2009).

In the years following the Kosovo crisis, there have been no substantial changes to the Security Council itself; however, as a result of the crises in Bosnia, Rwanda, Kosovo, and elsewhere, the United Nations undertook a series of reforms aimed at preventing future human rights abuses. In 2000, Canada convened a special panel, the International Commission on Intervention and State Sovereignty, to determine whether there are conditions under which states may supersede the sovereignty of another state in order to protect civilian populations. The panel's findings became the basis for the Responsibility to Protect (R2P) doctrine adopted by the UN at the 2005 World Summit. The R2P doctrine mandates that states have a moral and legal imperative to protect their populations from crimes against humanity. If the individual state is unable or unwilling to ensure these protections, R2P dictates that the international community "has the responsibility to use appropriate diplomatic, humanitarian and other peaceful means, in accordance with Chapters VI and VIII of the Charter, to help protect populations from genocide, war crimes, ethnic cleansing and crimes against humanity" (The International Coalition for the Responsibility to Protect 2015). The R2P doctrine would later be cited as justification for NATO's intervention in the 2011 Libyan crisis.

American officials used the 1999 Washington Summit to press the allies to strengthen their commitment to the alliance both politically and militarily. The United States insisted the alliance develop better command and control mechanisms and pushed the allies for more operational resources, citing the ongoing Kosovo operation as evidence of the alliance's shortcomings. As a result, the allies revised its Strategic Concept and, in following the end of OAF, established the Defense Capabilities Initiative (DCI) in December 1999 to overcome some of these challenges. The DCI worked to improve interoperability between the allies, ensure the rapid deployment of resources in emergencies, strengthen the alliance's ability to engage in sustained warfare over a longer period of time, and address the command and control difficulties experienced during OAF (NATO 1999).

The United States also benefited from its status as a hegemonic superpower in its relationship with NATO during the Kosovo intervention. When the NATO was founded in 1949, the United States used its status in the post-WWII era to establish itself in highly influential positions within the alliance. For example, the NATO Supreme Allied Commander Europe (SACEUR) has traditionally been a four-star American officer who serves in a dual role as NATO SACEUR and Commander, US European Command (USEUCOM). The NATO SACEUR is the head of the Allied Command Operations (ACO) and is responsible for the conduct of all NATO military operations (NATO 2014). Thus, even though the United States maintained a parallel command structure (under the direction of Lieutenant General Short), the United States exerted influence through NATO SACEUR and USEUCOM Commander General Clark. In addition to tensions between Lieutenant General Short and General Clark, Clark's dual position caused tension between the allies at times, as some challenged whether he had the authority to make some operational decisions. However, these tensions quickly subsided (Weitsman 2014).

Conclusion

President Clinton's decision to engage in a multilateral intervention in Kosovo was the sum of his personal preferences, domestic politics, the United States' relationship with its European partners and the NATO alliance, and the international political climate. Like the Afghanistan, Iraq, and Libya interventions, NATO's participation in Kosovo conferred legitimacy on the intervention. The legitimacy conferred by NATO participation was particularly important because the allies lacked an explicit authorization for the use of force in Kosovo. However, unlike the aforementioned cases, NATO's role in Kosovo also validated the alliance's existence for both political legitimization and military capability: the unity of the allies and their ability to execute the 'out-of-area' operation demonstrated the alliance's relevance in the post-Cold War environment. The lessons learned during Operation Allied Force also presented an opportunity for NATO to improve its utility for future operations, and gave the United States leverage to press the European allies for more defense spending and alliance contributions.

The dissolution of the Soviet Union left NATO searching for a purpose in the post-Cold War era. The Balkans conflicts reinvigorated the alliance, and both the United States and the European allies recognized the utility of the alliance, albeit for different reasons. For the European allies, NATO kept the United States actively involved in European security. Years of cuts to defense budgets, fewer reserve capabilities, and depletions in active duty troops left many states with large gaps in their ability to address threats to national security. The United States was capable of filling those gaps and committed to the allies by the Washington Treaty. Conversely, the United States enjoyed the legitimacy enhancement of NATO support for the air campaign. Although the intervention in Kosovo was ultimately deemed legitimate by UN officials and the international community, the success of the air-only campaign enhanced the United States' reputation within the alliance and set a precedent for future engagements and the US-NATO relationship: US officials could now justify using an air-only campaign to its fellow allies. By citing the success of both Bosnia and Kosovo air operations and the minimal numbers of friendly fire incidents and civilian casualties, the United States could use its influence to push NATO into future interventions to prevent or halt crimes against humanity.

NATO's first major operation in the post-Cold War period revealed the complexities of the US-NATO relationship, as well as the relationship between multilateralism, legitimacy, and the alliance's persistence in the absence of threat from the Soviet Union. There is strong evidence supporting each of the hypotheses regarding why NATO persistence is important to the United States. As previously demonstrated, NATO's role in Kosovo conferred a high degree of legitimacy on the operation, despite the absence of an authorizing UN Security Council resolution. This benefited the operation—which, in retrospect, was deemed "illegal but legitimate"—while also benefitting the alliance for future operations. The possibility of NATO missions outside of the United Nations' mandate influenced the United States' later decision-making—especially in Iraq, where the United States and others believed its actions would be retrospectively validated in a similar manner. US policymakers demonstrated both the United States' commitment to international norms and the allies' desire to transform norms concerning humanitarian interventions (as evidenced by the development of the R2P doctrine), confirming the second hypothesis on the importance of NATO persistence. From the perspective of the Clinton administration, a multilateral operation in Kosovo prevented some of the domestic political fallout of a unilateral strategy while still allowing the United States to exert a substantial influence on the alliance and take a leadership position over military operations.

The following chapters on the wars in Afghanistan and Iraq also provide some insight into what could have happened in Kosovo if the United States chose an alternative to Operation Allied Force. If the United States acted unilaterally in Kosovo, successfully convincing the European allies to undertake the necessary stabilization and reconstruction efforts would have been difficult, even if the combat operation was faster and more successful than OAF. Thus, the decision to stage a multilateral operation may have paid off, as European forces remain committed to stability in the Balkans today.

Operation Allied Force reinforced the importance of maintaining the alliance and provided opportunities to ensure its utility as predicted by the third hypothesis. The United States recognized the importance of NATO resources to its operations, despite the inability of all allies to contribute the necessary resources. Many allies still pushed to develop European security mechanisms that did not rely on the United States' participation, but because of the Balkans conflicts understood the importance of the United States' role in the short term. The European allies also recognized the growing technology gap and operational challenges facing the alliance. These initiatives affected the alliance's ability to respond to the Afghanistan war, as demonstrated in the following chapter. While NATO participation was important to the United States because of its operational contributions, there was an additional impetus for NATO leadership in Operation Allied Force: the alliance's credibility as a willing and capable mechanism for action was threatened if the allies did not act in unison and engage the alliance.

Finally, as evidenced here and in Chap. 7, the United States used its role as a leader in the alliance and its hegemonic status to influence the alliance's decision-making, consistent with the fourth hypothesis on NATO's importance to the United States. The decision to act without UN authorization, to refrain from a ground campaign at the outset of OAF, and to undertake major initiatives in light of the alliance's shortcomings in combat operations were influenced (and in some cases initiated) by the United States. NATO planners used American combat plans to formulate the OAF strategy, which was directed by US officers serving in dual US/NATO capacities. The Defense Capabilities Initiative (DCI) and intelligence, surveillance, and reconnaissance (ISR) reforms were spearheaded by the United States to enhance the alliance and overcome the shortcomings experienced in Kosovo.

REFERENCES

Allin, Dana H. 2002. *NATO's Balkan Interventions*. London: Routledge.

BBC News. Timeline: Breakup of Yugoslavia. Last Modified May 22, 2006. http://news.bbc.co.uk/2/hi/europe/4997380.stm. Accessed 1 Mar 2015.

Bjola, Corneliu. 2009. *Legitimising the Use of Force in International Politics*, Contemporary Security Studies. London: Routledge.

Buchanan, Allen. 2010. *Human Rights, Legitimacy, and the Use of Force*. New York: Oxford University Press.

Cimbala, Stephen J., and Peter Forster. 2005. *The US, NATO and Military Burden-Sharing*, Cass Contemporary Security Studies Series. London: Routledge.

Clinton, William J. Address to the Nation on Airstrikes Against Serbian Targets in the Federal Republic of Yugoslavia (Serbia and Montenegro). Last Modified Mar 24, 1999. http://www.presidency.ucsb.edu/ws/?pid=57305. Accessed 1 Mar 2015.

CNN. G-8 Ministers Draft Kosovo Peace Formula. Last Modified May 6, 1999. http://www.cnn.com/WORLD/europe/9905/06/kosovo.03/. Accessed 1 Mar 2015.

Cohen, Roger. 1994. U.S. Clashes with Russia Over Bosnia. *The New York Times*, May 18. http://www.nytimes.com/1994/05/18/world/us-clashes-with-russia-over-bosnia.html

Cohen, William S., and Shelton, Henry H. Joint Statement on the Kosovo After Action Review. Last Modified Oct 14, 1999. www.au.af.mil/au/awc/aecgate/kosovoaa/jointstmt.htm. Accessed 7 Feb 2015.

Daalder, Ivo H. 1998. Decision to Intervene: How the War in Bosnia Ended. *Foreign Service Journal* 73 (12): 24–31.

Daalder, Ivo H., and Michael E. O'Hanlon. 2000. *Winning Ugly: NATO's War to Save Kosovo*. Washington, DC: Brookings Institution Press.

Davidson, Jason. 2011. *America's Allies and War*. New York: Palgrave Macmillan.

Deighton, Anne. 2000. The European Union and NATO's War Over Kosovo: Toward the Glass Ceiling? In *Alliance Politics, Kosovo, and NATO's War: Allied Force or Forced Allies?* ed. Pierre Martin and Mark R. Brawley. New York: Palgrave.

Donfried, Karen. 1999. *Kosovo: International Reactions to NATO Air Strikes*. CRS Report for Congress, April 21. Washington, DC: Congressional Research Service.

Dunn, David. 2009. Innovation and Precedent in the Kosovo War: The Impact of Operation Allied Force on US Foreign Policy. *International Affairs (Royal Institute of International Affairs 1944–)* 85 (3): 531.

Hendrickson, Ryan C. 2000. The Constraint of Legitimacy: The Legal and Institutional Framework of Euro-Atlantic Security. In *Alliance Politics, Kosovo, and NATO's War: Allied Force or Forced Allies?* ed. Pierre Martin and Mark R. Brawley. New York: Palgrave.

———. 2005. Crossing the Rubicon. *NATO Review*, Autumn. http://www.nato.int/docu/review/2005/issue3/english/history_pr.html

Human Rights Watch. 2014. The Crisis in Kosovo. http://www.hrw.org/reports/2000/nato/Natbm200-01.htm. Accessed 7 Sept 2014.

Independent International Commission on Kosovo. 2000. *The Kosovo Report: Conflict, International Response, Lessons Learned*. New York: Palgrave.

Kaplan, Lawrence S. 2004. *NATO Divided, NATO United*. Westport: Praeger.

Karadis, Mike. 2000. *Bosnia, Kosova, and the West*. Sydney: Resistance Books.

Kupchan, Charles A. 2000. Kosovo and the Future of U.S. Engagement in Europe: Continued Hegemony or Impending Retrenchment? In *Alliance Politics, Kosovo, and NATO's War: Allied Force or Forced Allies?* ed. Pierre Martin and Mark R. Brawley. New York: Palgrave.

Lambeth, Benjamin S. 2001. *NATO's Air War for Kosovo: A Strategic and Operational Assessment*. Santa Monica: Rand.

Latawski, Paul C., and Martin A. Smith. 2003. *The Kosovo Crisis and the Evolution of Post-Cold War European Security*. Manchester: Manchester University Press.

Macleod, Alex. 2000. France: Kosovo and the Emergence of a New European Security. In *Alliance Politics, Kosovo, and NATO's War: Allied Force or Forced Allies?* ed. Pierre Martin and Mark R. Brawley. New York: Palgrave.

Menon, Andrew. 2006. From Out of Adversity: Kosovo, Iraq, and EDSP. In *The Transatlantic Divide: Foreign and Security Policies in the Atlantic Alliance from Kosovo to Iraq*, ed. Osvaldo Croci and Amy Verdun. New York: Manchester University Press.

NATO. Statement by the Secretary General Following the ACTWARN Decision. Last Modified Sept 24, 1998. www.nato.int/docu/pr/1998/p980924e.htm
———. Defence Capabilities Initiative (DCI). Last Modified Dec 2, 1999. www. nato.int/docu/comm/1999/9912-hq/fs-dci99.htm. Accessed 11 Nov 2014.
———. Peace Support Operations in Bosnia and Herzegovina. Last Modified Nov 11, 2014. http://nato.int/cps/en/natohq/topics_52122.htm?selected Locale=en. Accessed 1 Mar 2015.
———. Kosovo Force: Key Facts and Figures. Last Modified Feb 1, 2015a. http://www.nato.int/nato_static/assets/pdf/pdf_2013_12/131201-kfor-placemat-final.pdf. Accessed 5 Apr 2015.
———. NATO's Role in Kosovo. Last Modified Jan 6, 2015b. http://www.nato. int/cps/en/natolive/topics_48818.htm#. Accessed 1 Mar 2015.
Norris, John. 2005. *Collision Course: NATO, Russia and Kosovo.* Westport: Praeger.
Owen, Robert C. 2001. *Operation Deliberate Force: A Case Study on Humanitarian Constraints in Aerospace Warfare.* Paper Presented at Humanitarian Challenges in Military Intervention Workshop, November 29–30.
PBS. 2018. A Kosovo Chronology. http://www.pbs.org/wgbh/pages/frontline/shows/kosovo/etc/cron.html. Accessed 26 Aug 2018.
PBS Frontline. 2015. War in Europe: Facts and Figures. http://www.pbs.org/wgbh/pages/frontline/shows/kosovo/etc/facts.html. Accessed 1 Mar 2015.
Pew Research Center. Continued Public Support for Kosovo, but Worries Grow. Last Modified Apr 21, 1999a. http://www.people-press.org/1999/04/21/continued-public-support-for-kosovo-but-worries-grow/. Accessed 5 Apr 2015.
———. Support for NATO Air Strikes with Plenty of Buts. Last Modified Mar 29, 1999b. http://www.people-press.org/1999/03/29/support-for-nato-air-strikes-with-plenty-of-buts/.
Program on International Policy Attitudes. Americans on Kosovo: A Study of US Public Attitudes. Last Modified May 27, 1999. http://www.pipa.org/OnlineReports/Kosovo/Kosovo_May99/Kosovo_May99_rpt.pdf. Accessed 5 Apr 2015.
Reuters. What Happened During the War in Bosnia? Last Modified July 21, 2008. http://www.reuters.com/article/2008/07/21/idUSL21644464
Rice, Susan E., and Andrew Loomis. 2007. Evolution of Humanitarian Intervention. In *Beyond Preemption: Force and Legitimacy in a Changing World*, ed. Ivo Daalder. Washington, DC: Brookings Institution Press.
Riding, Alan. Conflict in the Balkans; Mitterand Will Send Troops Only to Protect Bosnia Relief. Last Modified Aug 14, 1992. https://www.nytimes. com/1992/08/14/world/conflict-balkans-mitterrand-will-send-troops-only-protect-bosnia-relief.html. Accessed 1 Mar 2015.
Smith, Mark. 2009. *The Kosovo Conflict: U.S. Diplomacy and Western Public Opinion.* Los Angeles: Figueroa Press.

The International Coalition for the Responsibility to Protect. Paragraphs 138–139 of the World Summit Outcome Document. Last Modified Mar 1, 2015. http://responsibilitytoprotect.org/index.php/component/content/article/35-r2pcs-topics/398-general-assembly-r2p-excerpt-from-outcome-document

The New York Times. 1999. Crisis in the Balkans: Statements on the United States' Policy on Kosovo. *The New York Times*, April 18.

U.S. Department of State Office of the Historian. The War in Bosnia, 1992–1995. Last Modified Oct 21, 2013. https://history.state.gov/milestones/1993-2000/bosnia. Accessed 1 Mar 2015.

———. 2015a. Bill Clinton, Boris Yeltsin, and U.S.-Russian Relations. https://history.state.gov/milestones/1993-2000/clinton-yeltsin. Accessed 1 Mar 2015.

———. 2015b. The Breakup of Yugoslavia. https://history.state.gov/milestones/1989-1992/breakup-yugoslavia. Accessed 1 Mar 2015.

———. 2015c. United States Relations with Russia: After the Cold War. http://2001-2009.state.gov/r/pa/ho/pubs/fs/85962.htm. Accessed 1 Mar 2015.

U.S. House of Representatives. 1999. *A Concurrent Resolution Authorizing the President of the United States to Conduct Military Air Operations and Missile Strikes Against the Federal Republic of Yugoslavia (Serbia and Montenegro)*. 106th Congress Session.

United Nations Department of Public Information. United Nations Protection Force. Last Modified Sept 1, 1996. http://www.un.org/en/peacekeeping/missions/past/unprof_b.htm. Accessed 1 Mar 2015.

United Nations Security Council. *UNSCR 753 Admission of a New Member: Croatia*, May 18, 1992.

———. *UNSCR 1160 on the Letters from the United Kingdom (S/1998/223) and the United States (S/1998/272)*, Mar 31, 1998a.

———. *UNSCR 1199 Kosovo (FRY)*, Sept 23, 1998b.

———. *UNSCR 1244 On the Situation Relating Kosovo*, June 10, 1999.

Wallack, Michael. 2006. From Compellence to Pre-Emption: Kosovo and Iraq as Responses to Contested Hegemony. In *The Transatlantic Divide: Foreign and Security Policies in the Atlantic Alliance from Kosovo to Iraq*, ed. Osvaldo Croci and Amy Verdun. New York: Manchester University Press.

Weitsman, Patricia. 2014. *Waging War: Alliances, Coalitions, and Institutions of Interstate Violence*. Stanford: Stanford University Press.

Weller, Marc. 1999. The Rambouillet Conference on Kosovo. *International Affairs* 75 (2): 211.

Williams, Michael J. 2008. *NATO, Security, and Risk Management*. Milton Park: Routledge.

Wintz, Mark. 2010. *Transatlantic Diplomacy and the Use of Military Force in the Post-Cold War Era*. New York: Palgrave Macmillan.

CHAPTER 4

September 11, 2001, and the War in Afghanistan

The narrative of September 11, 2001, is etched into the minds of millions of Americans who witnessed the tragic events of the day, beginning when American Airlines Flight 11 struck the North Tower of the World Trade Center (WTC) at 8:46 a.m. Nineteen al Qaeda operatives hijacked a total of four flights that day—Flight 11, United Airlines Flight 175, American Airlines Flight 77, and United Airlines Flight 93. Two planes flew into the two WTC buildings and a third crashed into the Pentagon. Passengers on the fourth flight overtook the hijackers and prevented the plane from striking its intended target, instead crashing into a field in rural Pennsylvania. The attacks killed 2977 people, injured 7000 more, and caused over $100 billion in direct economic damage to the US economy (Lansford 2012). In the days and weeks that followed, Americans felt an unprecedented sense of vulnerability and rallied around President George W. Bush, New York City Mayor Rudy Giuliani, and the first responders of the New York City fire, police, and EMT departments. They sought answers as to why and how these attacks occurred.

Americans were not the only to suffer the consequences of the September 11 attacks. Nearly 400 civilians from outside of the United States perished in the four strikes, and support from the international community abounded in the days and weeks that followed. The United Nations Security Council permanent members contacted President Bush to express their condolences and, in many cases, pledge their support for a US-led response to the attacks (Weitsman 2014). The Security Council

© The Author(s) 2020
J. Garey, *The US Role in NATO's Survival After the Cold War*,
Palgrave Studies in International Relations,
https://doi.org/10.1007/978-3-030-13675-8_4

also immediately passed a resolution explicitly condemning the attacks and pledging support for the United States, while NATO invoked Article 5 of the Washington Treaty for the first time in alliance history. Despite an outpouring of support from the United Nations, NATO, other international organizations, and individual states, the United States quickly decided that once the responsible parties were identified, it would engage in military operations with limited allied participation.

Seventeen years later, Afghanistan is the United States' most protracted conflict in history. Established in November 2014 and further legitimized by UN Security Council Resolution 2189, NATO's Resolute Support (RS) continues "to train, advise and assist the Afghan security forces and institutions" (NATO 2018). What began as a stopgap measure to restore stability at the end of NATO's International Security Assistance Force (ISAF) mission is still in operation, and four years later supported by an estimated 8400 American soldiers—nearly half of the total NATO forces deployed in Afghanistan (U.S. Department of Defense 2018). Further, in 2017 Trump administration officials acknowledged the presence of several thousand more troops engaged in temporary, covert, and counterterrorism activity, putting the United States' total presence closer to 11,000 personnel (Cooper 2017).

While much was documented about decisions and processes in the post-9/11 era, considerably less attention is paid to *how* the United States engaged the NATO alliance in particular, and *why* it pursued this engagement, or just how significant the alliance's first-time invocation of Article V of the North Atlantic Treaty would be in subsequent years. This chapter identifies the impacts of the war in Afghanistan on US-NATO relations, as well as changes to the alliance stemming from this relationship. Expanding the two-stage model developed by Sarah Kreps to understand American multilateralism in Afghanistan, I divide the war into three phases to analyze US-NATO relations in the same period (Kreps 2011). The first phase began on September 11, 2001, when the United States had a tremendous amount of support from its allies and much of the international community. Some of the United States' allies disagreed with the operational strategies of the United States, including the decision to engage only a small contingent of international forces, but few challenged the *necessity* of a military intervention against the perpetrators of the attacks.

The second phase is denoted by the commencement of Operation Enduring Freedom (OEF) on October 7, 2001. This operation was unique in important ways: Americans largely acted alone, and instead of engaging hundreds of thousands of ground troops, relied heavily on special operations forces (SOFs). Additionally, the United States' primary ally was the Northern Alliance, which posed a number of challenges to the mission's success. The third phase begins in December 2001, with the establishment of the International Security Assistance Force (ISAF). ISAF underwent several changes in the ensuing years, including a transition of leadership from individual states to the NATO alliance, and operated in conjunction with OEF operations.

Examination of each of these phases reveals important evidence to support or confirm all of the earlier hypotheses concerning US-NATO relations to varying degrees. Four factors led the United States to prefer limited military contributions from allies during OEF: the difficulties with command and control during the 1999 Kosovo operation, a growing divide of capabilities between the United States and NATO members, the preferences of members of the Bush administration in combatting international terrorism, and a widespread belief that the actions of the United States were both morally and legally legitimate. The United States did not perceive a need to campaign for legitimacy prior to OEF. Unlike the Kosovo and Iraq interventions, both the United Nations and NATO overwhelmingly supported the United States' decision to act in response to the 9/11 attacks. Thus, US policymakers believed the United States' military operations would be widely accepted as legitimate.

Previous scholarship, treating American decisions and interests in isolation from NATO decisions and interests, asserted the United States' decision to limit NATO engagement in the early stages of the Afghanistan war as indicative of the relationship's decline (Abyat and Moore 2010; Garden 2002; Goldgeier 2009; Rupp 2006; Talbott 2002). However, these analyses provide unsatisfactory explanations as to not only continued American support of NATO efforts, but also its investment in new programs designed to enhance NATO's capacity in light of Afghanistan and in spite of shortcomings in Kosovo. When the United Nations established the International Security Assistance Force (ISAF) mission in December 2001, the necessity of NATO participation was almost immediately evident. The United States advocated for NATO's leadership in ISAF in 2003, allowing the alliance to take responsibility for outreach, stabilization, and reconstruction. This led to the development of both military and nonmilitary resources within the alliance, but was not done to simply pass the buck, as previously assumed: throughout the entirety of OEF, the United States made sizable financial and resource contributions, including troops. In light of evidence presented here, this is consistent with an overarching perception of NATO's utility among American policymakers.

In terms of its capabilities, NATO developed much more aggressive antiterrorism and counterterrorism policies, including improving intelligence sharing to prevent terrorism, advancing technology to defend against and counterterrorist attacks, improving the alliance's chemical, biological, radiological, and nuclear (CBRN) defense systems, and ensuring the alliance had the necessary military equipment and interoperability for any threat to member states. As demonstrated here, these changes were largely consistent with American perspectives of both the causes of and adequate responses to terrorism, diverging from the European perspective—in spite of the alliance's consensus decision-making model—and corroborating the notion of American interests as pivotal to sustaining its alliance relationship, due to its influence over its evolution.

In addition to enhanced capacity to respond to threats, these actions further entrenched US interests in the alliance and cemented US-NATO relations. On the nonmilitary side the alliance worked to improve its relationships with non-NATO members through programs such as the Istanbul Cooperation Initiative (ICI) to further enhance information sharing and antiterrorism efforts. ISAF troops worked to build community relationships, engage nongovernmental actors and build stronger civil-military relations. It implemented literacy and education campaigns, worked to strengthen the Afghan National Army (ANA) and the Afghan National Police (ANP), reestablished a judicial system, and provided support for many other humanitarian missions within the country. This expanded American perspectives of NATO's capacity to fill both traditional military and nontraditional needs, and further supports hypotheses regarding US interests in multilateralism and the utility of multilateralism (perceived and real).

The Afghanistan conflict provided two unique opportunities to NATO. Firstly, it was able to demonstrate its utility to the United States and have an impact on the conduct of the war. Secondly, its ability to evolve to meet the demands of the new threat environment ensured that it would remain relevant and persist in the post-Cold War period. While the United States decided to largely forgo NATO participation in the first two phases of the war, it continued to contribute to the alliance to improve NATO's ability to engage in conflict. In the third phase of the war, the United States recognized the necessity of NATO engagement and advocated the alliance take a leading role in the ISAF mission, thus demonstrating both its interest and its role in the alliance's persistence.

BACKGROUND: UNDERSTANDING THE UNITED STATES, AFGHANISTAN, AND NATO BEFORE 9/11

Although a new chapter in US-Afghanistan relations began on September 11, 2001, it was hardly the United States' first encounter with bin Laden or al Qaeda. Though the organization—translated from Arabic to mean "the base"—was intended to create a centralized system for documenting the mujahedeen, visitors, and family members of the camps of Afghan fighters during the Soviet-Afghan war, bin Laden's vision for the future quickly morphed the organization into a global network for Islamic groups to focus attention on international jihad and engage in well-orchestrated acts of terror under the principles of radical Islamist fundamentalism (Scheurer 2011; Lansford 2012; PBS 2014). When Pakistan and Afghanistan signed the Geneva Accords in April 1988, the Soviet Union began to withdraw its troops from Afghanistan to finally end the war (Klass 1988). Bin Laden perceived the Soviet withdraw to be a victory for al Qaeda and sought to expand the organization's capacity to conduct global jihad in places like South Yemen, Somalia, Chechnya, Kosovo, and Kashmir. A devout Sunni Muslim, bin Laden was incensed by the actions of the Soviets during the war and, after the implementation of the Geneva Accords, turned his attention to the United States.

Bin Laden blamed American policymakers for the plight of Afghanistan after the Soviet war and representative of "the forces of evil that are bringing corruption and domination into the Islamic world" (Dobbs 2001) despite its support for the mujahedeen during the war. Meanwhile, the United States provided support for one of the largest anti-Taliban groups, the Northern Alliance, and initiated a secret plan to purchase anti-aircraft missiles and other weaponry from the Afghans. When the Taliban and al Qaeda conquered Kabul (the Afghanistan capital) in September 1996, increasing the Taliban's territorial control to nearly two-thirds, the United States and other Western nations continued to recognize the Afghanistan president, Burhanunddin Rabbani, as the legitimate leader of the country. These actions, as well as United States' sustained intervention in Afghanistan and other Islamic countries, further enraged bin Laden as he continued amassing considerable wealth and other necessary resources for continued pursuit of jihad through his organization al Qaeda (Coll 2004).

Despite its prevalence in eastern and southeastern Europe, the Middle East, and Central Asia, as well as its work alongside other anti-West groups to orchestrate terrorist attacks, al Qaeda's operations remained largely outside of the NATO alliance's area of operation in its early years. This changed with an attack on the World Trade Center, sovereign American soil, in 1993, in which six people died and more than a thousand were injured (FBI 2008). Additional attacks, including against UN peacekeepers and American soldiers in Mogadishu, Somalia, a foiled plot to assassinate the Pope and down a dozen airliners in 1995, challenged the existing US-NATO antiterrorism and counterterrorism efforts and highlighted a growing divide between the United States and its allies regarding the best path forward.

The United States' comprehensive policies for combatting terrorism during the Clinton administration were slow to change and were principally focused on domestic, law enforcement measures and terrorism more broadly, not bin Laden and al Qaeda specifically. In early 1995, President Clinton introduced to Congress the Omnibus Counterterrorism Act (OCA) of 1995 to establish clear federal jurisdiction over international terrorism, but the bill was never enacted (Clinton 1995). In response to the April 1995 domestic bombing of the Alfred P. Murrah Federal Building in Oklahoma City, Oklahoma—at the time, the single worst terrorist act on US soil, killing 168 and injuring hundreds more (FBI 2007)—the administration pushed again for stronger legislation, this time proposing the Antiterrorism Amendments Act (AAA) of 1995. The OCA and the AAA were combined and passed into law under the Antiterrorism and Effective Death Penalty Act of 1996. The legislation drastically expanded the authority of law enforcement officials to collect information and conduct electronic and financial surveillance (Clinton 1995).

The response to the threat of bin Laden and al Qaeda was also mixed. It primarily relied on diplomacy to pressure Saudi Arabia and Sudan to end their relationship with bin Laden. After the 1996 Khobar Towers attack and bin Laden's return to Afghanistan, the United States carried out airstrikes against known al Qaeda training facilities in Afghanistan and Sudan. In August 1998, al Qaeda-linked terrorists detonated two truck bombs at US embassies in Kenya and Tanzania, killing 234 people and injuring several thousand. The Clinton administration, believing al Qaeda to be supporting the group behind the attacks, issued an indictment for bin Laden and demanded the Taliban surrender him. Still, bin Laden eluded capture and continued to lead al Qaeda, coordinating additional attacks including the 2000 bombing of the USS Cole, which killed 17 sailors and injured dozens (Perl and O'Rourke 2001). In 1999, President Clinton signed Executive order 13129, which declared the threat posed by al Qaeda a national emergency and established sanctions against the Taliban because of its ties to bin Laden and al Qaeda (Exec. Order 13129). The Clinton administration also pushed the international community to become more aggressive in their antiterrorism and counterterrorism measures, as well as to strengthen policies regarding weapons of mass destruction (WMDs). After the 1996 Khobar Towers bombing, the G-7 convened in Lyons and pushed terrorism to the top of the agenda (Clinton 1996). The European Union consulted closely with the United States to develop extradition and mutual legal assistance programs, restrict fundraising opportunities for terrorist organizations, and engage in intelligence sharing (Clinton 1998). In response to the 1998 embassy bombings, the United Nations undertook efforts to locate and prosecute bin Laden. Under Chapter VII of the United Nations Charter, the UN Security Council established a sanction regime against al Qaeda beginning with UNSCR 1267.[1] The resolution demanded the delivery of bin Laden within 30 days, citing the United States' indictment of him for the 1998 embassy bombings. If the Taliban failed to deliver him, the resolution authorized a number of sanctions, travel restrictions, and trade embargos (similar to those in Clinton's executive order 13129) to be implemented (UN Security Council 1999).

The United Nations also worked to establish stability in Afghanistan after the 1989 Geneva Accords. In addition to the United Nations Special Mission to Afghanistan (UNSMA), the UN provided financial and food aid, construction materials to rebuild homes, basic healthcare provisions such as immunizations, and assistance with limiting the production of opium. After the US embassy attacks in 1998, the Security Council adopted resolutions 1193 and 1214, condemning the Taliban and demanding the immediate end of ties with international terrorist organizations (UN News Centre 2017).

Prior to the September 11, 2001, attacks, however, there was very little momentum for enhanced antiterrorism and counterterrorism planning in the NATO alliance. Declassified NATO committee communiques, ministerial

---

[1] Resolution 1267 (1999) was the first resolution to address al Qaeda. It was followed by Resolutions 1333(2000), 1390(2002), 1455(2003), 1526(2004), 1617(2005), 1735(2006), 1822(2008), 1904(2009), 1989(2011), 2083(2012) and resolution 2161(2014). Each of these resolutions addresses individuals, groups, and other entities with al Qaeda affiliations and is comprised of three elements: a travel ban, an arms embargo, and the freezing of assets. See: "Security Council Committee Pursuant to Resolutions 1267 (1999) and 1989 (2011) Concerning Al-Qaida and Associated Individuals and Entities," United Nations, accessed December 8, 2017, https://www.un.org/sc/suborg/en/sanctions/1267

communiques, summit declarations, and other documents from 1990–2001 and other documents indicate limited concern for terrorism relative to other potential threats to alliance members. Most discussions limited to the alliance itself linked terrorism to other threats, such as the use of illegal biological and radiological weapons. In the Euro-Atlantic Council, which brought 21 non-member states together with the allies to address issues of shared concern, terrorism was frequently included in the two-year planning agenda but largely lacked actionable directives. Russian actions in Chechnya brought terrorism and human rights into larger discussions in the NATO-Russia Council, and Serbian charges of terrorism against Kosovar Albanians brought condemnation from the North Atlantic Council (NATO 1990–2001). The 1991 and 1999 Strategic Concepts each mention terrorism only once, in a broad dialogue about supporting allies and protecting NATO member state assets with no substantive explanation or focus (NATO 1991, 1999). This is in contrast to the 2010 Strategic Concept, the first since the 9/11 attacks, wherein terrorism was a central focus of the alliance's prescribed mandate despite being drafted nearly a decade later (NATO 2010).

There are two explanations for NATO's limited focus on terrorism prior to 9/11. First, beginning in the mid-1990s, the allies were preoccupied by conflict in the Balkans, culminating in the 1999 Kosovo intervention. As demonstrated in the previous chapter, changes to the alliance, such as the 1999 Defense Capabilities Initiative, were in large part because of the challenges resulting from the command structure, capabilities disparity, and operational execution during the Kosovo intervention.

Second, though several allies experienced terrorist attacks in the 1990s, terrorism was considered a domestic problem, not an international one, and limited in its prevalence. From 1990–2001, nearly 2700 citizens of NATO members were killed in terrorist attacks, rivaling the number of people killed in the WTC bombings. However, there was no single attack (or group of attacks executed by one organization) causing such loss of life: most instances involved fewer than 100 casualties (Global Terrorism Database 2018). In many attacks, the organization was located domestically, creating the perception of the threat being localized, not regional or international. These groups—such as the IRA in the United Kingdom and the ETA in Spain—were not radicalized Islamic fundamentalists, and operated largely within the state they threatened. Though bin Laden continued to grow the al Qaeda network of Islamic extremist groups, it was not immediately clear that there was an imminent global threat. Thus, most states (including the United States) worked to strengthen domestic surveillance and law enforcement efforts, as well as further securing infrastructure likely to be targeted (such as airports). Efforts to work with allies on antiterrorism networks were aimed primarily at information sharing and limiting the access of nonstate actors to weapons of mass destruction.

THE SEPTEMBER 11 ATTACKS

When President Bush entered into office in January 2001, there was no evidence that his administration intended to change its policies toward Afghanistan, the Taliban, or al Qaeda. It appeared as though many of President Bush's closest foreign policy advisors lacked an intimate knowledge of the region, and this may have contributed to his decision to retain the Clinton administration's Director of Central Intelligence, George Tenet. Director Tenet regularly voiced his concerns about al Qaeda, briefing National Security Advisor (NSA) Condoleezza Rice and others in the months prior to the attacks about his concerns over al Qaeda's growing network (Coll 2004). Domestic issues on the administration's agenda took priority, forcing concerns over bin Laden, al Qaeda, and international terrorism to the back burner.

But on September 11, 2001, the United States was again under attack by international terrorists. President Bush and officials from the Department of Defense, the FBI, the CIA, the Justice Department, and numerous other organizations worked in the hours and days following the attacks to ascertain the information necessary to mount a counterattack. News quickly spread of the likely connection between the attacks and al Qaeda. For the most part, the American public was unaware of threat from al Qaeda prior to now; though videotapes of bin Laden calling for a holy war against the United States had been circulating for months and he was suspected in the 1998 embassy bombings and the 2000 bombing of the USS Cole, the organization never explicitly admitted any direct responsibility for previous attacks. Bin Laden denied responsibility for the attacks on the WTC buildings and the Pentagon, but praised the attackers' actions (CNN 2001).

In the days following the attacks, President Bush and others publicly asserted the likelihood that bin Laden orchestrated the attacks and their investigation into al Qaeda's role (Balz 2001). In his address to a joint session of Congress on September 20, 2001, the president confirmed these suspicions and announced the United States' intentions to go to war in Afghanistan. In the address, Bush made it clear that the intentions of the United States was to find bin Laden and bring him to justice, as well as eliminate the threat posed by al Qaeda. He issued demands to the Taliban:

Deliver to United States authorities all the leaders of Al Qaida who hide in your land...Close immediately and permanently every terrorist training camp in Afghanistan, and hand over every terrorist and every person in their support structure to appropriate authorities. Give the United States full access to terrorist training camps, so we can make sure they are no longer operating. These demands are not open to negotiation or discussion. The Taliban must act and act immediately. They will hand over the terrorists, or they will share in their fate. (Bush 2001)

The administration immediately undertook a number of domestic initiatives aimed at strengthening the United States' ability to track and prevent future terrorist attacks. The newly established Office of Homeland Security would be to bring together all of the agencies relevant to the war against terrorism. The Transportation Security Administration (TSA) was tasked with securing transportation systems and monitoring the transport of people and goods via land, air, and sea (U.S. Department of Homeland Security 2016). The administration underscored the authority of the National Security Administration (NSA) and worked to create legislation that would expand the domestic and international monitoring capabilities, including the Uniting and Strengthening America by Providing Appropriate Tools Required to Intercept and Obstruct Terrorism Act (Pub. L. No. 107-56, 115 Stat. 272 2001). Efforts to strengthen law enforcement officials' ability to use surveillance, money tracking, and information sharing technology were widely supported by Congress.

One of the most important pieces of legislation during this time was the 2001 Joint Authorization for the Use of Military Force (AUMF). The AUMF authorized President Bush to "use all necessary and appropriate force against those nations, organizations, or persons he determines planned, authorized, committed, or aided the terrorist attacks that occurred on September 11, 2001, or harbored such organizations or persons, in order to prevent any future acts of international terrorism against the United States by such nations, organizations or persons" (Pub. L. No. 107-40, 115 Stat. 224 2001). The bill passed the Senate 98-0, with vote abstentions from Senators Larry Craig (R-Idaho) and Jesse Helms (R-North Carolina). Only one representative in the House—Barbara Lee (D-California)—voted against the bill (Ibid). In some respects, the AUMF and the additional legislation was a contemporary manifestation of the 1964 Tonkin Gulf Resolution: the president had the overwhelming support of both Congress and the American public to prosecute the war on terror.

In addition to reaffirming the United States' resolve to bring those responsible to justice, President Bush and others worked to reassure the American public, shore up congressional and public support, and strategized ways to engage al Qaeda and the Taliban in a war in Afghanistan. Public opinion polls indicated 65–71 percent of those questioned supported military action, and when asked in later September 2001, 64 percent of respondents supported the use of ground troops in Afghanistan. This was due in part to the feelings of vulnerability after the attacks: prior to Operation Enduring Freedom, nearly 80 percent of Americans surveyed by CBS/NYT polls believed the United States was likely to experience terrorist attacks in the future (Huddy et al. 2002). President Bush's approval ratings skyrocketed to 86 percent after 9/11 as a result of both the attacks and the bipartisan congressional support for action (Larson and Savych 2005).

Within days of the September attacks, CIA teams and Operational Detachment Alpha teams deployed to Afghanistan, and a unilateral response to al Qaeda seemed imminent. President Bush and Secretary of Defense Donald Rumsfeld ordered military planners at the Pentagon to develop several plans for moving forward in Afghanistan. Rumsfeld pushed for the United States to adopt a strategy in Afghanistan that was consistent with the Revolution in Military Affairs (RMA) model he spearheaded prior to the attack. Central to the RMA was a belief the defense establishment had grown to be practically unmanageable and wholly inefficient, and support for the model was augmented by strategists' specific concerns about the mountainous terrain of Afghanistan and the nature of finding al Qaeda operatives (in areas that were predominately civilian).

In the wake of the 1998 embassy bombings military officials at US Central Command (USCENTCOM), responsible for developing strategies for any kind of event in the Middle East, North Africa, and Central Asia, including Afghanistan, developed options for striking bin Laden which included Delta Force-led covert operations, aerial bombing campaigns, and a land invasion. However, USCENTCOM lacked a comprehensive plan for dealing with both the Taliban and al Qaeda, citing operational roadblocks such as lack of available airfields in the region, poor infrastructure such as roads and electrical networks, as well as poor communications systems and inadequate water supplies. Because USCENTCOM did not have an existing plan for Afghanistan, its commander, Army General Tommy Franks, scrambled to meet the condensed timeline set by policymakers after the WTC attacks. This timeline, as well as the resulting USCENTCOM strategy that called for thousands more troops than Secretary Rumsfeld preferred, caused significant tension between General Franks and Rumsfeld (Lambeth 2005). Ultimately, Bush choose Rumsfeld's limited model over USCENTCOM's resource-heavy recommendations, thus the "Afghan model" was born. Planners devised an engagement relying heavily on US airpower, intelligence assets, and special operations forces (SOFs) (Biddle 2005/2006). The SOFs would work with indigenous allies to build relationships with village officials and locate suspected al Qaeda affiliates.

Phase 1: International and NATO Support After 9/11

The international community expressed widespread support in the wake of the attacks. In addition to calls from members of the UN Security Council expressing their condolences and pledging their support, there was a public outpouring of support for the United States. From the now-iconic *Le Monde* headline declaring "We are all Americans!" to the playing of "The Star Spangled Banner" at Buckingham Palace, the international public openly mourned alongside its North American ally (Lansford 2012). September 12th's UN Security Council Resolution 1368 condemned the attacks and expressed the Security Council's "readiness to take all necessary steps to respond…and to combat all forms of terrorism, in accordance with its responsibilities under the Charter of the United Nations" (United Nations Security Council, Resolution 1368 2001). A second resolution, UNSCR 1373, followed on September 28, 2001, which reaffirmed the UN Charter Article 51's self-defense provision.

Closer inspection of the period immediately following the 9/11 attack reveals three important indicators: how the allies conceptualized its support to whatever course of action American decision-makers pursued, how the United States valued this support, and the realized effects of both actors' decision-making on the war as well as the US-NATO relationship. During the pre-war period, the United States attempted to increase multilateral support for its larger war on terror, but did not consider multilateralism as necessary to combat operations. As noted previously, the alliance was in many ways unprepared to execute counterterrorism efforts due to a lack of attention and planning within the alliance and the emphasis on terrorism as a largely domestic threat. Still, allied support remained high and the United States' plans were generally accepted as both legally and morally legitimate.

For the first time in its history, NATO invoked Article 5 of the Washington Treaty, which states

…an armed attack against one or more of them in Europe or North America shall be considered an attack against them all and consequently they agree that, if such an armed attack occurs, each of them, in exercise of the right of individual or collective self-defence recognised by Article 51 of the Charter of the United Nations, will assist the Party or Parties so attacked by taking forthwith, individually and in concert with the other Parties, such action as it deems necessary, including the use of armed force, to restore and maintain the security of the North Atlantic area. (NATO 2014)

In his address to Congress on September 20, President Bush spoke to the role of other states, saying that the threat posed by terrorism was not a problem unique to the United States but rather threatened the international community. "The United States is grateful that many nations and many international organizations have already responded with sympathy and with support, nations from Latin America to Asia, to Africa, to Europe, to the Islamic world. Perhaps the NATO Charter reflects the best attitude of the world: an attack on one is an attack on all" (Bush 2001).

In addition to the support pledged by both the United Nations and NATO, several individual states approached the United States to offer resources for the United States' global war on terror. The United Kingdom, Australia, France, Italy, Turkey, Canada, Germany, and others offered troops, aircraft, and other necessary support to US operations (Weitsman 2014). While Secretary of State Colin Powell continued to work with the UN and NATO, President Bush personally rallied support from state leaders by contacting over 80 countries, gaining pledges of assistance from dozens of states. Bush also convinced 27 states to provide overflight and landing rights for US operations, citing USCENTCOM's pre-9/11 Afghanistan assessments (Lambeth 2005).

Interestingly, Russian President Vladimir Putin pledged support for both the US and NATO efforts. Noting their own experiences with terrorism, Russian policymakers pledged to share any pertinent intelligence information about the hijackings with the United States and to engage with NATO on an international mission against terrorism. Russian experts were sent to the CIA to share their experiences during the Soviet war, particularly in regard to Afghanistan's mountainous terrain. Russia agreed to allow the United States access to its airspace for humanitarian flights and pledged combat and rescue support. President Putin gave explicit permission for former Soviet republics in Central Asia to assist the United States as they saw fit. This allowed the United States to pursue basing support and air access from states such as Uzbekistan, Tajikistan, and Turkmenistan (Lambeth 2005).

The United States was initially reluctant to accept most of the military pledges of support, with one notable exception: the United Kingdom. Prime Minister Tony Blair believed the relationship to be integral to UK interests, and after the 9/11 attacks urged the United States to accept its offers of support and assemble a multilateral coalition. He also thought the assault against al Qaeda and the Taliban was necessary for securing the United Kingdom—the likelihood of future attacks was not limited to the United States and had the potential to be even more devastating in scope should the groups acquire weapons of mass destruction (Davidson 2011). Thus, he offered the Americans access to all of the United Kingdom's available resources—including the 20,000 British soldiers stationed in Oman—with few restrictions on how these resources could be used. British Special Forces were also able to engage alongside US SOFs prior to the commencement of the official operation (Weitsman 2014).

Outside of the United States' partnership with the United Kingdom, much of the military support pledged by states and international organizations went largely unaccepted by policymakers in the initial planning stage, including the support of NATO. Scholars offered three plausible explanations as to why this was the case. First, there was a prevailing concern that a second round of attacks was imminent. Any delay resulting from multilateral planning could result in the loss of more American lives, and policymakers wanted immediate action, even if it required a unilateral approach (Kreps 2011). Second, the United States was not eager to repeat the challenges of allied intervention like it had in Kosovo in 1999 (Davidson 2011). In addition to coordination problems with ground troops and resources, the engagement in Kosovo tested the alliance's cohesiveness. Many states placed caveats on the use of their troops and the geographic areas in which they could engage, limiting the effectiveness of the alliance's engagement (Auerswald and Saideman 2014).

Third, policymakers recognized that even if allied support was incorporated into the United States' strategy for Afghanistan, most states were unequipped with the necessary technology and resources to allow them to contribute. After Cold War, US policymakers argued with its European counterparts over the necessity of maintaining a robust and easily mobile

NATO force. Previous attempts at strengthening the alliance's military capabilities—such as the 1999 Defense Capabilities Initiative—were given low priority by many European allies (Sloan 2005). Changing demographics, the end of military conscription, and shrinking defense budgets in many states resulted in an inability to contribute to the alliance (Simon 2008).

American denial of the generous offers of its international partners implies prima facie a unilateral operation would commence. The Afghan model gave no real consideration to allied support and many officials believed the United States would have a relatively easy fight against a poorly trained, loosely organized enemy further, adding a plausible fourth explanation for limited international participation in the initial weeks after the 9/11 attack.

A closer look, however, shows otherwise. Condoleezza Rice, National Security Advisor, was one of the principal proponents of including NATO, while Vice President Richard Cheney articulated the need for the United States to avoid any alliance or coalition member who sought to exert control over the United States' actions. Both later remarked that despite the outcome, President Bush actually favored a more prominent role for the alliance (Cheney and Cheney 2012; Rice 2011). Some American policymakers were reluctant to use a NATO command structure in Afghanistan because of its experiences with command and execution difficulties in the 1999 Kosovo intervention, yet the United States requested a number of resources from its NATO allies including enhanced intelligence sharing, assistance to states with high levels of threat, clearance for air operations, air support (such as fueling), and additional security for facilities integral to US operations. The North Atlantic Council also pledged the support of its naval forces in the Eastern Mediterranean, as well as use of its Airborne Early Warning and Control Force (AWACs) to support operations (Sloan 2005). On October 9, 2001, in conjunction with the US Operation Enduring Freedom, NATO launched Operation Eagle Assist. The operation used AWACs to patrol US sovereign airspace in conjunction with the United States' Operation Noble Eagle, and was the first deployment of NATO resources over US territory in the alliance's history (NATO 2017).

Thus, with regard to how the allies perceived NATO's role in responding to the 9/11 attacks, there was clear support for a comprehensive commitment from both member and partner states as well as considerable access to shared allied resources. The value of these offers and NATO's initial response to 9/11 for the United States, however, is less clear.

Resource contributions were not valued as highly, caused significant concern at times, and limited in acceptance of country aid. Invocation of Article 5, widespread political support from allies and partners such as Russia, and relationship-building, however, provided political utility to the United States, which it then used as confirmation its actions would be perceived as legally and ethically legitimate in the eyes of the international community.

Operation Enduring Freedom

On October 7, 2001, the United States and the United Kingdom reported to the UN Security Council about their intention to use military force pursuant to Article 51 of the United Nations Charter. Operation Enduring Freedom commenced with aerial and cruise missile attacks, and was designed as both a preemptive and retaliatory strike: though the United States sought justice for the 9/11 attacks, it also hoped that removing the Taliban from power would prevent future regimes from aiding al Qaeda or other terrorist organizations (Williams 2008). The United States' aggressive air assault was intended to disrupt the Taliban's air defences, though it was later revealed that the administration also sought to scare al Qaeda operatives out of hiding and collect intelligence on bin Laden's whereabouts. In many respects, the United States' campaign during the first ten days was successful: no enemy fighters were ever able to be airborne during the entire war, and the United States sustained no casualties and minimal difficulties on the ground.

After ten full days of bombing, the second phase of the operation commenced with a more extensive ground campaign. The ground campaign largely consisted of US and Northern Alliance members, and ran in conjunction with a continued aerial campaign. Coalition and Northern Alliance members moved throughout the country to dismantle Taliban and al Qaeda resources and raise support from Afghan civilians. The ground campaign was considered by many to be slower moving and less successful than the aerial strikes. This was in part because US forces were under strict orders to pass any intended target through a long chain of command, for two reasons: officials wanted to minimize civilian casualties in the hopes of limiting anti-Americanism sentiments among the locals, and they hoped to preserve the existing infrastructure of Afghanistan for the stabilization and reconstruction phase of the war.

November 2001 was a turning point for Operation Enduring Freedom. Coalition and Northern Alliance fighters took the city of Mazar-e-Sharif back from the Taliban on November 9. The coalition then set its sights on the capital city of Kabul, and on November 13 were able to reclaim the city. After the fall of Kabul, the United States began a protracted guerilla war against al Qaeda and Taliban forces throughout the country. Kandahar, the second-largest city in Afghanistan and the last major city under Taliban control at the end of 2001, was seized shortly after. In early 2002, a major combat operation in the Shah-i-Kot valley took place. The coalition engaged and killed dozens of al Qaeda fighters over a two-week period. When US and Canadian troops finally withdrew on March 19, US officials declared its ground initiatives successful (PBS 2017a).

Phase 2: International and NATO Support at the Outset of Operation Enduring Freedom

When the United States finally launched its operations on October 7, the Bush administration highlighted resource contributions from over 40 states and pledges of support from dozens more. Some of the 70 states indirectly pledged their support via international organization membership, while others extended direct support in addition to the international organizations in which they participated. Some of these states were asked by US officials to provide specific types of support, while others pledged resources they believed to be paramount to the United States' operations. Additionally, many of these pledges were intentionally vague (Gerleman et al. 2001).

Despite this, the United States' initial engagement was largely unilateral. At the outset of Operation Enduring Freedom, only the United Kingdom and the Northern Alliance actually fought alongside the United States. Great Britain provided Tomahawk missiles, Royal Navy submarines, access to air force bases, and troops and support from the Royal Air Force. These contributions were particularly important to the United States' air campaign, as the British provided 20 percent of the necessary inflight refueling capacity for the operation. Great Britain also contributed 4200 personnel at the outset of the operation (Lambeth 2005).

Although its pre-war plans did not anticipate substantial multilateral engagement and it limited coalition support in the early days of the operation, American policymakers capitalized on the offers of support for its efforts shortly after the engagement commenced. Australia and Canada deployed both troops and aircraft. France supplied a number of aircraft, satellites and other intelligence and reconnaissance assets, as well as naval resources. French Special Forces were put on high alert and the French leadership pledged troops to support the ground offensive. Germany supplied armored vehicles designed for chemical, biological, and radiological (CBR) materials. The Germans offered 3900 military personnel for coalition operations. Australia, Canada, Denmark, France, Poland, and Germany all offered special operations forces, but were never considered by US planners. The Italians and Dutch supplied a variety of aircraft for both attack missions and reconnaissance. The end of 2001 brought major changes to coalition efforts: whereas the war had previously been waged primarily from the air, the United States transitioned to a ground effort. The United States continued to be receptive to allied participation, accepting support from more than 25 partners (Weitsman 2014). In mid-November 2001, Great Britain deployed 100 commandos to Bagram; however, the Afghan leadership argued this was a violation of their sovereignty and the United States put the deployment on hold. In all, there were 69 members of the OEF coalition, with military contributions from 21 of these states (Lambeth 2005; Kreps 2011; Hallams 2009).

NATO as a whole remained largely removed from the United States' strategy. It continued its patrol of American airspace as part of Operation Eagle Assist to allow US resources to be used elsewhere. In addition, NATO commenced patrolling efforts in the Mediterranean Sea to monitor shipping and to engage with any suspect ships. This operation—Operation Active Endeavour—was later expanded to escort nonmilitary ships through the Straits of Gibraltar (NATO 2016). NATO officials also agreed to reduce the ongoing mission in Kosovo to allow US troops to be restationed in Afghanistan. Of the 21 states that contributed military resources to OEF, 14 of these states were NATO members. Like in Kosovo, the United States was better equipped than the other allies and it provided most of the operation's military capabilities. Where the 1999 Kosovo and 2001 Afghanistan operations differed was the command structure: the United States was not restricted to a (sometimes arduous) NATO decision-making process. For his part, NATO Secretary General Lord George Robertson defended both NATO and the United States' decision to engage without the alliance's participation. He continually advocated for the United States to accept more of the allies' offers of assistance, particularly offers of humanitarian relief supplies into neighboring Central Asian countries (Hallams 2009; Lambeth 2005). In mid-November, NATO began developing plans for the anticipated humanitarian effort that would be undertaken after OEF completed, and these plans would serve as the basis of the UN peacekeeping effort (Lansford 2012).

Though the United States enjoyed a high level of political and military support for its operations in the pre-war phase, its reluctance to allow the full participation of other states in OEF resulted in tension amongst NATO allies. While France played a role in the operation, it expressed its concern over the United States' seeming willingness to act unilaterally. French officials were upset by the absence of international participation in the planning stages of the war, and expressed its concern about the stability of Afghanistan after the United States' operation. Days before Operation Enduring Freedom commenced, France appealed to the European Union to develop stabilization and reconstruction plans for Afghanistan after the Taliban was deposed. Some NATO allies, such as Italy, expressed their contempt regarding the United States' decision not to utilize the resources offered (Kitchen 2010). The United States' proposal to invade Iraq in 2002 exacerbated tensions over operations in Afghanistan. Though Green Parties across Europe began expressing their reservations about US actions against al Qaeda bases almost immediately after Operation Enduring Freedom began, concern about the long-term sustainability of the Afghanistan mission in light of the United States' proposed second war in Iraq worsened European sentiment (Kaplan 2004).

On the ground, a number of operational missteps also challenged OEF's success. Despite its efforts to maintain a rigorous targeting process and clear chain of command, locals reported incidents of civilian casualties and mistakenly bombed targets. In the first year of OEF, Human Rights Watch reported over 200 casualties, among which at least 15 were children (Human Rights Watch 2003). There were also several friendly fire incidents between the US and Canadian forces, as well as between British and American troops, igniting tensions between the allies. British troops were involved in a friendly fire incident in the Helmand province after they ordered US airstrikes because they believed they were being attacked by Taliban forces. However, the attack was actually by the Afghan police force, which also mistook the British troops for Taliban fighters. The incident killed 1 Afghan officer and wounded 12 others. There were several reports of accidental bombings of coalition assets and civilian buildings, including two separate bombings of a facility used by the International Committee of the Red Cross (ICRC) (Weitsman 2014; Leigh 2010; Lambeth 2005).

The contributions from and challenges to NATO and coalition support for the war reveal important answers as to how the United States perceived and valued allied contributions, how NATO perceived its own ability to contribute, and some of the effects this had on the US-NATO relationship. In isolation, failure to include NATO as part of its Afghan model—whether deliberate or inadvertent—suggests limited value was placed on allied participation. The United States enjoyed enough military capacity to choose between a Powell Doctrine-esque use of force and the Rumsfeld's RMA model, and demonstrated during the Clinton administration (including Kosovo) it was not only able but almost eager to forego land invasion, preferring instead to wage war (successfully) from the skies. As other factors are layered in, however, such as the United States' attempts to rally international support for its efforts and its warming to coalition and NATO support in later stages of OEF, a challenge to this assumption emerges, suggesting the United States' perceptions of multilateralism more accurately resembling a *necessary but not sufficient* image. President Bush's continual efforts to rally international support indicate that the United States placed a premium on the political value of alliance engagement, and the administration's willingness to accept resources are indicative of perceived military value. Though there were disagreements between allies, it is also clear there was a widespread perception regarding the legitimacy of American actions, which was undoubtedly enhanced by the United States' adherence to norms in NATO and the United Nations.

Legitimacy and Multilateralism in Phases 1 and 2

In the first two phases of the war—the pre-war planning phase and the initial combat operation OEF—the United States enjoyed a high level of support for its actions, which were widely accepted as legitimate. In the pre-war phase, the United States was responding to a clear violation of its sovereignty and attack on its homeland. Individual states and international organizations lined up behind the United States to offer political, economic, and military support for a retaliatory strike. Both domestic and international public opinions were also high. Though it quickly became evident that the United States intended to strike Afghanistan in a military operation that did not include widespread international participation, its plans to engage al Qaeda and the Taliban fell well within the parameters of Article 51 of the United Nations Charter (the self-defense clause). Thus, the United States' actions in this phase were considered by most to be morally and legally legitimate. During OEF, there were few challenges to the legal legitimacy of the operation. Questions about the moral legitimacy of US operations arose, but these questions were largely focused on concerns such as preventing civilian casualties, avoiding critical infrastructure, improving basic living conditions, and providing basic humanitarian aid such as access to healthcare, medicine, food, clean water, electricity, and education. Concerns regarding the moral legitimacy of the United States' actions against al Qaeda and the Taliban were almost nonexistent.

Legitimacy was both implicitly and explicitly conferred on US responses to 9/11 in the initial phases, and thus not a priority or value derived from engaging NATO. However, the United States' approach to—and value derived from—multilateralism differs. Kreps aptly describes the United States' decision to proceed without NATO participation in the early phases of the war in Afghanistan but then transition to more multilateral operations as resulting from two factors: a change in the expected timeline and changes to the necessary operational commitment (Kreps 2011). Many Bush administration officials acknowledged the likelihood of a protracted engagement in Afghanistan in the pre-war phase, but the vulnerability the United States experienced in the wake of the 9/11 attacks contributed to heightened anxiety and a perceived need to act quickly against those responsible for the attacks. In her later memoir, for example, then-US National Security Advisor Condoleezza Rice reflected on the United States' priorities vis-à-vis NATO:

> I have wondered many times if we somehow missed an opportunity to make the declaration of Article V have meaning for the Alliance. It is true that we were capable largely on our own to initiate war against the Taliban. It is also true that, after years of neglecting their military capabilities and concurrent failure to modernize for the war we'd eventually fight, most members of the Alliance were unable to move their military forces quickly. And we were single-minded, bruised, and determined to avenge 9/11 and destroy al Qaeda and its dangerous sanctuary as quickly as possible. Nonetheless, I've always felt that we left the Alliance dressed up with nowhere to go. (Rice 2011)

Additionally, the development of a counterterrorism strategy that emphasized utilizing special operations forces and airpower in lieu of a heavy ground presence—consistent with Secretary Rumsfeld's Revolution in Military Affairs (RMA) strategy—led policymakers to desire a direct decision-making structure and chain of command. Because the NATO command and control structure required a consensus from all NATO members, the United States feared it would not be able to convince all of the other allies in a timely manner, thus sacrificing operational efficiency. While the United States maintained a high degree of influence over the alliance, Bush administration officials were not eager to repeat the Clinton administration's experience in the 1999 Kosovo operation. Thus, hypotheses regarding derived value from legitimacy enhancement cannot be confirmed or rejected in the first two phases of the conflict. American officials did not foresee a need for additional legitimacy for its actions, beyond what was already offered by the United Nations (and in particular, the Security Council), as well as the vast majority of states.

With regard to hypotheses concerning the military and political value of multilateralism, phases 1 and 2 yield mixed findings. As the United States reformulated its approach to antiterrorism, both the Bush administration and Congress foresaw the need for a multilateral approach, emphasizing the NATO relationship, in maximizing defenses. Although members of each body disagreed with the ultimate direction NATO support should take, and whether it had the capacity to adequately address contemporary threats, prominent members of both political parties publicly voiced support for NATO engagement in the short and long term. As a senior member of the Senate Foreign Relations Committee, Senator Richard Lugar called for unity between the United States and its European allies in building not only effective antiterrorism measures but also cooperation in dealing with related issues such as chemical, biological, radiological, and nuclear (CBRN) weapons. Not only does terrorism and access to these materials transcend borders, Senator Lugar argued, but a challenge to the United States "will be less likely if the NATO allies stand shoulder to shoulder with the U.S. is pursuing such a counterterrorism policy" (Lugar 2002). Although he explicitly noted the alliance's shortcomings in Kosovo and elsewhere, as well as the ongoing debates regarding the future of NATO, he also foresaw a role for NATO should other states not comply with demands for transparency and accountability: "[W]hen such nations resist such accountability, or their governments make their territory available to terrorists who are seeking weapons of mass destruction, then NATO nations should be prepared to join with the U.S. to use force as well as all diplomatic and economic tools at their collective disposal" (Lugar 2002). This, Lugar argued, was paramount to American security, as well as European and more broadly global security.

Senator Lugar was hardly alone in championing a role for NATO in Afghanistan. His Democratic counterpart, Senator Joseph Biden, foresaw an opportunity for the United States to utilize NATO in its combat mission and the failure to do so in the early stages of the war as counterproductive to both trans-Atlantic relations and winning the war on terror and in Afghanistan. State Department officials applauded NATO's contributions to OEF and ISAF, and acknowledged a window of opportunity for adapting the alliance to fit the political, operational, and strategic needs of the United States. Under Secretary of State for Political Affairs Marc Grossman testified "NATO is no less important to our security today. Indeed, it is possible that NATO is more important to our security today" (U.S. Congress, Senate, Committee, The Future of NATO 2002). While acknowledging its many operational challenges prior to and during the response to 9/11, Under Secretary of Defense for Policy Douglas Feith said, "We are intent on bolstering, not cutting the transatlantic links of NATO. And we will do so in ways that serve the common interest in promoting defense transformation and streamlining NATO's Command structure" (Ibid).

Despite calls from prominent members of the administration and Congress, and noting how President Bush publicly championed multilateral support for its responses to the 9/11 attacks in the early phases, ultimately the United States did not give significant weight to multilateralism in its planning. Nonetheless, it welcomed limited NATO participation so long as it retained ultimate control of said participation, as well as the larger mission. NATO's engagement in OEF operations, as well as its overall engagement in the United States' response to 9/11 in the early phases, came with costs to the alliance and the US-NATO relationship. Combined with its concerns about the alliance's capacity as demonstrated in the Balkans and Kosovo, however, these costs did not exceed the benefits to including the allies in the early stages of Operation Enduring Freedom.

As the proceeding sections demonstrate, the United States' need for legitimacy as well as capability enhancement brought about by multilateral engagement shifted in latter phases of OEF, giving more than just lip service to the added benefits of NATO engagement. Prolonged challenges on the battlefield, as well as stabilization and reconstruction efforts, forced military officials and policymakers to reevaluate whether US resource allocation was sufficient and, if not, in what ways the alliance could assist American efforts. Shifting perceptions within and amongst the allies at times complicated the US-NATO relationship, but did not detract from the alliance's overall willingness to play a prominent role in the International Security Assistance Force (ISAF). The comprehensive benefits of this role, as well as the overall effects on the US-NATO relationship and the alliance as a whole, would not be fully realized until much later.

INTERNATIONAL SECURITY ASSISTANCE FORCE (ISAF)

One of the most important developments in the latter phase of Operation Enduring Freedom resulted from the conference held in Bonn, Germany, on November 27, 2001. The United Nations convened representatives from four of the major ethnic factions in Afghanistan to develop a plan for a new Afghan government. They established a 29-member interim government led by Pashtun leader Hamid Karzai, and agreed that this interim government would rule Afghanistan until the next meeting of the loya jirga in the spring. When the loya jirga met, it would select a transitional administration and begin drafting a new constitution. Despite reaching a consensus on these issues, there was much concern over who would be responsible for peacekeeping in Afghanistan. Prior experiences and ethnic tensions made the groups reluctant to allow an all-Afghan peacekeeping force led by the Northern Alliance (PBS 2017b).

The four groups finally reached an agreement: they would request that the United Nations Security Council lead a multinational peacekeeping force from Kabul. In return, the groups would remove all of their military units from both Kabul and any other area in which the UN force was deployed. The groups also requested that the multinational force participate in rebuilding Afghanistan's infrastructure (United Nations 2001). On December 20, 2001, the UN Security Council approved the requests made under the Bonn Agreement through UNSC Resolution 1386. The resolution established the International Security Assistance Force (ISAF), comprised of 3000–5000 personnel from nearly 20 different countries (United Nations 2017; Williams 2008). And on December 22, 2001, Northern Alliance President Rabbani officially handed over control to the Interim Afghan administration led by Karzai (Lansford 2012).

US officials were pleased by the outcomes of the Bonn Conference. The United States promoted Karzai as a "viable candidate" to lead the interim government and worked to include him in the negotiations (PBS 2017b). They also supported the establishment of ISAF under the leadership of the United Nations. Since ISAF's primary mission was peacekeeping, the

United States could focus on its combat operations without worrying about security, leaving the more experienced European countries to conduct humanitarian operations. As a result, OEF was reduced to 10,000–12,000 troops and reallocated its resources to the ISAF mission (Lansford 2012; Williams 2008). Both the United States and its coalition partners hoped the ISAF mandate would encourage Afghans to take an active role in the stabilization and reconstruction efforts, this allowing the international effort to be minimized.

In conjunction with combat operations and the ISAF mission, the United States also deployed Provincial Reconstruction Teams (PRTs) around Afghanistan, beginning in 2002. The PRTs were intended to represent a "whole of government" approach to rebuilding Afghanistan. Each team was funded by the United States and consisted of 100–200 members, with a mix of both civilian and military personnel. Although these PRTs were funded and initially led by the United States, the NATO alliance started to take control of its own PRTs in January 2004. By 2005, there were 25 PRTs throughout the country, all of which had NATO allies' soldiers assigned to them and 11 of which were led by NATO allies.

Phase 3: International and NATO Support for ISAF

The international community was also pleased by the outcome of the Bonn Conference and supported the establishment of ISAF. Great Britain agreed to lead the first deployment of the multinational force, which consisted of troops from Austria, Belgium, Bulgaria, Great Britain, Denmark, Finland, France, Germany, Greece, Italy, the Netherlands, New Zealand, Norway, Portugal, Romania, Spain, Sweden, and Turkey (United Nations 2001; Williams 2008). Each participating state served a six-month term as operations leader.

In January 2002, the United Nations led the International Conference on Reconstruction Assistance for Afghanistan over a two-day period in Tokyo, raising $4.5 billion in pledges (United Nations 2001). In April, the members of the G8 met in Geneva and agreed to a multinational security sector reform (SSR) for Afghanistan. The United States, Germany, Italy, the United Kingdom, and Japan would each take the lead on an issue area most related to their strengths. The United States would lead military reforms, while Germany would work to reform the police force and Italy the judicial sector. The United Kingdom would lead the effort to combat the rampant drug problems resulting from Afghanistan's opium production, while Japan would lead the effort for disarmament, demilitarization, and reintegration (DDR) (Kelly et al. 2011).

Although there was widespread international support for the UN mission in Afghanistan, within ISAF there was disagreement regarding the mission's leadership. When the German-Dutch leadership rotation took control in February 2003, they appealed to NATO to provide assistance to the ISAF mission. These appeals sparked a transition, and by August 2003, ISAF ended the six-month leadership rotation. Instead, NATO would lead the ISAF mandate, though it would remain under the direction of the United Nations. Under NATO leadership, the Security Council passed Resolution 1510 in October 2003, authorizing phased ISAF engagement into all regions of Afghanistan. The mission's control spread from the north in 2004, the western region in 2005, and finally to the south and east in 2006.

Changes to the leadership and scope of the ISAF mission led NATO to participate in other operations in Afghanistan. In January 2004, the alliance took command of its first PRT, and by June of 2004 had six PRTs throughout the country. Though NATO supported the efforts of both ISAF and the United States, some allies were reluctant to allow their troops to participate in the expansion of the ISAF mandate into less stable regions. There were also several incidents that concerned allies. British forces were outstretched, and both the United Kingdom and Finland reported friendly fire episodes resulting from poor communication among allies. Allies raised doubts about the private security firms operating throughout the country as well, and objected to the interim government's use of capital punishment. Despite these concerns, all 26 NATO member states (until the addition of Albania, Croatia, and Montenegro in 2009 and 2018) participated in the ISAF mission. Eleven additional countries also contributed to the mission, and by 2006 NATO increased the deployment to 36,000 troops and 25 PRTs. NATO also established a nonmilitary position, the NATO Senior Civilian Representative in Afghanistan, to assist with the country's political development (Hallams 2009; Kelly et al. 2011; NATO 2015; Peterson 2011).

In October 2006, the United Nations ceded control of the entire ISAF mission to NATO. Just prior to the transition, NATO also signed into an agreement with the Afghan government to establish a framework for cooperation between the two parties. The agreement outlined activities for each party to undertake, planning and implementation measures, and a mechanism for assessing progress. There was an added emphasis on making improvements in the Afghan National Army. The following month, NATO allies met at a summit in Riga, Latvia. The mission in Afghanistan dominated the agenda. Alliance participants argued that NATO had an obligation to its own citizens, as well as the citizens of Afghanistan, to continue supporting the Afghan Compact and ensure the establishment of democratic institutions, the Afghan National Army, the Afghan National Police, and civilian organizations. Summit participants also saw Afghanistan as a turning point in the internal politics of NATO: the alliance's future, they argued, was based on whether it could overcome coordination problems in Afghanistan and whether the mission would ultimately be successful (NATO 2006).

As ISAF continued its phased expansion into the more conflictual regions of Afghanistan, the NATO alliance struggled to address issues regarding burden-sharing, deployment levels, major disparities between allies in the number of troops engaged, and national caveats on the operational flexibility of troops (Weitsman 2014; Saideman and Auerswald 2012). Still, at the January 2010 NATO Summit in London, the alliance devised a strategy to transition responsibility for security to the Afghan National Security Force (ANSF), as well as an expansion of the NATO civilian mission. The Kabul Conference, held in July 2010, emphasized the continued economic and social challenges in Afghanistan. By July 2012, 50 countries were participating in ISAF. In spite of disagreements among allies, all 28 NATO member states contributed. Of the estimated 130,000 ISAF troops, 90,000 were from the United States (Weitsman 2014). In June 2013, NATO began the last phase of ISAF by transitioning responsibility of the security of the entire country to ANSF. Though it continues to support the development of Afghanistan in the noncombat mission Operation Resolute Support, NATO completed its ISAF mission in December 2014 (NATO 2014).

Legitimacy and Multilateralism in Phase 3

When the first phases of Operation Enduring Freedom were completed, the United States' operational needs changed. Though counterterrorism operations continued under US leadership, the United Nations, NATO, and the Bush administration recognized the need for a long-term plan to stabilize Afghanistan and begin reconstructing the state's infrastructure and governmental institutions. These efforts required open-ended commitments from many countries, both in terms of troop contributions and resource and financial contributions (Kreps 2011). More importantly, from the perspective of key American officials such as the USEUCOM Commander and NATO SACEUR Admiral James Stavridis, there was a recognition the Europeans were better equipped to conduct stabilization efforts (Stavridis 2015). Thus, US officials reversed the earlier decision to largely forego NATO participation and leadership and requested that NATO play a more pivotal role in the reconstruction and stabilization of Afghanistan (Hallams 2009). When NATO agreed to take over leadership of ISAF in 2003, President Bush applauded the alliance's decision, and the United States maintained its support for NATO leadership as responsibility for ISAF transitioned from the UN to NATO in 2006.

The December 2001 Bonn Conference revealed a legitimacy "gap" for the United States: despite its efforts with the Northern Alliance, long-standing ethnic rivalries prevented conference participants from reaching an agreement allowing one group to oversee peacekeeping. Thus, a greater multinational contribution than that under the OEF coalition was necessary if the United States wanted to stabilize Afghanistan and begin reconstruction efforts. The establishment of ISAF under UN Security Council Resolution 1386 gave substantial legitimacy to peacekeeping operations. Although the United States remained the largest contributor of troops and resources to NATO, it was the alliance's reputation that allowed it to assume responsibility for the ISAF mission and maintain the legitimacy of a multinational operation. As former SACEUR Admiral James Stavridis (USN) explained, NATO's efforts to engage in the community enhanced the ISAF mission's legitimacy (Stavridis 2015).

The legitimacy conferred on ISAF operations by NATO leadership was important to the United States' continued combat mission as well. Despite enjoying high levels of support for military operations at the outset, friendly fire incidents and disagreements between coalition members threatened the operation's legitimacy. As concerns over the United States' commitment to multilateralism grew, the legitimacy of the United States' actions was questioned. Compounding these concerns was the United States' announcement in late 2002 that it intended to pursue military operations in Iraq, against the wishes of many other UN Security Council permanent members to enact stronger sanctions against the Hussein regime. Prior to the 2004 Afghan election, US policymakers expressed concern that the failure to address some of the United States and its allies' shortcomings within ISAF operations would not only delegitimize the mission, but also "legitimize the warlords and drug traffickers" (Bereuter 2004).

Despite its vast technological advantages and capacity for warfighting, the United States chose to engage the alliance in OEF and ISAF operations. This is in part due to the legitimization effects NATO participation conferred, confirming hypotheses linking US-NATO relations to legitimacy enhancement. In spite of the challenges it faced in doing so, such as friendly fire incidents, burden-sharing disparities, command and control difficulties, and national caveats, the United States did not abandon the alliance's efforts in Afghanistan or elsewhere.

The coalition assembled during Operation Enduring Freedom symbolized a trend that began much earlier: the United States, unparalleled in defense spending and military resources and virtually unmatched by its European partners, would take the lead in determining the operational direction of the alliance's role in conflict engagement. It did not require the assistance of allies to achieve operational success in Kosovo or Afghanistan, but it perceived an added political and military value in engaging the alliance and its resources. US policymakers wanted to conduct a largely unilateral operation because of NATO's burdensome decision-making frameworks. However, President Bush, Secretary Rumsfeld, and others recognized that there were also significant benefits in forming a coalition. Firstly, it appeased allies who sought the political benefits of partnering with the United States. Secondly, it provided the United States with access to resources it lacked previously, particularly overflight and landing rights necessary to the United States' aerial campaign. Thirdly, it allowed US policymakers to boast of the near-70 member coalition it assembled, including military contributions from over 20 states, while doing most of the heavy lifting. It also allowed the United States to maintain a relatively unrestricted decision-making process and chain of command. This was politically advantageous to the United States as it campaigned for support for the Iraq mission, as well as to appease the domestic and international community.

Whereas the benefits of multilateralism seemed somewhat difficult to assess in the first two phases of the Afghanistan conflict, they were much more essential to the ISAF mission, thus confirming hypotheses on capability enhancement for US objectives as a driver of alliance engagement. The contributions of 40,000 troops from NATO members and other allies allowed the United States to divert troops and resources to its combat operations. Though some allies had substantial military resource disparities, the United States' operations benefited greatly from their knowledge of culture, religion, and languages. As Charles Barry notes, the ISAF mission allowed the United States and NATO to improve the interoperability of allies in multinational coalitions—what Barry terms the "coalition culture." The United States invested in providing allies access to the capabilities necessary to conduct ISAF operations, while improving the standardization of tactics, techniques, and procedures (TTPs) for future NATO operations (Barry 2012). NATO participation was also important to the transition of responsibility for the Provincial Reconstruction Teams (PRTs). Although the United States funded the PRTs and many remained under US leadership, the entire PRT structure was eventually transitioned to the ISAF mandate, with nearly half led by other NATO allies.

NATO participation in Afghanistan and leadership of the ISAF mission was not without controversy. Some believed that the United States' attempts to engage a multinational coalition were nothing more than empty rhetoric. Knowing it was outmatched in terms of military capabilities and seeking to avoid any impediments to action, the United States was willing and able to act unilaterally. Thus, it largely avoided NATO engagement in the first two phases of the war, and participation by other allies was seen as political appeasement, not a sincere attempt to engage international partners. Still, allies contributed political, economic, and military support to Operation Enduring Freedom, particularly in the third phase, and gave the United States an important advantage in conducting its aerial campaign. There is little evidence to suggest the absence of NATO participation hindered the effectiveness of the combat operation, or that there was any long-standing damage to US-NATO relations as a result.

NATO participation in and leadership of the ISAF mission was also criticized. Many states placed caveats on the use of its troops on the ground, particularly in the less stable regions of the country. This hampered the effectiveness of the ISAF mission, limiting its ability to engage the local communities. It also fostered resentment between allies, with those states placing fewer caveats on their troops feeling as though they carried a higher burden for ISAF operations (Warren 2010). However, national caveats were not unique to the Afghanistan mission—the ability of states to refrain from engagement is enshrined in the Washington Treaty, which allows states to decide the ways in which it will fulfill its obligations to the alliance (Saideman and Auerswald 2012).

Despite the many benefits of engaging in a multilateral operation, one of the most difficult obstacles for the United States and NATO missions was engagement with regional actors, particularly Pakistan. Prior to 9/11, Pakistan was one of only a few states to recognize the Taliban as the legitimate authority of Afghanistan. Additionally, because of the ongoing Kashmir dispute and high levels of corruption, many Pakistani officials were connected to terrorist organizations, including al Qaeda. Following the 9/11 attacks, Pakistan offered political support, military resources, access to air space, and a forward mounting base in Karachi for ISAF. However, it struggled to reconcile its cooperation with the West and its historical relationship with Afghanistan, the Taliban, and al Qaeda. When Pakistan froze the assets of several different terrorist groups, corrupted officials notified the groups ahead of time, allowing them to act in advance of the freeze. The domestic conditions and rugged terrain along the Pakistan-Afghanistan border also allowed many al Qaeda operatives to find a safe haven in Pakistan. Despite both the US-led coalition and the NATO-led ISAF efforts, the Taliban and al Qaeda's relationships with regional actors could not be overcome (Fair 2004).

Another point of contention regarding the ISAF mission and NATO's utility in Afghanistan was the PRTs. The PRTs were not wholly successful, and many of them experienced difficulties coordinating with combat operations in the same area. The United States funded all of the PRTs, and the structure of each unit varied widely. Although the PRTs were intended to balance between military and civilian personnel, most were dominated by military personnel and were frequently criticized for not providing the intended services. Allies also struggled to combat the narcotics problems in Afghanistan, establish the necessary security and governance bodies, and maintain public support within their own countries for continued NATO participation (Morelli and Belkin 2009). Despite these obstacles, the ISAF mission (through the PRTs) helped to build important infrastructure throughout Afghanistan, including 3500 schools that service nearly 7 million students, as well clinics and other healthcare facilities that provide healthcare to 85 percent of the population (Warren 2010).

CONCLUSION

As demonstrated here, NATO's participation in US operations in Afghanistan benefited the United States, particularly in regard to the ISAF mission. The engagement also resulted in improvements to the alliance, detailed in Chaps. 7 and 8, thereby improving the odds that NATO would persist after the war ended. Though the Bush administration was frequently criticized for being too willing to act unilaterally, the United States pursued multilateralism in all phases of the Afghanistan effort. In the early phases, this pursuit was primarily for political reasons, although coalition members provided valuable resources for the United States' efforts. It declined to pursue the war through the NATO command structure based on a number of factors, including a reticence to repeat the mistakes of Kosovo, the invention of the RMA, and the post-9/11 environment. In the later phase of the war, however, the United States' commitment to multilateralism was much more sincere, as it recognized real benefits to the inclusion and leadership of NATO. As Daniel Fried, Assistant Secretary European And Eurasian Affairs in the State Department, testified before members of the House Foreign Affairs Committee, the prevailing belief of policymakers in the Afghanistan conflict was that "NATO has critical value to the United States. NATO is in action now and will be in the future. And if NATO did not exist, we would have to invent it. NATO, simply put, is the great security arm of the transatlantic alliance of democracies" (U.S. Congress, House, Committee, The Future of NATO 2007).

The United States enjoyed the legitimacy NATO leadership conferred on ISAF operations. Legitimacy was particularly important to the stabilization and reconstruction efforts, as the perception of NATO as "an alliance with a solid reputation and altruistic intentions" (Warren 2010) worked to gain the trust of the Afghan people. The United States maintained its autonomy in combat operations under OEF, but was also able to take a leadership role in ISAF and PRT missions as the strongest NATO member. NATO also proved its utility to the United States' mission by providing resources the United States was incapable or unwilling to provide. Previous experience with stabilization, reconstruction efforts, and an understanding of the cultures, religions, and languages of Afghanistan enhanced the United States' efforts to mobilize the civilian population and establish legitimate security and governance institutions.

As the alliance's first "out-of-area" mission, Afghanistan also demonstrated that NATO could adapt and persist in the post-Cold War periods House Foreign Affairs Committee Chairman Tom Lantos suggested "NATO's efforts [in Afghanistan] since 2001 demonstrate that the United States and the Europeans are willing to conduct tough combat operations and do so in a country outside of Europe" (United States 2007). As indicated here, the ISAF mission provided a number of improvements in the security and prosperity of Afghanistan by establishing the ANA and the ANP, establishing a justice system, facilitating elections, building schools, opening healthcare facilities, and continuing an open dialogue between the PRTs and Afghan citizens (Ibid).

Additionally, allies worked to improve the alliance's relationships with non-NATO states and developed extensive antiterrorism and counter-terrorism measures. Both the Bush administration and Obama adminis-tration paid careful attention to the impacts of the conflict on US-NATO relations, considering the impact of each decision on the alliance. When the United States decided in 2012 to push for drawing down the ISAF mission and bringing it to a close, defense Secretary Leon Panetta and Secretary of State Hillary Clinton met with the allies' foreign ministers. Later, Secretary Panetta reflected how the United States' measured decisions were received by the allies:

> Our allies appreciated [the decision to reconceptualize the mission instead of completely withdrawing], and expressed relief that we were resisting the urge to pull out precipitously, which they feared would tumble Afghanistan backward and leave open a path for the Taliban's return. Instead, we offered a measured plan to draw down while at the same time bolstering Afghanistan's security capacity. Our European allies were happy to join us. We were, as we said, "in together, out together". (Panetta 2014)

Afghanistan provided the alliance an opportunity to learn from the mis-takes of the Kosovo operation by improving the interoperability of allied forces and fostering the "coalition culture" (Barry 2012). The challenges the alliance experienced in Afghanistan—such as a renewed debate over burden-sharing—were not unique to the Afghanistan mission, and it is difficult to say that they proved to be any real threat to US-NATO rela-tions or NATO persistence.

Both legitimacy and the utility of multilateralism were pivotal to the United States' Afghanistan mission, confirming each hypothesis. The United States pursued the alliance's support and invested in its ability to engage in conflict for legitimacy enhancement. As evidenced by both the initial coalition and the later NATO leadership of ISAF, the Bush admin-istration also understood the importance of adherence to international norms. Additionally, NATO provided valuable resources for the US and ISAF efforts, confirming the utility of alliance engagement for the United States. The United States also capitalized on its influence in the alliance to encourage improvements to the alliance and the "coalition culture" by emphasizing experiences in Afghanistan.

Although hypotheses concerning why the United States would engage the alliance in combat are largely confirmed by the Afghanistan case, in some ways the analysis leaves more questions than answers. Despite having adequate military, political, and economic resources to rid Afghanistan of both the Taliban and al Qaeda, contemporary observations suggest the end of Operation Enduring Freedom is hardly indicative of the US and NATO's success. Roughly 8400 US troops are part of a 13,000 NATO contingent still embedded in Afghanistan as part of Resolute Support (NATO 2018). According to the Department of Defense, 2351 American military personnel were killed in Operation Enduring Freedom (U.S. Department of Defense 2018), alongside more than 1100 allied troops (Crawford 2018). Estimates of Afghan soldiers and security forces are more difficult to discern as many of the total figures are kept secret, but 2018 estimates suggest at 50–60 a day (Nordland 2018). The Watson Institute of International Affairs' "Costs of War" Project estimates 104,000 civilians have also been killed, and most of the country lacks access to basic necessities such as clean drinking water, adequate food supplies, education, and healthcare (Watson Institute 2016). A resurgent Taliban now controls an estimated 44–61 percent of the country (Nordland 2018).

As Chap. 7 demonstrates, the significance of the alliance's role in Afghanistan was not isolated to the ISAF mission. Instead, both the challenges and successes of the mission were institutionalized via a number of operational and political changes to the alliance. Further, its ability to adapt to the demands of American policymakers contributed to NATO's continued persistence and relevance in the twenty-first century strategic environment. The evidence presented in this chapter builds the foundation upon which the hypotheses concerning US influence over the development of the alliance and the importance of US-NATO relations to alliance persistence are confirmed.

REFERENCES

Abyat, Gulnar, and Rebecca R. Moore. 2010. *NATO in Search of a Vision.* Washington, DC: Georgetown University Press.

Auerswald, David P., and Stephen Saideman. 2014. *NATO in Afghanistan: Fighting Together, Fighting Alone.* Princeton: Princeton University Press.

Balz, Dan. 2001. Bush Warns of Casualties of War. *The Washington Post,* September 18.

Barry, Charles. 2012. Building Future Transatlantic Interoperability Around a Robust NATO Response Force. *Transatlantic Current* 7: 1–14.

Bereuter, Doug. 2004. *Grace Shortfalls in NATO's International Security Assistance Force in Afghanistan.* U.S. House of Representatives, June 3.

Biddle, Stephen D. 2005. Allies, Airpower, and Modern Warfare: The Afghan Model in Afghanistan and Iraq. *International Security* 30 (3): 161–176.

Bush, George W. 2001. Address Before a Joint Session of the Congress on the United States Response to the Terrorist Attacks of September 11. Last Modified September 20, 2001. http://www.presidency.ucsb.edu/ws/index.php?pid= 64731. Accessed 30 Nov 2017.

Cheney, Richard B., and Elizabeth Perry Cheney. 2012. *In My Time*. New York: Threshold Ed.

Clinton, William J. Message to the Congress Transmitting Proposed Legislation to Combat Terrorism. Last Modified May 3, 1995. www.presidency.ucsb.edu/ ws/print.php?pid=51310. Accessed 15 Nov 2017.

———. Remarks with President Jacques Chirac of France on the G-7 Response to Terrorism and an Exchange with Reporters in Lyons. Last Modified Jun 27, 1996. www.presidency.ucsb.edu/ws/print.php?pid=53001. Accessed 15 Nov 2017.

———. European Union/United States Joint Statement on Shared Objectives and Close Cooperation on Counterterrorism. Last Modified May 18, 1998. www.presidency.ucsb.edu/ws/print.php?pid=55984. Accessed 15 Nov 2017.

CNN. Bin Laden Says He Wasn't Behind Attacks. Last Modified Sept 17, 2001. http://edition.cnn.com/2001/US/09/16/inv.binladen.denial/index. html?iref=storysearch. Accessed 8 Dec 2017.

Coll, Steve. 2004. *Ghost Wars: The Secret History of the CIA, Afghanistan, and Bin Laden, from the Soviet Invasion to September 10, 2001*. New York: Penguin Books.

Cooper, Helene. 2017. U.S. Says It Has 11,000 Troops in Afghanistan, More than Formerly Disclosed. *The New York Times*, August 30. https://www. nytimes.com/2017/08/30/world/asia/afghanistan-troop-totals.html

Crawford, Neta C. Human Cost of the Post-9/11 Wars: Lethality and the Need for Transparency. Last Modified Nov 2018. https://watson.brown.edu/cost-sofwar/files/cow/imce/papers/2018/Human%20Costs%2C%20Nov%20 8%202018%20CoW.pdf. Accessed 22 Nov 2018.

Davidson, Jason. 2011. *America's Allies and War*. New York: Palgrave Macmillan.

Dobbs, Michael. 2001. Bin Laden: A 'Master Impresario'. *The Washington Post*, September 13. http://www.washingtonpost.com/wp-dyn/content/article/ 2010/03/12/AR2010031201552.html

Executive Order 13129, 64 Fed. Reg. 36759 (July 4, 1999). https://fas.org/irp/ offdocs/eo/eo-13129.htm

Fair, C. Christine. 2004. *The Counterterror Coalitions*. Santa Monica: RAND.

Federal Bureau of Investigation. 2007. Terror Hits Home: The Oklahoma City Bombing. November 15. http://www.fbi.gov/about-us/history/famous-cases/ oklahoma-city-bombing

———. 2008. First Strike: Global Terror in America. February 26. https:// archives.fbi.gov/archives/news/stories/2008/february/tradebom_022608

Garden, Timothy. 2002. NATO in Trouble. *The World Today* 58 (11): 17–18.

Gerleman, David J., Jennifer E. Stevens, and Steven A. Hildreth. 2001. Operation Enduring Freedom: Foreign Pledges of Military and Intelligence Support. CRS Report for Congress. October 17.

Global Terrorism Database. 2018. *National Consortium for the Study of Terrorism and Responses to Terrorism (START)*.

Goldgeier, James. 2009. NATO's Future: Facing Old Divisions and New Threats. *Harvard International Review* 31 (1): 48–51.

Hallams, Ellen. 2009. The Transatlantic Alliance Renewed: The United States and NATO Since 9/11. *Journal of Transatlantic Studies* 7 (1): 38–60.

Huddy, Leonie, Nadia Khatib, and Theresa Capelos. 2002. The Polls – Trends: Reactions to the Terrorist Attacks of September 11, 2001. *Public Opinion Quarterly* 66 (3): 418–450.

Human Rights Watch. Afghanistan: U.S. Military Should Investigate Civilian Deaths. Last Modified Dec 14, 2003. http://www.hrw.org/news/2003/12/12/afghanistan-us-military-should-investigate-civilian-deaths. Accessed 8 Dec 2017.

Kaplan, Lawrence S. 2004. *NATO Divided, NATO United*. Westport: Praeger.

Kelly, Terrence K., Nora Bensahel, and Olga Oliker. 2011. *Security Force Assistance in Afghanistan*. Santa Monica: RAND.

Kitchen, Veronica M. 2010. *The Globalization of NATO: Intervention, Security and Identity*. New York: Routledge.

Klass, Roseanne. 1988. Afghanistan: The Accords. *Foreign Affairs* 66 (5): 922–945.

Kreps, Sarah E. 2011. *Coalitions of Convenience: United States Military Interventions After the Cold War*. New York: Oxford University Press.

Lambeth, Benjamin S. 2005. *Air Power Against Terror*. Santa Monica: Rand.

Lansford, Tom. 2012. *9/11 and the Wars in Afghanistan and Iraq*. Santa Barbara: ABC-CLIO.

Larson, Eric V., and Bogdan Savych. 2005. *American Public Support for US Military Operations from Mogadishu to Baghdad*. Santa Monica: RAND.

Leigh, David. 2010. Afghanistan War Logs: Friendly Fire Deaths Plagued Invasion from the Start. *The Guardian*, July 10. http://www.theguardian.com/world/2010/jul/25/friendly-fire-deaths-toll-afghanistan

Lugar, Richard. 2002. NATO's Role in the War on Terrorism. January 18. http://avalon.law.yale.edu/sept11/lugar_001.asp

Morelli, Vincent, and Paul Belkin. 2009. *NATO in Afghanistan: A Test of the Transatlantic Alliance*. Washington, DC: BiblioGov.

NATO. 1991. The Alliance's New Strategic Concept, 07-Nov.-1991. Accessed May 30, 2019. https://www.nato.int/cps/en/natohq/official_texts_23847.htm?

———. The Alliance's Strategic Concept. Last Modified Apr 24, 1999. https://www.nato.int/cps/en/natolive/official_texts_27433.htm. Accessed 6 Feb 2014.

————. Riga Summit Declaration. Last Modified Nov 29, 2006. https://www. nato.int/docu/pr/2006/p06-150e.htm. Accessed 9 Apr 2015.

————. 2010. The Alliance's New Strategic Concept. Last Modified August 26, 2010. https://www.nato.int/cps/en/natohq/official_texts_23847.htm

————. Resolute Support Mission (RSM): Key Facts and Figures. Last Modified Sept 2018. https://www.nato.int/nato_static_fl2014/assets/pdf/pdf_2018_09/20180903_2018-09-RSM-Placemat.pdf. Accessed 30 Oct 2018.

————. ISAF's Mission in Afghanistan. http://www.nato.int/cps/en/natohq/topics_69366.htm. Accessed 15 Dec 2014.

————. NATO's Operations: 1949 – Present. http://www.aco.nato.int/resources/21/NATO%20Operations,%201949-Present.pdf. Accessed 8 Dec 2017.

————. Operation Active Endeavour. http://www.nato.int/cps/en/natolive/topics_7932.htm. Accessed 9 Dec 2016.

————. Resolute Support Mission in Afghanistan. https://www.nato.int/cps/en/natohq/topics_113694.htm. Accessed 22 Nov 2018.

————. The North Atlantic Treaty. http://www.nato.int/cps/en/natolive/official_texts_17120.htm. Accessed 15 Oct 2014.

————. North Atlantic Council Fonds, 1990–2001. NATO Online Archives, Brussels, Belgium; NATO Secretary-General Fonds, 1990–2001. NATO Online Archives, Brussels, Belgium; NATO Military Committee Fonds, 1990–2001. NATO Online Archives, Brussels, Belgium; NATO International Secretariat/International Staff Fonds, 1990–2001. NATO Online Archives, Brussels, Belgium; Defence Committee Fonds, 1990–2001. NATO Online Archives, Brussels, Belgium.

Nordland, Ron. 2018. The Death Toll for Afghan Forces Is Secret. Here's Why. *The New*, September 21. https://www.nytimes.com/2018/09/21/world/asia/afghanistan-security-casualties-taliban.html

Panetta, Leon. 2014. *Worthy Fights*. New York: Penguin Group (USA) LLC.

PBS Frontline. 2014. A Biography of Osama Bin Laden. http://www.pbs.org/wgbh/pages/frontline/shows/binladen/who/bio.html. Accessed 22 Oct 2014.

————. 2017a. Campaign Against Terror March 2002: Operation Anaconda. http://www.pbs.org/wgbh/pages/frontline/shows/campaign/etc/epilogue.html. Accessed 8 Dec 2017.

————. 2017b. Campaign Against Terror Filling the Vacuum: The Bonn Conference. Last modified Dec 8, 2017. http://www.pbs.org/wgbh/pages/frontline/shows/campaign/withus/cbonn.html

Perl, Raphael, and Ronald O'Rourke. 2001. *Terrorist Attack on USS Cole: Background and Issues for Congress*. Congressional Research Service.

Peterson, James W. 2011. *NATO and Terrorism: Organizational Expansion and Mission Transformation*. New York: Continuum.

Rice, Condoleezza. 2011. *No Higher Honor*. New York: Crown.

Rupp, Richard E. 2006. *NATO After 9/11: An Alliance in Continuing Decline.* New York: Palgrave Macmillan.

Saideman, Stephen M., and David P. Auerswald. 2012. Comparing Caveats: Understanding the Sources of National Restrictions upon NATO's Mission in Afghanistan. *International Studies Quarterly* 56 (1): 67–84.

Scheurer, Michael. 2011. *Osama Bin Laden.* New York: Oxford University Press.

Simon, Jeffrey. 2008. NATO's Uncertain Future: Is Demography Destiny? *Strategic Forum* 236, October.

Sloan, Stanley R. 2005. *NATO, the European Union, and the Atlantic Community.* Lanham: Rowman & Littlefield.

Stavridis, James (USN-Ret., Former Commander, USEUCOM, NATO SACEUR). Interview with Author, Jan 5, 2015.

Talbott, Strobe. 2002. From Prague to Baghdad: NATO at Risk. *Foreign Affairs* 81 (6): 46–57.

U.S. Department of Defense. 2018. *Enhancing Security and Stability in Afghanistan.*

———. Casualty Status. https://dod.defense.gov/News/Casualty-Status/. Accessed 22 Nov 2018.

U.S. Department of Homeland Security. 2016. History. https://www.dhs.gov/history. Accessed 30 Nov 2017.

United Nations. 2001. Agreement on Provisional Arrangements in Afghanistan Pending the Re-Establishment of Permanent Government Institutions (the Bonn Agreement). May 12. https://peacemaker.un.org/afghanistan-bonnagreement2001

———. 2017. Afghanistan and the United Nations. http://www.un.org/News/dh/latest/afghan/un-afghan-history.shtml. Accessed 8 Dec 2017.

———. Security Council Committee Pursuant to Resolutions 1267 (1999) and 1989 (2011) Concerning Al-Qaida and Associated Individuals and Entities. https://www.un.org/sc/suborg/en/sanctions/1267. Accessed 8 Dec 2017.

United Nations Security Council. *UNSCR 1267 On the Situation in Afghanistan,* Oct 15, 1999.

———. *UNSCR 1368 Threats to International Peace and Security Caused by Terrorist Acts,* Sept 12, 2001.

UN News Centre. 2017. Afghanistan & the United Nations. www.un.org/News/dh/latest/afghan/un-afghan-history.shtml. Accessed 9 Dec 2017.

United States. 2002. Congress. Senate. Committee on Foreign Relations. *The Future of NATO. Hearing Before the Committee on Foreign Relations United States Senate, One Hundred Seventh Congress Second Session.* Washington: U.S. Government Printing Office.

———. 2007. Congress. House. Committee on Foreign Affairs. *The Future of NATO: How Valuable an Asset? Hearing Before the Committee on Foreign Affairs, House of Representatives, One Hundred Tenth Congress, First Session.*

United States Congress. S.J. Res. 23 *Joint Authorization for the Use of Military Force, Pub. L. no. 107–40, 115 Stat. 224,* 107th Congress Session, 2001. https://www.govtrack.us/congress/bills/107/sjres23

Uniting and Strengthening America by Providing Appropriate Tools Required to Intercept and Obstruct Terrorism Act of 2001, Pub. L. No. 107–56, 115 Stat. 272 (2001).

Warren, Tarn D. 2010. *ISAF and Afghanistan: The Impact of Failure on NATO's Future.* Washington, DC: National Defense University.

Weitsman, Patricia. 2014. *Waging War: Alliances, Coalitions, and Institutions of Interstate Violence.* Stanford: Stanford University Press.

Williams, Michael J. 2008. *NATO, Security, and Risk Management.* Milton Park: Routledge.

CHAPTER 5

The 2003 Iraq War

The execution of the 2003 Iraq War, like the war in Afghanistan, resulted from changes to US foreign policy and policies of intervention in the post-9/11 period. However, unlike Afghanistan, the United States lacked widespread support for intervention. When the United Nations failed to authorize the use of force, the Bush administration looked first to its NATO allies and then to individual states to form its ad hoc "coalition of the willing." The consequences of these decisions have since occupied a prominent space in discussions of the Bush legacy, as well as American foreign policy more broadly. While the processes and logic behind the coalition's assembly are now well-known, the consequences of these decisions are less so. Importantly, the decisions in late 2002 and early 2003 continue to impact both the United States and NATO today. The alliance evolved as a result of American preferences for conflict engagement, in a manner consistent with but also distinct from changes stemming directly from the Balkans and Afghanistan operations. Perhaps more importantly, American policymakers and their European counterparts continue to face the realities of their actions in the continued instability plaguing Iraq and the rise of groups such as the Islamic State of Iraq and Syria (ISIS).

This chapter begins with a brief introduction to the disputes between the United States, the UN, and NATO over the appropriateness of military action in Iraq in 2002. Bush administration officials believed the United States' actions in Iraq would be retroactively legitimized if the United States discovered weapons of mass destruction (WMDs) and thwarted an impend-

© The Author(s) 2020

J. Garey, *The US Role in NATO's Survival After the Cold War*,
Palgrave Studies in International Relations,
https://doi.org/10.1007/978-3-030-13675-8_5

ing attack. The international community—including many of the NATO allies—was less convinced of the imminence of an attack, as well as Saddam Hussein's access to WMDs, and sought diplomatic alternatives to the United States' proposed invasion. Though the United States engaged in a public and at times visceral debate over the prudence of the Iraq War, it maintained its relationship to the NATO alliance while working to strengthen the alliance's capabilities in Afghanistan as well as in the broader war on terror.

The remainder of this chapter further addresses the questions of legitimacy during the Iraq War, as well as the multilateral value derived from operations despite NATO's limited participation. I demonstrate that the United States first pursued international support via the United Nations, then multilateral support through NATO, and finally assembled the coalition because it wanted to enhance the legitimacy of its actions. The legitimacy of the United States' actions in Iraq was not significantly challenged by the absence of NATO for two reasons. First, many of the United States' NATO allies participated in some capacity during combat operations. Second, although they provided small contributions, the operation did not substantially differ from the Kosovo and Afghanistan operations wherein NATO was a major participant but the United States carried much of the burden.

NATO's limited participation during the Iraq War is regularly cited as evidence of a fractured US-NATO relationship. Political discourse in the time leading up to combat operations is consistent with this, but militarily, NATO's actions were not a far deviation from the norm of multilateral operations led by the United States. Further, the Bush administration's decision to lead a coalition of the willing in the absence of widespread NATO support had minimal impact on US-NATO relations in the long term. The United States' continued engagement with NATO served a practical purpose—because the allies were fully engaged in Afghanistan, the United States could divert additional resources to the Iraq effort. Further, as demonstrated in Chaps. 7 and 8, the prolonged discussions about NATO's willingness and ability to engage in Iraq gave American policymakers leverage to encourage substantive changes to the alliance.

THE UNITED STATES PREPARES FOR WAR, AND THE INTERNATIONAL COMMUNITY RESPONDS

The United States kept a close watch on Saddam Hussein and his regime in Iraq in the years following the 1990 Gulf War. When Iraq invaded Kuwait in August 1990, the United Nations Security Council moved rapidly to pass resolutions condemning the use of force and authorizing an intervention, led by the United States, to restore Kuwait's sovereignty and dispel the occupying Iraqi forces. Though the war lasted only 40 days, the UN continued to pass resolutions and enforce sanctions against the regime in the hopes of securing the region and preventing humanitarian abuses (Smith 2003). The UN Monitoring, Verification and Inspection Commission (UNMOVIC), established by UNSCR 1284 in 1999, led Iraq's disarmament and demanded compliance with the numerous UN resolutions passed after the 1990 Iraq-Kuwait war. UNMOVIC inspectors worked with Iraqi government officials to establish mutually agreeable terms of compliance. The lack of full compliance with UN demands, combined with Hussein's efforts to extract oil revenues, made many states uncomfortable as to Iraq's future ambitions (Bjola 2009). In the post-9/11 period, the UN took further action to strengthen sanctions and express its concern about the Hussein regime.

There is little evidence that the George W. Bush administration intended to drastically change its policy toward Iraq before 9/11 (Kreps 2011). But growing concerns over weapons development were thrust into the spotlight after the attacks, causing the United States to begin an international campaign aimed at regime change. In a September 2002 speech at UN Headquarters, President Bush called member states to action. He invoked memories of the Gulf War and asserted that in the years since, Iraq demonstrated it had no respect for international law. Without action, Bush insisted Iraq would continue to disregard the rule of the United Nations, develop its weapons arsenals, and act as a bully to its neighbors. Many perceived the language of President Bush's speech as an unequivocal call for armed intervention. Within days of his speech, the Iraqi government announced it would again allow inspectors to return. The Bush administration rebuffed the offer, arguing Saddam Hussein would simply continue to circumvent the inspectors (Davidson 2011).

How to respond to the uncertainty over Iraq's intentions was a major cause of divergence between the United States and its global partners. To those opposed to using force in Iraq, the United States seemed determined to go to war regardless of what the UN accomplished with its inspections. Some states felt the UN had no choice but to assist the United States or get out of its way (Rupp 2006). When Iraq announced it would allow unconditional access to UNMOVIC inspectors, France and others asserted that if given enough time, Iraq would eventually comply with UN demands. But the United States continued to appeal to the greater dangers posed by

Iraq's noncompliance—the proliferation of weapons of mass destruction (WMDs), the possibility Hussein could decide to support terrorist organizations, the threat Iraq posed to regional stability—to build both domestic and international support (Shimko 2006).

The United Kingdom, one of the United States' closest allies in the pre-war period, strongly urged the United States to continue its UN campaign. Prime Minister Tony Blair stressed the importance of international support to enhance the operation's legitimacy, and although the United States continued to push for additional UN support, it also threatened to bypass any agreement or resolution not expressly authorizing military intervention in the event Iraq did not comply (Borger 2002). Negotiations over a Security Council resolution continued for nearly two months as a result of the tensions between the United States and other Security Council members. The result of these negotiations was resolution 1441. UNSCR 1441 was seen as a compromise for both sides, despite the 15–0 vote in favor. UNSCR 1441 did not provide the authorization for military intervention the United States sought, but did allow for all UN involvement in Iraq to be accompanied by a military presence. US officials were convinced that Iraq would never meet the resolution's demands and would eventually require military intervention. France (supported by China and Russia) believed a significant military contingency in Iraq would only exacerbate tensions and would lead the UN Security Council to war. Thus, the French leadership was unhappy with this clause of the resolution. However, the French agreed to the terms of UNSCR 1441 because it prevented the United States from engaging immediately and unilaterally with force. They believed if UNMOVIC failed under the new resolution, the United States would return to the Security Council for additional resolutions (Rupp 2006; Gordon and Shapiro 2004).

Within days of UNSCR 1441, the Iraq government submitted a letter to UN Secretary General Kofi Annan, acknowledging its acceptance of the resolution's terms but denying it possessed WMDs. The regime could not account for the chemical and biological materials previously documented by UN inspectors, and the Bush administration used this information as an indication of Saddam Hussein's unwillingness to comply with the demands of the UN. However, the United States lacked the support of its fellow Security Council members for a second resolution (authorizing the use of force for enforcement), and continued to appeal to the international community for its Iraq plan by engaging international partners such as NATO.

Efforts to engage NATO began in earnest at the 2002 Prague Summit, just a few weeks after the negotiations on UNSCR 1441. At the summit, President Bush pushed states to recreate the alliance to make it more effective for combatting new threats such as terrorism (Gordon 2002). NATO allies were asked to make improvements in areas such as intelligence sharing, securing facilities, and providing support for states facing additional threats (Sloan 2005). Utilizing the "lessons learned" from the Kosovo and Afghanistan engagements, the summit centered on the establishment of the NATO Response Force and reform of the military command structure.

The United States did not directly request support for Iraq intervention during the summit. Though the NATO allies agreed the Iraqi government was not in compliance with international law, and that the consequences of a noncompliant Iraq were severe, they disagreed with the United States on the necessity of immediate military intervention. The French and German leadership wanted to give weapons inspectors more time to either persuade Iraq to comply or to find more substantial evidence of their weapons stockpile, and they were concerned about the United States' apparent determination to go to war (Sloan 2005; Kreps 2011).

US Deputy Secretary of Defense Paul Wolfowitz went to NATO headquarters two weeks after the Prague Summit and formally requested assistance for the defense of fellow ally Turkey. Wolfowitz asked primarily for nonmilitary assistance, knowing from NATO's earlier engagements that most allies would be incapable of providing the necessary military resources. Debate over NATO's involvement continued into January 2003, when the United States made six formal proposals for assistance (Gordon 2002). The United States' requests were met with support from several members, including Great Britain, Spain, Italy, Denmark, Portugal, the Czech Republic, Hungary, and Poland; however, the French and Germans maintained their opposition. Belgium and Luxembourg also expressed concern over the US proposals and sought to block NATO action. In addition to support from existing NATO members, the United States' plan for Iraq was also publicly supported by the "Vilnius 10." Seven of these states—Bulgaria, Estonia, Latvia, Lithuania, Slovakia, Slovenia, and Romania—were invited to join NATO at the earlier Prague Summit, and though they lacked the capacity to provide military contributions, their support for the United States influenced policymakers to support a quick membership approval process.

French and German officials were vocal about their skepticism of US proposals, believing the Bush administration was simply using aid to Turkey as a way to implicitly authorize and legitimize the Iraq invasion. Said one French representative, "If we are not yet deciding to go to war in the Security Council, we cannot decide to go to war at NATO. Once the Security Council authorizes force against Iraq, it will be very easy to send matériel to Turkey right away" (Weisman 2003). As the Council debate progressed, President Chirac emphasized France's lack of support by publicly announcing France would veto a second resolution (to UNSCR 1441) authorizing military action (Black and White 2003). Despite the agreement of other member states on the need to uphold its commitment to member state Turkey, opposing states contended that the United States' proposals were insincere. Even if the intentions of the United States were sincere, opposing states argued, accepting the United States' proposal would commit the alliance to an intervention that could easily become prolonged (Rupp 2006).

Because of both continued debate in the North Atlantic Council (NAC) and the declarations of the French and German leadership, NATO Secretary General Robertson moved the Turkey debate to the Defense Planning Council (DPC) in the hopes of reaching a resolution. France, who had separated itself from the military structure of NATO in 1966, was not a party to the DPC, and Secretary General Robertson's move caused both Belgium and Germany to drop their opposition (NATO 2012). On February 19, 2003, the DPC formally authorized NATO to provide aid to Turkey (Rupp 2006). But the damage to the relationships between individual decision-makers was evident: the heated, sometimes confrontational exchanges of President Chirac, German Chancellor Gerhard Schroeder, and President Bush (or more frequently, Secretary Rumsfeld) led to anger and distrust between the alliance partners. Additionally, Turkey maintained that the United States would not be permitted to offload its ships in Turkey and enter Iraq through the north, cutting off the United States' entryway and limiting the United States' efforts to secure the area (Barbero 2015).

When the United States finally commenced Operation Iraqi Freedom on March 20, 2003, it did so with a "coalition of the willing." Unable to secure a second UN Security Council Resolution because of the objections of France, Russia, and China, the United States remained convinced that its actions would be legitimized once it was proved that Saddam Hussein was hiding WMDs. Its closest supporter of intervention, the

United Kingdom, provided the most significant contribution for the combat phase of the operation by mobilizing 46,000 of its troops. Contributions of the United States and the United Kingdom constituted 95 percent of both the troop support and financial backing. Additionally, the United Kingdom was the only coalition member to engage in the planning and implementation stages of the operation, and the United States maintained its control over every aspect of the operation (Kreps 2011). Australia and Poland also provided troops to Operation Iraqi Freedom. Of the 40 participating countries, most provided political support or supplied additional resources. Very few provided combat troops, and even when they did, their participation was highly conditional (Weitsman 2014).

On May 1, 2003, President Bush infamously stood aboard the USS Abraham in front of a "Mission Accomplished" banner and addressed the gathered crowd, declaring the major combat phase of the invasion complete and touting the United States' overwhelming successes in Iraq. In the period immediately following President Bush's announcement, the administration sent a mixed message to the international community about the stabilization and reconstruction phases of the war. Bush sent former Secretary of State James Baker on a tour of Europe in the later months of 2003 to ask states such as France, Germany, and Russia to forgive Iraqi debt from before the war. However, just days before he was set to present the US requests, the administration released a memorandum authorizing 61 states to place contract bids for reconstruction projects in Iraq. The French, German, and Russian administrations—all of whom had interests in participation in the reconstruction phase—believed this to be a direct commentary on their nonparticipation, as the memorandum expressly prohibited the participation of noncoalition partners. Meanwhile, states that had supported the United States were seen as being rewarded for their support (Sloan 2006; Jehl 2003).

The capture of Saddam Hussein on December 13, 2003, allowed the United States to devote even more time and effort to stabilizing Iraq. In addition to Turkey's request for assistance during the initial months of the invasion, the United Kingdom and Poland had been two of the most active members of the coalition. NATO was extremely reluctant to support Poland's commitment to the operation, and some member states remained resentful toward the United States' decision to engage without UN authorization. When the alliance refused to take over Polish efforts in late 2003 and early 2004, US policymakers' expectations for support in the post-war reconstruction phase dropped (Rupp 2006). However, realizing the need for additional international support, the United States again turned to NATO in the hopes it would deploy peacekeeping forces. When it refused peacekeeping support, the administration undertook an aggressive campaign to regain the support of individual allies (Allen and Wright 2004).

In January 2004, Jaap de Hoop Scheffer, a politician from the Netherlands, succeeded Lord Robertson as NATO Secretary General. Scheffer openly criticized the Bush administration for what he believed to be a cherry-picking use of the alliance: only when it directly suited the administration's efforts, he argued, did Washington involve the alliance in Afghanistan and Iraq. Despite the lack of support for a NATO-led training mission in Iraq, Scheffer insisted that NATO had an obligation to fulfill the requests of the Iraqi interim government with full US participation (Sciolino 2004). The United States used the June 2004 Istanbul Summit as an opportunity to request support for training Iraqi security forces. France, Belgium, Germany, and Spain immediately refused to provide forces for the training mission, but other allies agreed to assist US efforts (Rupp 2006).

When the United Nations Security Council passed UNSCR 1546 on June 4, 2004, recognizing the request of the Iraqi government for a multinational force (MNF) to assist in the reconstruction effort, it also established a framework from which NATO began preparations for NATO training mission-Iraq (NTM-I) (United Nations Security Council 2004; NATO 2015). Several alliance members feared that if the United States was given too much control over the NATO mission, the alliance would effectively be endorsing the United States' actions (Rupp 2006). NATO's presence increased from under 100 to nearly 400 personnel during its operation, but the alliance maintained its concentration on training Iraqi forces. NATO officially ended its mission in December 2011, coinciding with the withdrawal of the last US forces in Iraq (NATO 2015).

The strain on President Bush's relationships with his most vocal opponents demonstrated the United States' re-evaluation of its relationship with some of its NATO partners, but not its relationship with the collective alliance. As Stanley Sloan writes, "although the unilateral U.S. approach to Iraq was the instigating event for the crisis in U.S.-European relations, French President Jacques Chirac and German Chancellor Gerhard Schroeder helped make it a full-blown crisis that produced deep divisions among Europeans as well as between Europeans and the U.S." (Sloan 2005). The dissent from NATO partners France and Germany did not threaten the alliance either, and in some respects was unsurprising. Though the United States had enjoyed unprecedented support in the post-9/11 period, the French had been vocal in the belief that European security should not be tied to US security since the inception of NATO. When Charles de Gaulle rose to prominence in the late 1950s, eventually winning the presidency, he was adamant that the United States would not maintain its commitment to Western Europe in the event of an attack—especially one requiring the United States to deploy its nuclear weapons. He also noted how the United States had much longer, well-established ties to its interests in Asia and the Pacific, and argued it would be absurd for Europe to tie its security so closely to the United States. As a result, in 1963, de Gaulle announced France would withdraw its fleet from the Supreme Allied Command Atlantic (SACLANT) and would, after one year from the date of notification, remove itself from all of NATO's military operations (Kaplan 2004).

In the post-Cold War era, France continued to lead the charge for Europe to divorce its security from the United States and to build a similar collective defense alliance in either the Western European Union (WEU) or the European Union (EU). As evidenced in the earlier Kosovo case, French officials were also steadfast in their conviction that any NATO operation should have explicit UN authorization, and the United States lacked any kind of Security Council approval. Like Germany, the Iraq War was another opportunity for France to demonstrate that its actions would not always be the result of US demands (Ibid.). That the DPC was able to come to an agreement on what kind of assistance to provide to Turkey when it invoked Article IV was largely the result of nonparticipation in the DPC by the French.

However, even in light of the Iraq War, France has also sought to maintain close ties to NATO. In 2009, it recommitted fully to NATO military operations. Additionally, it led the campaign to utilize NATO in 2011, when the international community considered intervention in Libya, and was a key contributor to both the US-led Operation Odyssey Dawn and NATO-led Operation Unified Protector (Dempsey 2011). Therefore, though the Iraq intervention strained relations between the United States and NATO in large part because of French opposition, the actions of the French did not necessarily signal the alliance (or the United States' relationship to it) would result in the end of the US-NATO partnership.

As demonstrated in the previous chapter, the United States also continued to play an active role in the development of other NATO programs related to the war on terror as well as efforts in Afghanistan. After the

2002 NSS was published, Rice urged the United States to exercise caution in initiating preventative, coalition-based warfare too often, favoring that diplomatic means be used whenever possible (Fukuyama 2006). In April 2003, Powell testified in front of the Senate foreign relations committee, arguing that while the United States and Europe disagreed on the connection between WMDs and terrorism, the United States had an obligation to convince them as well as a need to work in conjunction to most effectively combat terrorism (Powell 2003).

After the November 2002 Prague Summit, Secretary Rumsfeld proposed the establishment of a "NATO Response Force" (NRF) in a meeting of the defense ministers. The proposal addressed the shortcomings of the 1999 Defense Capabilities Initiative (DCI), established in the wake of the 1999 Kosovo intervention. Though the DCI was intended to modernize NATO's military capabilities, the initiative failed to meet many of the goals as member states refused to increase defense spending (Ek 2007). The proposal for a response force called for a lightweight military force with roughly 20,000 ground soldiers, flexible communication and strikes capabilities, and the ability to combat nuclear, biological, and chemical threats (U.S. Department of Defense 2002). The force was modeled after the Fourth Marine Expeditionary Brigade (MEB), established by General James L. Jones (U.S. Marine Corps) (Mihalka 2005). The United States intended for the NRF to complement both the NATO Allied Rapid Reaction Corps and the EU European Security and Defense Policy (ESDP), and to serve as a secondary force for short-notice operations lasting no longer than 30 days.

The United States' proposal for an NRF reflected growing concerns about the utility of the NATO alliance to the United States. While NATO participation could increase the political legitimacy of intervention, there existed a large gap between the military needs of the United States and the alliance's military capabilities. For the United States, the NRF proposal was intended to augment its own fighting capabilities and reflected the lessons learned from Afghanistan. Writes Michael Mihalka, "A more plausible scenario (for the use of the NRF) would be one where the United States is tied down in a major conflict (such as Iraq) when a transnational terrorist group conducts a mass casualty attack...the NRF would be tasked to take out the training camps of the transnational terrorist group" (Ibid). When asked about the likelihood of the United States seeking NATO assistance in Iraq, Rumsfeld said, "(the issue is) seeing if we can have more of our capabilities available in days or weeks rather than months or years.

If we can have a larger fraction of our capabilities agile and able to get in and out of places and move around in places with a smaller footprint. This is something that NATO countries are perfectly capable of doing if they decided to do it" (Graham and Kaiser 2002). Rumsfeld hoped NATO would adopt the proposal, thus creating a rapidly deployable force embodying his domestic Revolution in Military Affairs (RMA) campaign and creating a deployable unit to use in Iraq.

The United States' proposal was formally presented at the November 2002 Prague Summit and approved by the Allied Ministers of Defense in June 2003. By June 2004, the NRF was fully operational, and US officials commented that the NRF could allow the alliance to overcome some of the operational challenges it faced in the contemporary threat environment (Miles 2004). At the Riga Summit in 2006, NATO leaders announced the NRF was fully operational and has been adjusted in the time since to "provide a more flexible approach to force generation, thereby facilitating force contributions which were being hampered by the enduring high operational tempo arising from Iraq, Afghanistan and other missions" (NATO 2014). The formation and maintenance of the NRF, as well as the Mediterranean Dialogue, the Istanbul Cooperation Initiative, and other counterterrorism operations also led the Bush administration to voice its support for the alliance's evolution.

The disagreement between US policymakers over Iraq exacerbated the perception that United States no longer valued NATO. While Rumsfeld pursued a unilateral, RMA strategy first in Afghanistan and then Iraq, Secretary of State Colin Powell and NSA Advisor Condoleezza Rice urged President Bush to seek multilateral support. Rumsfeld was skeptical of the alliance's ability to support US operations, recognizing the capabilities of the United States were far superior to what the alliance could offer. Though the alliance had taken steps to modernize under the Defense Capabilities Initiative in the years prior to Iraq, declining European contributions to the alliance fed Rumsfeld's perception that the alliance was not of any utility to the United States if it wanted to "move around in places with a smaller footprint" in places like Afghanistan and Iraq (Graham and Kaiser 2002). Powell, conversely, stressed the importance of multilateral action and of winning the political support of both its UN and NATO allies.

Despite disagreement within the administration, there is little evidence suggesting the United States valued the alliance less than before the war. US financial contributions to NATO grew from $371.5 million in 2002 to $880.4 million in 2011 (the last year of the NTM-I). US contributions to the three main areas of NATO funding (the civil budget, the military budget, and the Security Investment Program, or NSIP) accounted for 20–25 percent of all NATO contributions during the same period. Additionally, members of the administration continued to applaud the alliance's modernization efforts while downplaying the fervent debates on Iraq. In a speech in early 2004, Rice acknowledged these conflicts, saying, "I will not deny that there is a lot of noise and chatter among the world's great powers. But this noise is obscuring one of the most striking facts of our time: the world's great powers have never had better relations with one another."

Legitimacy and Multilateralism

The Bush administration insisted the use of force in Iraq was morally and legally legitimate, though it emphasized the latter. Concern for the legal legitimacy of military intervention resulted from the absence of UN authorization. Although the intervention did not have the explicit consent of the Security Council, the United States claimed intervention was a matter of self-defense. The erratic behavior of Saddam Hussein also bolstered the United States' case that military intervention was the only viable option left for addressing the regime: anything short of fundamental regime change would result in the continued oppression of the Iraqi people by a brutal dictator who also posed a threat to the peace and security of the international community (Bjola 2009). Additionally, although the United States enjoyed the legitimization of the Security Council endorsement for the war in Afghanistan, its actions in the 1999 Kosovo operation demonstrated that policymakers did not believe a Security Council resolution was imperative to act. The Kosovo operation was ultimately deemed "illegal but legitimate" and led policymakers to believe the same retroactive evaluation could occur in Iraq when the United States successfully located the WMDs and proved Saddam's intentions to act aggressively.

Those who did not support the use of force argued the Security Council could take further action if Hussein failed to comply with UNSCR 1441, including authorizing the use of force, but insisted inspectors be allowed to collect more evidence demonstrating the imminence of threat. During his reelection campaign in 2002, German Chancellor Schroeder was vocal about his opposition to a possible US invasion of Iraq (Graham and Kaiser 2002). French President Jacques Chirac, a Gaullist, demanded the United States first take action through the UN and threatened to veto any resolution that appeared to legitimize the use of force. The Chirac administration did not believe Iraq posed an immediate threat to its interests, and did not feel its international standing would be damaged by not supporting US efforts (Davidson 2011). US Defense Secretary Rumsfeld fielded the two states' concerns, arguing against giving the Iraqi government more time to mislead inspectors, and insisting only a military operation could result in compliance with UN demands. He also attempted to downplay opposition in the media, labeling them part of "Old Europe" and highlighting widespread support from other NATO members as indication of a shift in power and priorities to Eastern Europe (Richburg 2003; Shanker 2003).

As Philip Gordon and Jeremy Shapiro observe, the Bush administration made it clear in addresses to both the UN and NATO that if states failed to support the United States, the United States would proceed unilaterally, noting "many American actions, statements, and policies prior to and following (US appeals for assistance) suggested that the multilateral approach was pure form – it was not about collective decision making or even real consultations, but simply an effort to win legitimacy for decisions that had been and would be taken by Washington alone" (Gordon and Shapiro 2004). The assembled "coalition of the willing" lacked credibility as a legitimate military coalition. Not only were states unable (and in some cases, unwilling) to match the capabilities of the United States, only one state (the United Kingdom) was given a substantive role in the pre-war planning stage.

Though the United States made no secret of its intentions to act unilaterally if the international community refused to recognize the necessity of regime change in Iraq, it did not purposefully seek to act unilaterally. Instead, it appealed first to the UN, which would lend the most legitimacy to its operations. When those appeals failed, the United States sought NATO support. Policymakers knew that NATO would not have the operational capacity necessary to fight the efficient war Secretary Rumsfeld and others advocated for—the 1999 Kosovo War had demonstrated the alliance's weaknesses in adapting to the post-Cold War environment. Because US policymakers were so vocal in expressing their displeasure with the operational difficulties experienced in Kosovo, and because the United States had been so definitive in their willingness to proceed unilaterally if necessary, scholars mistook the United States' actions as evidence that it no longer valued NATO and the legitimation for the use of force resulting from multilateral action (Hendrickson and Tucker 2004).

The moral legitimacy of the United States' actions was also questioned. Europe was skeptical of the "war on terror" and its connection to Iraq. Though public opinion polls reflected a great concern about the threat posed by terrorism, they did not believe the United States' plans fit with the reality—combatting terrorism, in the eyes of many Europeans, was a prolonged battle requiring a multi-pronged approach, not preemptive conflict (Sloan 2005). Many European states believed that states should devote more of their resources to *combatting* terrorism domestically while developing strategies to address the root causes of terrorism internationally, causing further tension (Gordon 2002).

Some policymakers attempted to frame the need for immediate action by applying the same humanitarian frameworks employed in Kosovo in 1999, hoping it would enhance the moral legitimacy of the operation. Despite the absence of a UN endorsement, NATO staged Operation Allied Force in Kosovo to stop widespread humanitarian abuses by Serbian forces, led by Slobodan Milosevic. Though OAF was not authorized by the UN and resulted in thousands of casualties (from both Serbian forces and the NATO bombing campaign) and millions of displaced Kosovars, the Independent International Commission on Kosovo acknowledged the moral imperative that drove NATO's response (Independent International Commission on Kosovo 2000). The lack of UN endorsement resulted from permanent members Russia and China refusing to authorize any external intervention on the basis of humanitarianism (Williams 2008). Many leaders, including UN Secretary General Kofi Annan, believed the Kosovo intervention signified a need for new international law justifying humanitarian intervention, authorized by the Security Council, even when it violated the organization's commitment to protecting state sovereignty (Buchanan 2010). US Secretary of State Madeline Albright and others hoped that the lesson learned in Kosovo would catalyze the necessary legal reforms. While states preferred the UN to take action under the Responsibility to Protect (R2P) doctrine, Kosovo demonstrated the willingness of states to apply unconventional methods (in this case, acting through a regional organization) in the event the UN Security Council could not reach a consensus (Kramer 2007).

Policymakers attempted to apply the same argument to the Iraq case: the international community was widely aware of Iraq's use of chemical weapons in the Iran-Iraq War and the continued human rights abuses under the Hussein regime. However, as Corneliu Bjola correctly identifies, reports coming out of Iraq in the years prior to the war indicated slightly improved conditions, thus suggesting that the immediate use of force was unwarranted (Bjola 2009). This weakened the argument that the United States' use of force was morally legitimate.

The United States sought domestic and international support for its efforts in Iraq in two distinct phases: the first when it appealed to the international community via the United Nations for an endorsement for the invasion and the second when it requested political and military support, initially from NATO and later from individual states for its coalition of the willing.

Phase 1: Pre-War Planning

The Bush administration initially enjoyed strong domestic support for pursuing further action against Iraq. The Bush administration used the 2001 Congressional AUMF to bolster its case connecting Saddam Hussein to anti-Western terrorist groups. In a speech given in Cincinnati, Ohio on October 7, 2002, Bush spoke to the likely connection between the two:

> We know that Iraq and the Al Qaida terrorist network share a common enemy—the United States of America. We know that Iraq and Al Qaida have had high-level contacts that go back a decade. Some Al Qaida leaders who fled Afghanistan went to Iraq. These include one very senior Al Qaida leader who received medical treatment in Baghdad this year, and who has been associated with planning for chemical and biological attacks. We've learned that Iraq has trained Al Qaida members in bomb-making and poisons and deadly gases. And we know that after September the 11th, Saddam Hussein's regime gleefully celebrated the terrorist attacks on America. (Bush 2015)

The administration continued this rhetoric to successfully shore up additional support from the public and from Congress for the Iraq intervention, despite its intention to act unilaterally and without public or congressional support (Holsti 2011).

Though the Bush administration enjoyed overwhelming congressional support for the global war on terror in the early stages, there were lingering questions as to whether proceeding in Iraq without international support was the best course of action. Prominent US democratic leaders, including former President Bill Clinton and Senators Edward Kennedy, John Kerry, Carl Levin, and Representative Nancy Pelosi, expressed their beliefs that Iraq was in possession of WMDs and agreed Iraq posed a serious threat and demanded immediate attention. However they and members of the Bush administration, including Secretary of State Colin Powell, disagreed with the administration's plans to act unilaterally and without the support of UN and NATO member states (Kreps 2011). Much of the debate centered not on the severity of threat but rather the administration's fighting campaign. Former National Security Advisor Brent Scowcroft, former Secretary of State James Baker, both of whom had served under the George H.W. Bush administration, argued that overthrowing the Hussein regime without a real reconstruction plan was dangerous. The Council of Foreign Relations, the State Department, and the National Intelligence Council provided detailed reports to the administration on the negative consequences of engagement, which were all but ignored by Secretary Rumsfeld and White House officials planning the invasion. Army Chief of Staff Erik Shinseki repeatedly voiced his concerns over Rumsfeld's estimates for troop mobilization, claiming the administration was grossly underestimating how many would be required to establish security and stability, only to be later ridiculed by Rumsfeld and Wolfowitz (Holsti 2011).

When the Bush administration released the September 2002 National Security Strategy (NSS), it was evident that the administration intended to parlay its domestic support and act with or without international participation to invade Iraq. The NSS advanced the neoconservative agenda of preemption and preventative war, advocated for by many in the administration, including Vice-President Cheney, Secretary Rumsfeld, Deputy Secretary Paul Wolfowitz, and National Security Advisor Condoleezza Rice. However, the administration maintained a high level of support from both the public and Congress, due in part to the massive PR campaign it undertook to capitalize on the sense of vulnerability Americans experienced after the 9/11 attacks. According to Brian Schmidt and Michael Williams, "the Bush administration depicted a threat environment radically different from which existed during the Cold War...In the climate of fear that existed after 9/11, and intentionally inflamed by neoconservative pundits appearing on MSNBC and Fox News, scenarios of rogue states or terrorists armed with WMD were deemed unacceptable by Bush administration officials" (Schmidt and Williams 2008).

The Bush administration experienced a rally-around-the-flag effect from the public in the wake of 9/11, a trend that continued in the first phases of the Iraq invasion. Though the initial surge in support declined in late 2002 and early 2003, presidential approval ratings remained above 50 percent, and surged to over 70 percent when the United States announced its invasion on March 20, 2003 (Gallup 2014). However, there was some dissent from the public and a growing anti-war movement began to emerge as the United States moved forward with planning. The movement objected to intervention and contended that the money and resources would be better utilized for improving homeland security and building (domestic) social programs (Lansford 2012).

Both congressional and public support were key elements to the Bush administration's case for intervention to the international community, and officials worked to bolster domestic support in the hopes it would give leverage to the United States in its negotiations with the United Nations (Ibid). Pushing the need for immediate action in the event the UN authorized an intervention in Iraq, the administration successfully campaigned for a second congressional resolution authorizing the use of force. In September, President Bush sent a draft resolution to Congress, and in October 2002, Congress passed its own joint resolution. The Joint Resolution on the Authorization for Use of Military Force in Iraq (P.L. 107–243) addressed the long list of international law violations Iraq had committed since the 1990 invasion of Kuwait and insisted the United States take action to prevent the proliferation of WMDs and fulfill its commitment to the international community. Moreover, the resolution asserted that the authorization of military force was vital to US national security—specifically, the likely connection between Saddam Hussein and al Qaeda meant the Bush administration's proposals to use force against Iraq were consistent with its global war on terror. Though the second resolution did not enjoy as much overwhelming support in both chambers, it received more than the necessary approval in both the House (296–133) and the Senate (77–23).

Although the administration received the necessary authorization from Congress, the importance of international endorsement was still acknowledged by both Congress and the public. Bush's resolution draft gave little mention to the role of the United Nations and was met with concern by members of both parties in Congress. Senate Democrats, including Senate majority leader Tom Daschle (MN), were concerned about the president's willingness to act without UN authorization as well as congressional support. On the resolution draft, Daschle was quoted as saying "We don't want to be a rubber stamp…but we want to be helpful. We do want to be supportive." Senator Russ Feingold (WI) expressed concern over the wording of the resolution: "It is incredibly broad. Not only does it fail to adequately define the mission in question, it appears to actually authorize the president to do virtually anything anywhere in the Middle East" (Kornblut and Milligan 2002). Both parties worked to dispel the notion that dissent against the president's draft resolution or authorization for US efforts in Iraq was the result of partisan politics, instead attributing the concern to the lack of congressional input during the planning process (Shribman 2002). The final legislation emphasized the need for an active UN presence in Iraq. It called for the United States to enforce UN sanctions and any decisions made by the Security Council, but also implored the President to work through the UN to "obtain prompt and decisive action by the Security Council to ensure that Iraq abandons its strategy of delay, evasion and noncompliance and promptly and strictly complies with all relevant Security Council resolutions regarding Iraq" (H.J. Res. 114 2002).

As evidenced here, the Bush administration enjoyed high levels of support for both its global war on terror and intervention in Iraq from Congress. While President Bush often insisted public opinion did not factor in to his decision-making process, he often courted public support for his decisions, and the Iraq War was no exception (Holsti 2011). The Bush administration's decision to seek congressional support for the intervention indicates the administration's belief that domestic acceptance of its Iraq plan would bolster the support of the public as well as support for other political and military ambitions. The administration used the anxiety and feelings of vulnerability in the post-9/11 period to rally public support for the Iraq invasion by carefully connecting Saddam Hussein, weapons of mass destruction, and al Qaeda.

Even though public opinion tended to favor the engagement of allies in US military action, the administration's rhetoric about the necessity of immediate action successfully convinced many to support the United States. To further improve domestic public support, the administration downplayed the concerns of the European publics and connected European leaders' dissent to either economic concerns (both the French and the Germans had trade relationships with Iraq, and France had established oil agreements that were challenged by the UN sanctions against Iraq) or to anti-Americanism (Gordon and Shapiro 2004). Thus, domestic support was not wholly contingent on the international community's participation, and there was relatively little question as to the legitimacy of the invasion. The limited domestic debate focused primarily on Rumsfeld's RMA strategy, with former National Security Advisor Brent Scowcroft, former Secretary of State James Baker, and Army Chief of Staff Erik

Shinseki all campaigning against what they believed to be unrealistic estimates of the necessary resource and troop commitments (Holsti 2011). This debate did not focus on the moral or legal legitimacy of invading Iraq's sovereignty, deposing Saddam Hussein in the hopes of a complete regime change, and implementing institutional reforms aimed at democratizing Iraq.

The administration hoped that the high levels of domestic public support would bolster support from the international community as it attempted to win favor in the United Nations and challenge the Security Council to take action. Though there was a very public debate between Secretary Powell and those urging the United States to pursue legitimacy enhancement, and Secretary Rumsfeld who insisted the United States already had the moral and legal authority to act, President Bush expressed optimism the UN would understand its own survival was in question. When asked by a reporter from the Associated Press about the likelihood of allied support, Bush said, "I think you're going to see a lot of nations – that a lot of nations love freedom. They understand the threat. They understand that the credibility of the United Nations is at stake. They heard me loud and clear when I said 'Either you can be the United Nations, a capable body, a body able to keep the peace, or you can be the League of Nations.' And we're confident that people will follow our lead" (Bush 2002).

However, he made his belief that the United States had the authority to act without international support clear. "At the United National Security Council, it is very important that the members understand that the credibility of the United Nations is at stake...And if the United Nations Security Council won't deal with the problem, the United States and some of its friends will" (Ibid). However, unlike its successes in shoring up domestic support from both Congress and the public, the administration was unable to convince UN members that its proposed intervention was legitimate. During the lengthy debate over Resolution 1441, the United States repeatedly insisted there was just cause for intervention: not only was the Iraqi regime developing and stockpiling WMDs, but it repeatedly and deliberately failed to meet the existing UN guidelines. According to the United States, this posed an immediate threat to its national security and fell squarely within the parameters of Article 51 of the UN Charter. As Bjola notes, the administration failed to provide sufficient evidence that an attack was imminent "on the grounds that in the post-9/11 environment the nature of the evidence required to give a state the right to launch a military attack had sufficiently changed" (Bjola 2009). There was also longstanding evidence of serious human rights abuses in Iraq, but in the pre-war planning phase the Bush administration focused most of its argument on weapons development and the need for collective security (Ibid).

The administration's inability to obtain an endorsement from the United Nations for intervention in Iraq threatened the legitimacy of the operation. While policymakers enjoyed high levels of domestic support, it did not receive widespread international support. Theories as to why the United States was unable to secure international legitimization for its operations fall into one of a few major themes that are collectively more plausible (Bjola 2009; Kitchen 2010; Daalder 2007). The evidence presented in the earlier part of this chapter demonstrates that the United States differed with its UN partners over the imminence of the threat, the motivations for and necessity of intervention, and the proportionality of the use of force. Because of these disagreements, the United States did not obtain the necessary authorization for the invasion from the UN. However, instead of proceeding unilaterally, the United States continued to court international allies first through NATO channels and then by appealing to individual states for support. As earlier interventions demonstrated, multilateral coalitions were unlikely to enhance the operational capacity of the United States' efforts. However, the United States pursued these allies to enhance the operation's legitimacy, which it believed necessary for the success of the mission and for maintaining the United States' international reputation.

Phase 2: The Great NATO Debate

When efforts to build legal legitimacy for the Iraq invasion through obtaining a UN endorsement fell short under UNSCR 1441, domestic and international pressure mounted for the United States to pursue multilateral support via NATO. As previously demonstrated, there was a widespread belief that Saddam Hussein's regime posed a threat to both the United States and the international community, and some evidence that NATO allies would be supportive of US efforts. The publics of major NATO allies Great Britain, France, Germany, and Turkey expressed concern of Iraq as a threat to world peace, but were less inclined to support their home state's involvement with the US intervention. Majorities in France and Germany believed the United States' efforts were to control Iraqi oil, while Americans and the British believed the United States wanted to eliminate the threat to security posed by Hussein (Pew Global Attitudes 2002). Opposing allies were skeptical of the appropriateness of using force to depose Saddam Hussein, instead arguing disarmament without regime change could successfully be pursued.

The 1999 Kosovo intervention had, in some respects, set a precedent for the United States' efforts to move the debate from the UN to NATO in the hopes that the international community would see its actions as legitimate. In appealing to its NATO partners, the United States cited Kosovo as providing the necessary precedent for the alliance to circumvent the UN Security Council deadlock in the hopes that the alliance's participation would enhance the legitimacy of the intervention. But the United States' attempts to parallel the two cases were weakened by several factors, damaged by its own rhetoric as well as international perceptions of the Kosovo intervention. As demonstrated in Chap. 3, the United States was publicly critical of NATO's inefficiencies in combat and repeatedly called for increased contributions and more proportionate burden-sharing within the alliance in the years following Operation Allied Force. The United States and NATO were also criticized for engaging in an air campaign that killed hundreds of civilians on the ground and resulted in continued violence against Kosovars by the Serbian forces. The United States pointed to the Iraqi regime's obfuscation of weapons inspectors as evidence Saddam intended to use chemical agents in the immediate future, but as intrastate violence declined slightly in the years leading up to the war, its engagement plan was seen as hasty and imprudent. In addition, much of the United States' rhetoric regarding the need for action in Iraq focused on how the proliferation of WMDs and "likely" connections to terrorist organizations threatened US security and international peace, not on the humanitarian crimes against Iraqi civilians.

Despite earlier calls for legal reform and the human rights abuses committed by Saddam Hussein's regime, the precedent set by Kosovo did not result in support for NATO to supersede the authority of the UN and intervene in Iraq. As previously demonstrated, both France and Germany's opposition to the war carried over to the North Atlantic Council debates. A consensus for NATO support to ally Turkey was only reached after Secretary General Lord Robertson moved the debate to the Defense Planning Council (of which France was not a member). While the collective alliance disagreed with the United States' plans, individual member states were not deterred from pledging their support to the United States. The war's opponents openly criticized the participation of all seven states seeking NATO membership—Bulgaria, Estonia, Latvia, Lithuania, Romania, Slovakia, and Slovenia—while ignoring the possible motivations for their cooperation with the United States (such as the retention or increase in foreign aid). The United States lauded their efforts, with Secretary Rumsfeld referring to those supporting the United States as "New Europe" and implying that the efforts of Germany and France to block US action resulted from entrenched (and incorrect) ideas of European security threats (Kitchen 2010). NATO officials urged both sides to end the public rhetorical battles to ease tensions within the alliance (Ricks 2003). When the Iraq coalition was formed in 2003, 12 of the 47 participating states were NATO members (not including the United States). The aforementioned states seeking alliance membership also participated in the coalition. A total of 22 NATO states participated in the reconstruction efforts, and 23 made some contribution to the NATO training mission-Iraq (NTM-I).

Polls conducted by Gallup, Pew, CBS/*New York Times*, and others in the same period indicated the American public's preference for allied support: the majority of the public preferred the US engagement of its international partners to bring down the Iraqi regime. In the aftermath of Congress's joint resolution, over 55 percent of Americans polled favored military action in Iraq for regime change purposes; however, nearly half of those conditioned their support on the participation of allies. Support for US engagement in Iraq peaked in January 2003, with 68 percent favoring military engagement. But as support grew, so did the demand for multilateralism, with 37 percent demanding the United States act only if their allies agreed to fight alongside. In a poll conducted by Pew on the eve of the invasion (March 13–16, 2003), 59 percent supported military action against Hussein; however, of those supporting military action, only 16 percent insisted their support was conditional on allied participation, marking a shift in US attitudes (Holsti 2011).

International public opinion was most supportive of military interventions conducted through the UN or NATO. Interestingly, respondents believed that NATO enhanced intervention legitimacy to almost the same degree as the UN. The "Transatlantic Trends" 2003 report found that 43 percent of European respondents supported an intervention with NATO involvement, versus 34 percent or 39 percent who would support US unilateralism or US and allies, respectively. Support for intervention with the UNSC rose to 46 percent. American respondents were more favorable to US unilateralism (63 percent) and US and allies (64 percent) than their

European counterparts, but increased their support more when asked about NATO (73 percent) and UNSC (74 percent) intervention.

When NATO partners struggled to come to an agreement over the amount and type of aid it would provide to Turkey as part of the United States' operations, the United States temporarily abandoned its efforts to win the alliance's support. Though it had made its willingness to operate unilaterally abundantly clear, policymakers chose instead to pursue an ad hoc "coalition of the willing." Historically, ad hoc coalitions allowed the United States to customize its efforts to a particular conflict much easier than working through an alliance with pre-existing political and military decision-making structures (Weitsman 2010). Because Secretary Rumsfeld's plans for the Iraq invasion were based on the RMA—which was relatively successful in the earlier operation in Afghanistan with limited international participation—the ad hoc coalition seemed to meet the United States' operational needs.

Proponents of the coalition cited four factors for pushing ahead with the operation using a coalition in lieu of NATO and UN support: (1) the United States' actions would be found morally and legally legitimate in retrospect—just as in Kosovo—because of the danger posed by WMDs and terrorism; (2) the United States' military strength and hegemonic status demanded it act with or without international support; (3) despite disagreement in the Security Council and NATO, the allies did support taking action against the regime, and major allies such as Great Britain supported the United States' plan for regime change; (4) the anticipated timeline and necessary force was minimal, as the Iraq military was considerably weakened during the 1990 Kuwait invasion with no large-scale rebuilding after the war. The administration was willing to act unilaterally because it was powerful enough to do so, and because it was serving the common interest of the international system by maintaining stability.

But the assembled coalition did not have the desired legitimation effects. Though several member states (and the seven "Vilnius 10" member states seeking membership) participated in the United States' coalition of the willing, the coalition did not carry the same legitimacy as NATO participation would; instead, it seemed to many to be an ill-informed attempt at multilateralism with no sincere desire to work with its international partners. Sarah Kreps argues the United States attempted to engage smaller states (such as Palua and Micronesia) as part of coalition, despite their inability to make significant military or political contributions, for "the political validation they – at least in the aggregate – might offer to the coalition." She and others identify these efforts as an "alternate method of multilateralism" (Kreps 2011). Many believed most of the coalition members participated because of the financial or political incentives of having supported its most important ally: the United States. Writes Patricia Weitsman, "the coalition of the willing was largely composed of states with something to gain by standing shoulder to shoulder with the United States, rather than being motivated by outright fear or threat generated by the Hussein regime" (Weitsman 2014). Additionally, the coalition was financially and politically costly for the United States, with no measurable benefit to fighting effectiveness (Ibid).

Though President Bush declared the initial phase of Operation Iraqi Freedom an overwhelming success in May 2003, the United States' mission in Iraq continued to suffer from legitimacy and operational problems stemming from a number of issues. Firstly, though US troops quickly gained control of Baghdad, Saddam Hussein and several members of his administration were able to evade capture until December 2003. Secondly, the dispatched teams of WMD inspectors known as the Iraq Survey Group (ISG) spent $400 million in the first year only to find no evidence of a current WMD program (Lansford 2012). States like France and Germany, opposed to the war from the outset, used the lack of WMDs as reason to refrain from proving a retrospective UN resolution or NATO endorsement. Thirdly, in deposing the Baath Party, the United States fired thousands of individuals including young men serving in the Iraqi army, leaving the government incapable of providing basic services and giving rise to an anti-American insurgent movement. The Bush administration overestimated the level of support that US troops would receive from Iraqi civilians, how willing the three major groups in Iraq (Shiites, Sunnis, and Kurds) would be to work together, and underestimated how difficult it would be to prevent insurgency and ensure a stable, functioning, and peaceful government (Holsti 2011). Lastly, although the assembled coalition was initially successful at securing victory, its successes were seen not as the result of a carefully conceived and executed multilateral strategy, but rather as the "profound capability asymmetry between the coalition and Saddam Hussein's forces" (Weitsman 2014).

Deadlock in the United Nations was broken in June 2004, with the passing of UN Security Council Resolution 1546. From the resolution, and as a result of the request from the Iraqi Interim Government, NATO prepared to launch NATO training mission-Iraq (NTM-I). The United States was willing to provide security and funding for the NATO effort in exchange for a training schedule coinciding with the United States' time-tables, as well as command over the mission (Rupp 2006). However, because it was a noncombat mission, NATO maintained political control of its forces, which fell under the command of the US mission's Deputy Commanding General for Advising and Training (NATO 2015). As previously demonstrated, many NATO members believed the United States' demands for leadership in NTM-I indicated its unwillingness to cede control to the alliance; thus, while all NATO member states contributed to the mission, several states (including France and Germany) refused to allow their troops in Iraq to prevent them from falling under US command (Weitsman 2014).

According to Lieutenant General Michael Barbero, the US Army officer who commanded the NTM-I from 2009 until 2011, the disagreement between the NATO allies over the NTM-I mission (and US leadership) did not necessarily inhibit the NATO operation's success. Several of the allies, including Turkey, Great Britain, and Italy, played an integral role in training the Iraqi leaders and police force. In addition to the symbolic value of a NATO presence, the allies contributed real capabilities to the NTM-I; General Barbero cited Turkey's acceptance of dozens of military leaders into slots in their schools and the Italian Carabinieri's (military police) establishment of a training school to teach tactical skills, professionalism, and investigative skills as examples of allied capabilities contributions that enhanced the United States' OIF and the NTM-I (Barbero 2015).

Despite the contributions of over 40 coalition partners, the eventual UN Security Council resolutions designed to facilitate stabilization and reconstruction, and NATO's support through the NTM-I, the United States' war in Iraq suffered from the lack of legitimization from the international community. Additionally, the absence of weapons of mass destruction and the United States' underestimation of the tremendous commitment needed to rebuild a stable Iraqi government led to the erosion of domestic and international public support (Holsti 2011).

CONCLUSION

There are many possible explanations for why the Iraq War is treated as a unique case in the US-NATO relationship and frequently cited as evidence of both the alliance's ineffectiveness and inevitable demise. All of these explanations, however, obscure the possibility that the case, when considered in the context of post-Cold War interventions, provides a greater understanding of several key issues. The Iraq War illuminated a growing gap between the United States and its European allies regarding terrorism and international security. However, it did not indicate a change in US preferences for multilateralism, nor did it indicate that the United States would abandon the alliance.

In many respects, the Iraq case challenged fundamental beliefs about US-NATO relations in the post-Cold War period. US policymakers repeatedly voiced concerns about the alliance's ability to effectively engage in modern warfare, noting the growing disparities in NATO contributions by member states, the shrinking defense budgets of many states, and the challenges in Kosovo resulting from the growing capabilities gap. Despite NATOs offer for assistance after 9/11 and the invocation of Article 5 of the Washington Treaty, the United States developed a strategy for Afghanistan with little regard for international participation. Perceiving the Afghanistan mission a success, policymakers pushed for a similar approach in Iraq.

The United States' decision to employ this strategy in Iraq was disputed domestically and internationally, as critics repeatedly warned the Bush administration about the long-term consequences of regime change in Iraq. However, as the evidence presented here demonstrates, the international community was not wholly opposed to taking action against Saddam Hussein. Many believed the Baathist regime had committed humanitarian abuses against its own population, continued to develop weapons of mass destruction in light of international sanctions, and posed a threat to the international community. They did not dispute the need for action, and their objection to the United States' efforts did not come from its desire to act using the Afghan model. Instead, they argued over the necessity of the United States' expedited timeline: while the potential threat of Iraq was quite real, states such as France and Germany wanted further verification of Iraq's weapons development programs before authorizing intervention. The necessity of regime change was also disputed, as skeptics of the US plan believed Saddam Hussein could effectively be disarmed but remain in power.

These disagreements led to vociferous debates in the international community, first in the United Nations and later in NATO. But there is no evidence these debates caused permanent damage to US-NATO relations. While Secretary Rumsfeld and others were outspoken in their criticism of NATO, the United States continued to push for reforms to the alliance's ability to respond to crises in light of the Kosovo intervention, the war in

Afghanistan, and the new threat environment. These efforts resulted in the establishment of the NATO Response Force. Both the Bush and Obama administration continued US military and financial contributions to the alliance and pursued legitimacy enhancement for its Iraq efforts via the alliance. The American public also maintained support for US-NATO efforts, with many indicating a preference for any US conflict engagement to include NATO participation and in the wake of the Iraq War a desire to restore the United States' international reputation (Holsti 2011).

Despite the absence of NATO participation in the United States' primary operation in Iraq, the evidence presented here (and in particular, during the planning stages of the war) confirms the hypotheses that the United States pursues alliance participation for legitimacy enhancement and adherence to international norms. The Bush administration also requested NATO participation for the alliance's utility, and the alliance demonstrated its capability to enhance the US mission through the NTM-I, confirming the hypotheses on the utility of NATO. Furthermore, the United States continued to encourage reforms to the alliance, even though it largely refused the administration's requests in the early stages of the Iraq war.

The United States' plan for Iraq suffered from a lack of legitimacy from the beginning phase of planning, and the lack of an endorsement from both the United Nations and NATO only compounded the problem. During the 2002 campaign to rally support, the United States successfully gathered domestic support for the Iraq invasion despite inconclusive evidence of weapons of mass destruction. This was due in large part to the sense of vulnerability the public experienced in the aftermath of the 9/11 attacks and congressional efforts to unite behind the president and be resolute in the war on terror. The Bush administration played to this support, framing the Iraq threat as imminent and asserting the necessity for regime change led by the United States (Ibid). The administration hoped the widespread domestic acceptance of its plan for engagement, combined with its political strength in the international system, would lead to both an endorsement by the UN Security Council and the legitimization of the invasion. When it failed to secure a second resolution, the United States turned its attention to NATO in the hopes that alliance participation would lead the international community to retrospectively deem the invasion morally and legally legitimate as it had in Kosovo. However, it failed to secure overwhelming NATO support and was forced to draw on the support of individual member states for its coalition of the willing.

Of course, the lack of legitimacy for the United States' Iraq efforts did not result exclusively from its inability to rally international support. The United States' rhetoric about the need for immediate action against an imminent threat was repeatedly challenged by those who were critical of the United States' plan. Writes Ole Holsti, "The American invasion of Iraq was based on two elements of 'worst case' analysis – that Saddam Hussein possessed weapons of mass destruction and that, because he had intimate ties to the al Qaeda terrorist organization that had carried out the September 11 attacks on New York and Washington, Saddam was also complicit in those attacks" (Ibid). Both of these elements were discredited in the early parts of the invasion. No WMDs were discovered, and the United States failed to produce conclusive evidence demonstrating the ties between Saddam and al Qaeda. These revelations effectively weakened the United States' future efforts for rallying international support for the war. Writes John Mueller, "Had the invasion been a success…the venture, despite the very considerable misgivings, even hostility of the international community, would probably have been accepted as legitimate in time" (Mueller 2005). Though the UN Security Council would pass a set of resolutions authorizing a multinational force, it would do so primarily to prevent instability and ensure the establishment of a cohesive, functional government while protecting Iraqi civilians.

The other impediment to legitimacy enhancement was the United States' strategies for what to do once Saddam was disposed. The success of Rumsfeld's RMA—the Afghan model—in Afghanistan led members of the Bush administration to disregard some of the recommendations of military advisors as to the necessary troop commitment. Though the Iraqi military never fully recovered from the first Gulf War and was far outmatched by US military capabilities, American policymakers failed to realize how unstable Iraq would be during the reconstruction process. They believed Iraqi civilians would be favorable to the American presence because of the severity of brutality experienced at the hands of the Baathists, led by Saddam. They also believed leaders from each of the main groups within Iraq would unite around the common goal of reconstructing a more democratic government. For these reasons, the United States believed the assembled coalition of the willing would be sufficient for both conflict engagement and legitimacy enhancement, despite the lack of assistance from the UN and NATO (Kreps 2011).

However, the lack of international support for the intervention was incredibly damaging to US legitimization efforts, particularly in the planning phases of the war. While NATO participation would not confer the same degree of legitimacy as a Security Council resolution, there is clear evidence demonstrating Congress, the American public, and the international community likely would have perceived the United States' actions as more legitimate had NATO agreed to participate. The Kosovo precedent could have been applied to legitimacy in Iraq had the operation been successful at locating WMDs, connecting Saddam to terrorist organizations, and installing a stable democratic Iraqi government. The absence of legitimacy for the intervention made US efforts to rally support for the post-war reconstruction phase more difficult. Additionally, when NATO failed to fulfill US requests for assistance, the administration was forced to offer costly political and military incentives to individual states in exchange for participation in the coalition of the willing. Because of this, the resulting coalition lacked fighting efficiency, cohesion, and, most importantly, the legitimacy of an alliance-backed operation.

It is difficult to infer from the Iraq case the United States' value for multilateralism in the post-Cold War period. There are two competing narratives on the importance of multilateralism under the Bush administration that emerge from the evidence presented in this chapter. The first suggests the United States never actually intended to act multilaterally, and only sought international support because of the legitimacy enhancement. From this perspective, the United States' continued pursuit of allies after the initial invasion was purely strategic. Having faced much more difficulty in establishing a stable Iraqi government than initially anticipated, as well as executing the simultaneous war in Afghanistan, the United States recognized how difficult it would be to proceed unilaterally. Thus, the administration sought international participation for the reconstruction and stabilization phase so it could turn its attention to its larger war on terror and focus its combat abilities. The Bush administration's rhetoric—about the United States' confidence in the severity of threat posed by Saddam Hussein, the necessity of regime change, and the international dissent resulting from the debates in the UN and NATO—reinforced the perception that US primacy led policymakers to prefer unilateralism.

The second narrative suggests the Bush administration valued multilateralism, despite its claims the United States would pursue unilateral action if necessary. The evidence presented here indicates this assessment is more accurate. In the case of Iraq, the United States did not pursue multilateralism to enhance its military abilities: US capabilities were unmatched and the Iraqi army was so weakened, an American victory was certain. None of its efforts to assemble a multilateral coalition was to enhance the fighting effectiveness of the United States, and none was because the United States felt international support was integral to its success on the battlefield. Instead, the efforts to include the international community reflected US beliefs about legitimacy enhancement. If the UN or NATO endorsed the United States' efforts, it did not matter what kind of military or operational support was provided: the United States needed endorsement from these organizations to make their actions morally legitimate in the eyes of other states and in the eyes of the public. That the United States did not seek support from other alliances or organizations as vehemently as it did in the UN and NATO reveals in part the value of legitimization the alliance holds for the United States.

The tensions between the United States, France, Germany, and others regarding the United States' willingness to intervene in Iraq without an authorizing resolution from the UN Security Council did not significantly alter the United States' relationship with the alliance. The United States continued to support efforts to improve the alliance's ability to engage in Afghanistan and elsewhere. The United States' actions indicated the Bush administration believed the alliance, though not engaged in Iraq, was still useful to the United States' objectives. The United States spearheaded the establishment of the NATO Response Force, repeatedly engaged in efforts to mobilize allies around shared security concerns (such as terrorism and cybersecurity), supported the alliance's membership expansions, and continued to sustain its financial and resource contributions to the alliance.

REFERENCES

Allen, Mike, and Robin Wright. 2004. Bush Seeks NATO Help on Iraq. *The Washington Post*, June 25.

Barbero, Michael (USA-Ret., Former Commander NTM-I). Interview with Author, Jan 15, 2015.

Bjola, Corneliu. 2009. *Legitimising the Use of Force in International Politics*, Contemporary Security Studies. London: Routledge.

Black, Ian, and Michael White. 2003. Chirac Pledges to Veto New Resolution. *The Guardian*, February 17. http://www.theguardian.com/world/2003/feb/18/iraq.france/print

Borger, Julian. 2002. Straw Threat to Bypass UN Over Attack on Iraq. *The Guardian*, October 18. http://www.theguardian.com/world/2002/oct/19/iraq.foreignpolicy

Buchanan, Allen. 2010. *Human Rights, Legitimacy, and the Use of Force.* New York: Oxford University Press.

Bush, George W. Remarks Following a Meeting with Secretary of State Colin L. Powell and an Exchange with Reporters. Last Modified Sept 19, 2002. www. presidency.ucsb.edu/ws/print.php?pid=73123. Accessed 8 Apr 2015.

———. Address to the Nation on Iraq from Cincinnati, Ohio. Last Modified Oct 7. http://www.presidency.ucsb.edu/ws/print.php?pid=73139. Accessed 8 Apr 2015.

Daalder, Ivo H. 2007. *Beyond Preemption.* Washington, DC: Brookings Institution Press.

Davidson, Jason. 2011. *America's Allies and War.* New York: Palgrave Macmillan.

Dempsey, Judy. 2011. Beginning of the End for NATO. *The New York Times,* June 14. http://www.nytimes.com/2011/06/14/world/europe/14iht-letter14. html?ref=libya

Ek, Carl. 2007. *NATO's Prague Capabilities Commitment.* Washington, DC: Congressional Research Service.

Fukuyama, Francis. 2006. *America at the Crossroads: Democracy, Power, and the Neoconservative Legacy.* New Haven: Yale University Press.

Gallup. 2014. Presidential Approval Ratings – George W. Bush. Last Modified July 14. http://www.gallup.com/poll/116500/presidential-approval-ratings-george-bush.aspx

Gordon, Phillip H. 2002. NATO and the War on Terrorism a Changing Alliance. *The Brookings Review* 20 (3): 36–38.

Gordon, Philip, and Jeremy Shapiro. 2004. *Allies at War: America, Europe, and the Crisis Over Iraq.* New York: McGraw Hill.

Graham, Bradley, and Robert G. Kaiser. 2002. On Iraq Action, US Is Keeping NATO Sidelined. *The Washington Post,* September 24.

Hendrickson, David C., and Robert W. Tucker. 2004. The Sources of American Legitimacy. *Foreign Affairs* 83: 18–32.

Holsti, Ole R. 2011. *American Public Opinion on the Iraq War.* Ann Arbor: University of Michigan Press.

Independent International Commission on Kosovo. 2000. *The Kosovo Report: Conflict, International Response, Lessons Learned.* New York: Palgrave.

Jehl, Douglas. 2003. U.S. Bars Iraq Contracts for Nations that Opposed War. *The New York Times,* December 9. http://www.nytimes.com/2003/12/09/international/middleeast/09CND-DIPL.html

Kaplan, Lawrence S. 2004. *NATO Divided, NATO United.* Westport: Praeger.

Kitchen, Veronica M. 2010. *The Globalization of NATO: Intervention, Security and Identity.* New York: Routledge.

Kornblut, Anne E., and Susan Milligan. 2002. President Seeking Free Hand on Iraq Congress Asked to Endorse Unilateral Action in Region. *Boston Globe,* September 20.

Kramer, Anne. 2007. What the World Thinks. In *Beyond Preemption: Force and Legitimacy in a Changing World*, ed. I.H. Daalder. Washington, DC: Brookings Institution Press.

Kreps, Sarah E. 2011. *Coalitions of Convenience: United States Military Interventions After the Cold War*. New York: Oxford University Press.

Lansford, Tom. 2012. *9/11 and the Wars in Afghanistan and Iraq*. Santa Barbara: ABC-CLIO.

Mihalka, Michael. 2005. NATO Response Force: Rapid? Responsive? A Force? *Connect* 4 (2): 67–80. https://www.jstor.org/stable/26323172

Miles, Donna. 2004. NATO Response Force Ready for Duty, Rumsfeld Says. June 27. http://www.defense.gov/News/NewsArticle.aspx?ID=26194. Accessed 6 Apr 2015.

Mueller, John. 2005. Force, Legitimacy, Success, and Iraq. *Review of International Studies* 31: 109–125.

NATO. The Defence Planning Committee (Archived). Last Modified Mar 28, 2012. http://www.nato.int/cps/en/natolive/topics_49201.htm. Accessed 20 June 2014.

———. NATO Response Force. http://www.nato.int/cps/en/natolive/topics_49755.htm. Accessed 24 July 2014.

———. NATO Assistance to Iraq. Last Modified Sept 1, 2015. https://www.nato.int/cps/en/natohq/topics_51978.htm

Pew Global Attitudes Project. What the World Thinks in 2002. Last Modified Dec 4, 2002. http://www.pewglobal.org/files/2002/12/2002-Report-Final-Updated.pdf. Accessed 8 Apr 2015.

Powell, Colin. 2003. *An Enlarged NATO: Mending Fences and Moving Forward on Iraq, Hearing Before the Comm. On Foreign Relations*. 108th Cong. United States Senate.

Richburg, Keith B. 2003. NATO Blocked on Iraq Decision: France, Germany Lead Opposition to War. *The Washington Post*, January 23.

Ricks, Thomas E. 2003. NATO Allies Trade Barbs Over Iraq. *The Washington Post*, February 9.

Rupp, Richard E. 2006. *NATO After 9/11: An Alliance in Continuing Decline*. New York: Palgrave Macmillan.

Schmidt, Brian C., and Michael C. Williams. 2008. The Bush Doctrine and the Iraq War: Neoconservatives Versus Realists. *Security Studies* 17 (2): 191.

Sciolino, Elaine. 2004. NATO Chief Says Iraq and Afghanistan Are Doomed Without World Cooperation. *The New York Times*, July 2.

Shanker, Thom. 2003. Rumsfeld Rebukes the UN and NATO on Iraq Approach. *The New York Times*, February 9.

Shimko, Keith L. 2006. *The Iraq Wars and America's Military Revolution*. Cambridge: Cambridge University Press.

Shribman, David M. 2002. President Gambles, with Odds in His Favor. *Boston Globe*, September 5.

Sloan, Stanley R. 2005. *NATO, the European Union, and the Atlantic Community.* Lanham: Rowman & Littlefield.

———. 2006. Transatlantic Security Relations. In *The Transatlantic Divide: Foreign and Security Policies in the Atlantic Alliance from Kosovo to Iraq*, ed. Osvalso Croci and Amy Verdun. New York: Manchester University Press.

Smith, Edward M. 2003. Collective Security, Peacekeeping, and Ad Hoc Multilateralism. In *Democratic Accountability and the use of Force in International Law*, ed. Ku Charlotte and Harold K. Jacobson. New York: Cambridge University Press.

U.S. Department of Defense. U.S. Will Propose a New, Agile Military Response Force for NATO. Last Modified Sept 24, 2002. http://iipdigital.usembassy. gov/st/english/article/2002/09/20020920183018porth@pd.state. gov0.751034.html#axzz3EozjCWk2. Accessed 14 July 2014.

U.S. House of Representatives. 2002. H.J. Res. *114 Authorization for use of Military Force Against Iraq Resolution of 2002.* 107th Congress Session.

United Nations Security Council. Security Council Endorses Formation of Sovereign Interim Government in Iraq (Resolution 1546) [Press Release]. Last Modified Aug 6, 2004. https://www.un.org/press/en/2004/sc8117.doc.htm

Weisman, Steven R. 2003. Fallout from Iraq Rift: NATO May Feel a train. *The New York Times*, February 11. http://www.nytimes.com/2003/02/11/ international/middleeast/11ASSE.html

Weitsman, Patricia. 2010. Wartime Alliances Versus Coalition Warfare. *Strategic Studies Quarterly* 4 (2): 113–136.

———. 2014. *Waging War: Alliances, Coalitions, and Institutions of Interstate Violence.* Stanford: Stanford University Press.

Williams, Michael J. 2008. *NATO, Security, and Risk Management.* Milton Park: Routledge.

CHAPTER 6

The 2011 Libyan Intervention

Unlike the preceding cases, the 2011 Libyan crisis did not stem from longstanding ethnic tensions, an attack on a NATO ally, or a potential immediate threat to international security. Instead, the Libyan peoples' growing frustration with the 42-year rule of the authoritarian Colonel Muammar Qaddafi became the powder keg waiting for the spark of the Arab Spring. The growing discontent with economic disparities, advances in communication and the advent of social media, and a series of international events inspired an uprising of Libyan intellectuals, students, and oil workers. Although the international community was closely monitoring the Arab Spring uprisings, an intervention was not imminent until the Qaddafi regime's brutal response to relatively peaceful protests in mid-February.

Although the response to potential violations of humanitarian law and the central tenants of the Responsibility to Protect (R2P) doctrine were swift, restoring peace and stability in Libya was not. As with many interventions resulting in the overthrow of the governing regime, today Libya faces the consequences of the power vacuum left when Colonel Qaddafi was killed seven months after the initial US-led operation, Odyssey Dawn. The Islamic State (IS, or ISIS) has challenged the internationally recognized Government of National Accord (GNA), and in areas under its control, imprisoned, tortured, and murdered those in opposition. Several hundred thousand have fled, seeking asylum in Europe and elsewhere, while an estimated 193,000 remain internally displaced (UNHCR 2018; Salama 2018).

© The Author(s) 2020
J. Garey, *The US Role in NATO's Survival After the Cold War*,
Palgrave Studies in International Relations,
https://doi.org/10.1007/978-3-030-13675-8_6

The GNA lacks the legitimacy and resources to successfully defend against ISIS and other groups challenging its legitimacy, provide basic necessities to its civilian population, and develop badly needed governmental infrastructure to support the rule of law (Human Rights Watch 2017).

The Obama administration lauded Operation Odyssey Dawn (OOD) and Operation Unified Protector (OUP) missions in 2011 and 2012 a military success as the United States suffered no casualties from either the US-led or NATO-led operation. The NATO allies also highlighted their success by championing their ability to avoid combat casualties, limit civilian casualties, and engage in a technologically advanced precision air campaign which, from the alliance's perspective, also limited collateral damage. NATO Secretary General Anders Fogh Rasmussen publicly lauded the alliance's efforts in *Foreign Affairs*, while simultaneously seizing the opportunity to press allies for more:

> First, to those who claimed that Afghanistan was to be NATO's last out-of-area mission, it has shown that unpredictability is the very essence of security. Second, it has proved that in addition to frontline capabilities, such as fighter-bombers and warships, so-called enablers, such as surveillance and refueling aircraft, as well as drones, are critical parts of any modern operation. And third, it has revealed that NATO allies do not lack military capabilities. Any shortfalls have been primarily due to political, rather than military, constraints. In other words, Libya is a reminder of how important it is for NATO to be ready, capable, and willing to act. (Rasmussen 2011)

Yet a consensus on the effectiveness of the operations, and on the utility of multilateralism to US goals, has not been reached. Estimates of civilian deaths from NATO strikes are disputed (Human Rights Watch 2012), but regardless of the final tally, these deaths are indicative of the alliance's shortcomings in its persistently reiterated goal to avoid civilian casualties through the use of precision airstrikes. Further, as with the operations in Kosovo, Afghanistan, and Iraq, NATO skeptics foresaw Libya as indicative of the alliance's ever-looming demise (O'Donnell and Vaisse 2011; Kuperman 2015; Hunter 2011). Even President Barack Obama found fault in the ways in which allies participated in Libya, despite his resounding insistence on a multilateral effort from the outset and the criticism he faced for "leading from behind" (Goldberg 2016). The failures of Libya, he and others argued, was not the fault of the United States or its successful air campaigns in OOD and OUP; rather, it was the fault of imagination, long-term planning, or commitment from outside of the United States.

Thus, in addition to the questions regarding US-NATO relations and NATO persistence, the case of intervention in Libya, taken in conjunction with the Kosovo, Afghanistan, and Iraq cases, raises new questions about alliance participation and mission success from the American perspective, NATO perspective, and even the perspective of the international community. To address the first set of questions, this chapter analyzes the US-NATO response to the Libyan revolution. As in the other cases, I divide the crisis into three phases. The pre-intervention phase, from February to March 2011, is much shorter than the other three conflicts. Concerned about the possibility of a humanitarian crisis in Libya and spillover into other states in North Africa and the Middle East, the international community acted quickly to formulate plans for a possible intervention. The second phase, mid- to late March 2011, explains Operation Odyssey Dawn (OOD). Led by the United States, Operation Odyssey Dawn was a multilateral coalition effort to enforce the conditions of UNSCR 1973, including a no-fly zone, arms embargo, and the protection of Libyan civilians through an aerial bombing campaign. I demonstrate how the United States' reluctance to lead a prolonged campaign in Libya led the Obama administration to pursue a multilateral operation led by the NATO alliance. The third phase of the intervention is Operation Unified Protector, the NATO-led campaign to continue enforcement of UNSCR 1973. The operation enabled the rebels to overthrow the Qaddafi regime in late August 2011 and capture Colonel Qaddafi two months later. NATO officially ended Operation Unified Protector in October 2011.

Analysis of these three phases reveals the US-NATO relationship under the Obama administration and the benefits of NATO participation to the legitimacy of the Libyan intervention. The legitimizing effects of NATO factored into the United States' decision to pursue NATO leadership during the planning of Operation Unified Protector—many US officials believed NATO leadership would lend more legitimacy to the operation than a coalition of states or an individual state. However, legitimation of the operation was a *secondary* concern for the United States, as its primary reason for pushing the alliance's leadership was to alleviate the military and political burden on the United States. During the pre-intervention phase, the United States made its preference for multilateralism and its unwillingness to lead a prolonged operation clear. It sought a transition from the US-led operation to a NATO-led operation because the alliance provided the necessary political and military infrastructure for executing a coalition operation. In the early months of Operation Unified Protector, the administration rebuffed several requests to provide more resources. But as OUP continued, the alliance's weaknesses and the Europeans' inability to end the operation without substantial support from the United States became clear and the administration was forced to increase its contributions to effectively end operations.

Finally, this chapter concludes by introducing preliminary findings from the Libyan case to the latter set of questions regarding short- and long-term benefits of NATO-induced multilateralism. These questions are then further explored in the book's remaining chapters.

Background: Setting the Stage for Revolution— And Intervention

On paper, Colonel Qaddafi's 42-year tenure reads as a collection of contradictions, and as Alison Pargeter aptly details, punctuated by his treatment of Libya as a "giant laboratory" for "a litany of bizarre whims and half-baked political and economic experiments, which had plunged the country into a permanent state of chaos" (Pargeter 2012). As he transitioned from reluctant leader in the wake of the 1969 coup to what President Obama would later call a "dictator" ruling under "the dark shadow of tyranny" (Obama 2011a), Qaddafi constantly criticized the global powers as imperialists and regularly challenged their militaries to engage in conflict. He instituted highly repressive policies to preserve his power, based on his personal understandings of socialism, Arabism, and Islam. He chronicled his political, economic, and social philosophies and distributed them to the population in his now infamous *Green Book*. Yet to understand the 2011 uprising and subsequent Western intervention, it is imperative to contextualize these events in Qaddafi's historical relationship with the United States and the international community.

For much of his reign, Qaddafi's Libya was relatively isolated from the international community and treated as a threat to international stability. The greater the isolation, the more hostile Libya became to the United States. In 1981, two Libyan aircrafts challenged US forces over the Gulf of Sirte. In response, the United States shot down both planes. In early April 1986, Libyans attacked a Berlin disco and killed three people, including two US servicemen. The attack was later traced back to Qaddafi (BBC 2015; Malinarich 2001). In retaliation for his role in planning the club attack, the United States bombed military and residential facilities (including Qaddafi's house) in Tripoli and Benghazi, killing 101 people. In 1988, under the direction of Colonel Qaddafi, a Libyan intelligence officer, Abdel Basset Ali al-Megrahi, placed a bomb on Pan Am Flight 103. The plane exploded over Lockerbie, Scotland, killing all 270 people on board, 190 of whom were Americans. However, the United States was not the only target of Qaddafi's hostility. In 1984, a British police officer was killed outside the Libyan embassy in London during anti-Qaddafi protests, leading the United Kingdom to break its diplomatic ties with Libya. In the 1980s and 1990s, Qaddafi also engaged in several acts of state-sponsored terrorism.

In response to his global reach, the United States, Great Britain, and others pushed for international action. As evidence surfaced implicating Qaddafi in orchestrating the Lockerbie bombing attack, American and British policymakers pushed the UN Security Council for punitive measures against Libya. In 1992, the Security Council imposed sanctions against Libya for its participation in state-sponsored terrorism. In 1994, the Security Council implemented further restrictions on air travel and arms sales to Libya after Qaddafi refused to turn over two suspects implicated in the Lockerbie bombing by the United States and Great Britain (CNN 2014; BBC 2015).

In the late 1990s, however, Colonel Qaddafi had a change of heart regarding Libya's relationship with the West. In the hopes of generating new economic opportunities, Qaddafi agreed in 1999 to turn over the Lockerbie bombing suspects. During the US invasion of Iraq in 2003, Libya also agreed to abandon its weapons of mass destruction (WMDs) program, formally denounced terrorism, and accepted responsibility for the Pan Am 103 bombing in a letter to the United Nations. Subsequently, the United Nations removed Libya from list of states sponsoring terrorism and lifted sanctions against the regime. Libya's relationships with the United States, the United Kingdom, France, and the European Union improved as the parties worked to restore diplomatic ties. The West became the largest consumers of Libyan oil, which had lower production costs than oil from Norway and Russia. Prior to the 2011 crisis, an estimated 85 percent of Libyan oil was sold in the European markets (BBC 2015; Chivvis 2014; Engelbrekt and Wagnsson 2014).

Although the state improved trade relationships and increased its oil revenues, conditions for the working classes did not improve—only the regime and those closest to Qaddafi (including many of his children) benefitted from the political and economic expansion (Pargeter 2012). Despite its growing relationships with Western liberal democracies and the economic opportunities its improved reputation created, Libya remained one of the most oppressive countries in the world, according to Freedom House and other human rights organizations (Chivvis 2014). The economic disparities between the Libyan elite and the rest of the population sparked resentment toward Qaddafi and his regime, and these tensions provided the foundation for the 2011 revolution.

THE ARAB SPRING REACHES LIBYA, AND THE UNITED STATES RESPONDS

The 2011 Libyan revolution began as a result of both international and domestic conditions. Domestically, high levels of corruption and inequality, poor housing and employment opportunities, and other repressive policies of the regime fueled anger toward Qaddafi. The regime's oil revenues also prompted resentment, as only those closest to Qaddafi benefitted from Libya's newfound prosperity. Internationally, the Libyan conflict was sparked by a larger series of rebellions in the Middle East and North Africa, known as the Arab Spring. The Arab Spring rebellions, beginning with the self-immolation of fruit vendor Mohamed Bouazizi in December 2010, when many took to the streets to protest the regime of the Tunisian regime, led by President Zine el-Abidine Ben Ali (Fahim 2011). The protests quickly spread to Egypt, Algeria, Yemen, Jordan, Bahrain, Lebanon, Saudi Arabia, Syria, and other states. Citizens, in part informed and empowered by new technologies such as social media, took to the streets as well to fight back against their own authoritarian regimes, many of which had been in power for decades (Blight et al. 2012). In Libya, Colonel Qaddafi appeared unconcerned about the possibility of a similar uprising. When Tunisian president Ben Ali fled to Saudi Arabia in January 2011, Qaddafi blamed Wikileaks and a false sense of security for the protestors' success in deposing the president. He criticized the demonstrations and spoke of the harsh repercussions Libyans would face if they attempted a similar revolution (Chivvis 2014).

Despite Qaddafi's warnings, the Arab Spring protests ignited in Libya in February 2011. On February 15, protestors took to the streets of Benghazi to protest the arrests of Fathi Terbil, a human rights lawyer, who famously advocated for victims of the riots at the Abu Salim prison in 1996. Though the protests started with a small group of fellow lawyers, hundreds of residents quickly joined the demonstrations, throwing rocks and gasoline bombs at buildings and riot police. As the crowd grew, police began using water cannons. When word of the protests in Benghazi spread, similar protests in the cities of Zentan and Al Beyda commenced (Cowell 2001). In addition to the street protests, activists rallied online via social media websites such as Facebook, organizing more demonstrations and demanding changes to the Libyan constitution. Anti-Qaddafi rebels rallied for a self-proclaimed "day of rage" on February 17, and protests expanded to other cities including Misrath, Sirte, and the capital, Tripoli. The police fired machine guns at the crowds, killing 200 protestors and wounding 900 others in just a few short days. However, despite the aggressiveness of the police and the high number of civilian casualties, by February 21, all of Qaddafi's forces either retreated from Benghazi or abandoned their posts (Chivvis 2014).

As Kjell Engelbrekt and Charlotte Wagnsson note, the characteristic feature of the protests in mid-February was "the immediate and unrelenting" assault of the security forces, which forced the protestors to arm themselves. The protestors—mostly students, oil workers, and human rights activists—gained the sympathy of many citizens who had become tired of living under Qaddafi's rule. As support for the opposition grew, so did the number of rebel fighters—regular army and foreign fighters began to defect from Qaddafi's forces to join the protests (Engelbrekt and Wagnsson 2014). In addition to Benghazi, the rebels quickly took control of two more cities, Baida and Tobruk.

On February 21, Colonel Qaddafi appeared on television, pleading with the regime's loyal followers to fight back against the rebel forces. Referring to the protestors as "cockroaches" and "rats," Qaddafi told his followers, "Come out of your homes, attack them in their dens. Withdraw your children from the streets. They are drugging your children, they are making your children drunk and sending them to hell." He went on to say that he would "cleanse Libya house by house," and declared his intentions to remain in power: "I am not going to leave this land. I will die as a martyr at the end...I shall remain, defiant. Muammar is leader of the revolution until the end of time" (Spencer 2011; Gardner 2011). Speculation of a possible international intervention in Libya began following the protests in Benghazi on February 15–17, and Qaddafi's subsequent television appearance hastened the perception of a need for intervention.

In early March, the makeshift governments of rebel-controlled Libyan territories united to form the National Transitional Council (NTC). The NTC, comprised mostly of tribe leaders, former prisoners, human rights activists, lawyers, intellectuals, and expatriated individuals, was led by

Mustafa Abdel Jalil, a defected justice minister. On March 5, the NTC proclaimed itself the sole representative of Libya and sent two members to meet with foreign governments in the hopes of gaining international recognition as the legitimate representative of Libya. While the NTC worked to establish its legitimacy, the Qaddafi forces launched a major counteroffensive to combat rebels trying to take the capital of Tripoli. The counteroffensive consisted of both a ground and limited aerial campaign in the towns of Brega, Ras Lanuf, and Zaniyah. The regime's efforts were successful in shifting control of the fighting from the rebels back to Qaddafi.

On February 22, the UN Security Council convened for an emergency meeting after Qaddafi deployed snipers, gunships, and planes in an extensive and violent crackdown on the protestors. President Obama followed the emergency meeting with a speech demanding Qaddafi to end the violence. He cited Qaddafi's actions as violations of international law, and reiterated the condemnation of not only the Security Council, but also of the European Union, the Arab League, and the Organization of the Islamic Conference. He also noted the United States would implement efforts to remove its personnel from Libya, and work through multilateral institutions to take further action against Qaddafi if the violence continued (Obama 2011c). In the following days, President Obama consulted with the leaders of France, Great Britain, and Italy as all four states moved to pull its citizens out of Libya (Chivvis 2014). On February 25, the United States closed its embassy in Tripoli as it announced new sanctions against the Libyan government, including freezing assets belonging to Colonel Qaddafi and other high-ranking officials participating in the crackdown and a travel ban. Although the sanctions exerted diplomatic pressure on Qaddafi, the Obama administration refrained from publicly acknowledging any plans for a military intervention (Cooper and Landler 2011).

As it became clearer Qaddafi would not capitulate, the international community began to consider additional diplomatic and military options, including the establishment of a no-fly zone. Following a NATO defense ministerial meeting on March 10, US Secretary of Defense Robert Gates indicated the Obama administration would consider enforcing a no-fly zone but the United States was unwilling to commit to further military action. At a National Security Council (NSC) meeting on March 15, President Obama expressed discontent with the no-fly zone plan because he did not believe it would stop Qaddafi from continuing the violent campaign against the rebels. After the NSC meeting, US military advisors began preparing plans for an intervention, with a somewhat novel approach: NATO would take the lead role, and the United States would fulfill its obligation to the alliance while refraining from taking a leadership position in the operation (Michaels 2014; Engelbrekt and Wagnsson 2014). While the Obama administration felt pressure from the international community to respond to Qaddafi's successes in early March, the American public and political elites both expressed concern over the possibility of a US intervention in Libya. In a Pew poll conducted March 10–13, 2011, only 27 percent of those surveyed believed the United States had a responsibility to address the fighting in Libya. Although a small majority (51 percent) agreed the United States should increase the economic and diplomatic sanctions against Qaddafi, only 44 percent supported enforcement of a no-fly zone. Only 16 percent approved of bombing Libyan air defenses, and 82 percent opposed sending in ground troops (Pew Research 2011). Political leaders from both parties were divided on how to address the growing conflict. Secretary Gates, as well as Vice-President Joe Biden, National Security Advisor Tom Donilon, and Deputy NSA Denis McDonough, expressed reservations about enforcing the no-fly zone and argued it would require additional military operations, which could drag the United States even further into the Libyan conflict. However, congressional leaders such as Senator Joe Lieberman, Senator John McCain, and Senator John Kerry cited an imperative need for intervention to prevent a humanitarian crisis like those experienced in the 1990s in Rwanda and the Balkans (Chivvis 2014).

On March 17, the UN Security Council passed a second resolution on Libya. UNSCR 1973 detailed to the inability of the Libyan government to protect innocent civilians, condemned the gross actions and flagrant human rights violations by the Qaddafi regime, and demanded an immediate ceasefire. The resolution also authorized a no-fly zone, arms embargo, additional freezing of assets, and a flight ban (United Nations Security Council, Resolution 1973 2011b). Two of the Security Council permanent members, China and Russia, abstained from voting, as did NATO ally Germany and two other rotating members (United Nations 2011). The following day, President Obama addressed the nation, stating the United States' intention to act with its international partners to enforce UNSCR 1973. President Obama also explicitly stated the United States would not deploy ground troops into Libya and stressed the United States' continued coordination with the United Nations, the European Union, the Arab League, and individual allies—especially France and Great Britain (Obama 2011d). On March 19, 2011, the United States launched Operation Odyssey Dawn to enforce the no-fly zone.

International and NATO Support in Phase 1: Pre-Combat Planning

Unlike the Afghanistan and Iraq cases, the United States was not at the forefront of calls for international intervention. Instead, France and Great Britain were the two biggest advocates for some kind of action beyond a broad condemnation. British Prime Minister David Cameron voiced concern that Libya could become a humanitarian crisis similar to the Bosnian and Kosovo conflicts of the 1990s. French President Nicolas Sarkozy argued inaction posed a danger to the West's values, and the necessity for action fell well within the parameters established under both international law and the UN Responsibility to Protect (R2P) doctrine (Engelbrekt and Wagnsson 2014). The Libyan conflict posed a potential threat to European security and stability, as well as the flow of oil and natural gas to Europe. As Christopher Chivvis notes, "This joint Franco-British pressure was essential in generating diplomatic momentum for intervention...In retrospect, French and British pressure to intervene in Libya had at least as much to do with perceived threats to security and economic interests as with domestic and international power politics" (Chivvis 2014). After following the lead of the United States in evacuating their citizens, France and Great Britain presented the UN Security Council with a framework for implementing extensive sanctions against the regime, as well as for language establishing the conditions under which other states would be empowered to use force.

On February 26, the United Nations Security Council unanimously passed Resolution (UNSCR) 1970, the first of two resolutions to stem the violence in Libya, predicated on Great Britain and France's earlier proposals. UNSCR 1970 condemned the actions of the Libyan government, called for an international commission to investigate any potential human rights abuses, and referred the case to the International Criminal Court (ICC). Additionally, the resolution imposed a travel ban, arms embargo, and listed a number of financial and political sanctions. It referred the case to the International Criminal Court, for review of possible crimes against humanity and violations of international law. UNSCR 1970 also noted the widespread condemnation of Qaddafi's actions by international organizations such as the Arab League, the African Union (AU), and the Organization of the Islamic Conference (UNSCR 1970 2011a). Rallied by its members, the European Union shared in the condemnation of Qaddafi and expressed its concerns over spillover effects such as refugee slows and other externalities of the conflict on its members (BBC 2011a).

On February 25, one day before the UN Security Council passed UNSCR 1970, NATO convened an emergency meeting of the North Atlantic Council in response to Qaddafi's harsh crackdown on the protestors. NATO military officials prepared to assist in evacuating citizens from allied countries and to support humanitarian efforts undertaken by the UN or NATO allies. There was, however, some disagreement in the NATO alliance as to the role NATO should play in enforcing a no-fly zone or carrying out strikes against the Qaddafi forces. While the French pushed for a multilateral intervention, it was reluctant to endorse NATO participation as it feared the alliance's presence would undermine support from the Arab League and other states threatened by the alliance's "aggressive" reputation (Cowell and Erlanger 2011). The United States and Great Britain, as well as Italy and Norway, insisted the alliance should play an integral in any kind of operation. Germany, however, wanted to avoid any kind of military engagement, and instead argued in favor of increasing sanctions and taking additional diplomatic measures. Turkey worried the West's interest in Libya was driven by access to its natural resources and was reluctant to consider NATO intervention. There was also concern among all of the allies about NATO resources being stretched too thin as operations in Afghanistan continued (Michaels 2014).

In early March, several NATO allies increased their intelligence collection in Libya to better monitor the ground situation as hostilities escalated. On March 10, the same day the NATO defense ministers met and began formal consideration of enforcing the no-fly zone, NTC leaders met with French President Nicolas Sarkozy. NATO Secretary General Anders Fogh Rasmussen indicated the alliance would also discuss whether it should pursue additional military action, and would continue consulting regional organizations including African Union and the Arab League, as well as the UN and the EU (NATO 2011a). The following day, March 11, President Sarkozy raised the prospect of airstrikes to its European allies at an EU summit in Brussels. On March 12, the Arab League formally requested a mandate for a no-fly zone from the UN Security Council.

Because Qaddafi's offensive in mid-March successfully shifted control of the conflict away from the rebels, the allies agreed NATO should ensure the rebel forces would be able to maintain their defensive position and eventually shift back to an offensive position. Both the United States and Great Britain insisted NATO participation was crucial to the legitimacy of any operation and would be greater than a coalition effort while attracting non-NATO partners and other regional organizations. Additionally, the alliance provided the necessary operational framework with its well-established military command structure and access to regional facilities such as airfields (and over flight access). However several states, including Germany, Poland, Turkey, and the United States, maintained that the alliance should not undertake military operations outside of the no-fly zone. They also repeated concerns of what impact a Libyan operation would have on the ISAF mission in Afghanistan. The allies could not reach a consensus on the need for additional intervention planning and conceded to plan only for a supporting mission to enforce a no-fly zone, if mandated by the UN Security Council. The allies did, however, agree to reconsider if the conditions in Libya deteriorated further and the international community (and international law) supported intervention at a later time (Michaels 2014; Chivvis 2014).

When the Security Council ratified UNSCR 1973 on March 17, the requirements for reconsidering NATO participation in an intervention were fulfilled. In addition to having the support of the Arab League and the African Union for the no-fly zone and some kind of international intervention, the United Nations explicitly authorized the intervention. However, the alliance was unprepared to undertake immediate action. Thus, the United States launched its own operation, Operation Odyssey Dawn, with the assistance of France, Great Britain, and several other NATO and non-NATO allies.

Legitimacy and Multilateralism in Phase 1

Whereas the Bush administration sought legitimacy for its actions in Iraq, the Obama administration faced an international community more closely resembling the post-9/11 era: the president enjoyed a high level of support for a US or NATO-spearheaded intervention in Libya, and its decision to enforce a no-fly zone, implement an arms embargo, and expand sanctions was largely legitimized by the United Nations as well as several other international organizations. The decision to use force by conducting airstrikes was also legitimized—even requested, in some cases—by the allies, and avoided an immediate domestic political fallout. Although Obama frequently championed the virtues of multilateral engagement, the US-Operation Odyssey Dawn was born less out of the need for legitimacy and multilateralism than the reluctance of American policymakers to use force (Obama 2015). Unlike the 9/11 era, however, President Obama initially resisted the call to arms. US officials such as UN Ambassador

Susan Rice highlighted the unanimous vote on the UNSC 1970 resolution as evidence of the international community's commitment to resolving the Libyan crisis and its resolve to protect civilians from continued humanitarian abuses. Rice also confirmed the administration's belief that the diplomatic efforts would be sufficient to stopping Qaddafi—a belief not championed by those leading the charge for intervention, and ultimately, inconsistent with Qaddafi's actions following the late-February resolution (Rice 2011).

Although the United States' multilateral engagement was not bore out of the necessity for legitimacy enhancement, the proceeding section demonstrates how allied engagement transpired and the utility of the United States' NATO engagement. The NATO alliance itself would not play a pivotal role in executing Operation Odyssey Dawn, but individual allies would. Further, within less than two weeks, OOD transitioned into a more capable and versatile Operation Unified Protector, led by NATO. Perceptions of the alliance's capacity shaped the decision to transition to a NATO-led mission instead of the United States continuing its leadership or transitioning to another ally. Further, NATO's actions during Operation Unified Protector revealed its utility to the United States not only in transitioning responsibility but also successfully commanding the mission.

Operation Odyssey Dawn

When the United States launched Operation Odyssey Dawn (OOD) on March 19, 2011, it was joined by a coalition of states including the United Kingdom, France, Belgium, Spain, Denmark, Norway, Canada, Italy, Netherlands, Qatar, and the UAE. The primary objectives of OOD were to enforce the no-fly zone mandated by UNSCR 1973 and to conduct an aerial campaign to destroy Libya's long-range air defenses that protect the United States and its allies from retaliatory strikes (Weitsman 2014). The United States also aimed to damage any military units posing a threat to rebel positions. In the first few days of fighting, the coalition ran under separate US, British, and French commands as three parallel operations: Operation Odyssey Dawn (the United States), Operation Ellamy (the United Kingdom), and Operation Harmattan (France). The United States moved quickly to consolidate the effort under the US Africa Command (AFRICOM), led by US Army General Carter Ham. US Navy Admiral Samuel J. Locklear maintained control over the execution of OOD, serving in a dual role as Commander of the US Naval Forces Europe and Africa as well as the Commander of Allied Joint Force Command for NATO missions in the Mediterranean. Coalition forces remained under the control of their respective countries.

In the first few days of airstrikes, the United States and the coalition effectively eliminated the Qaddafi regime's long-range missile capabilities, struck a number of strategic military installations, and bombed several buildings, including one in Colonel Qaddafi's compound. Although the airstrikes successfully struck several targets, the aerial campaign did not convince Qaddafi to concede: on March 20, he spoke on state TV, saying "We will exterminate every traitor and collaborator with America, Britain, France and the crusader coalition. They shall be exterminated in Benghazi or any other place" (Dagher et al. 2011). Following the first few days of strikes, Obama administration officials reiterated the importance of international participation in a sustained effort in Libya. OOD, officials argued, was intended to be a preliminary operation to make it easier for NATO or a coalition effort to take over leadership of US operations. President Obama insisted the United States would continue its participation, but not in a leadership capacity. He demanded that responsibility for the Libya operation be transferred as quickly as possible, preferably to the NATO alliance.

Prior to Operation Odyssey Dawn, several congressional leaders acknowledged the need for an intervention on humanitarian grounds, and on March 1, 2011, the Senate unanimously agreed to Resolution 85, condemning the actions of Qaddafi and the human rights violations committed by the Libyan regime. The resolution also called for the United Nations Security Council to impose the no-fly zone over Libya. However, when President Obama officially notified Congress about the deployment of military personnel and equipment on March 21, members of both parties in the House and Senate chided the president's decision. Democratic Representatives Jerrold Nadler, Barbara Lee, and Michael Capuano argued the president exceeded his constitutional authority when he consented to engaging American troops without congressional authorization. Republican Senators Rand Paul and Richard Lugar issued statements condemning the president's actions as well.

As the United States increased the rhetorical pressure for other states to take the lead in Libya, the NATO allies continued to debate whether OOD should become an alliance mission. The alliance took several steps to improve its capability of taking responsibility for Libya operations. On

March 23, it moved ships and aircrafts in the Central Mediterranean to prevent the shipment of arms to Colonel Qaddafi's army. The allies also instituted a search and seizure order of all incoming ships. On March 24, NATO finally agreed to take control of the multinational effort in Libya, at the behest of several states and international organizations, including the Arab League and other non-NATO partners (NATO 2012). On Sunday, March 31, the United States officially ended Operation Odyssey Dawn.

During the 12-day operation, the United States deployed multiple resources from the Navy, Air Force, and Marine Corps, including, Arleigh Burke-class, guided-missile destroyers *USS Stout* and *USS Barry;* submarines *USS Providence, USS Scranton,* and *USS Florida; 110+ Tomahawk cruise missiles* (used by both the United States and the United Kingdom), 19 US warplanes (including Marine Corps Harrier jets); Air Force B-2 stealth bombers, F-15, and F-16 fighter jets; and US Navy EA-18 Growlers (U.S. Navy 2011; Shaughnessy 2011). These resources were supplemented with refueling aircraft and reconnaissance and rescue resources, as well as a number of CIA intelligence assets on the ground in Libya and neighboring states. Additionally, although the OOD mission did not include NATO participation, Joint Task Force (JTF) resources, including the USS Kearsarge (LHD 3) and the USS Ponce (LPD 15), were employed during the operation. The total operational expenditure for OOD was $550 million dollars (Michaels 2014).

International and NATO Support for Operation Odyssey Dawn: Phase 2

The NATO alliance as a whole was not a participant in the initial US-led Operation Odyssey Dawn. However, as previously noted, several NATO allies played an important role in the coalition. France was the first state to initiate airstrikes against Libya on March 19, shortly after heads of state convened to finalize preparations for enforcement of the no-fly zone and strategic aerial strikes. In the first three days of operations, France deployed 20 aircraft and conducted nearly 60 sorties. By the end of the OOD, French aircraft flew 150–200 sorties per day. Great Britain also deployed a number of aircrafts, including ten Eurofighter Typhoons and several Tornados, supported by the 907 Expeditionary Air Wing (whose resources included VC-10 tanker aircraft, Nimrod and Sentinel surveillance and reconnaissance planes, E-3D Airborne Warning and Control System (AWACS), and C-17 and C-130 transports). Additionally, the Royal Navy deployed a submarine and two frigates, HMS Cumberland and HMS Westminster (Gertler 2011).

Although the Arab League and other regional organizations strongly supported the establishment of a no-fly zone over Libya, the American operation was criticized by several states. The Arab League criticized OOD airstrikes as outside of the UN mandate, while China, who abstained from voting on UNSCR 1973, publicly acknowledged that it made a mistake in not vetoing the UN authorization (Dagher et al. 2011). Among NATO allies, Turkey and Germany remained the most critical of US and coalition efforts. When NATO moved its ships and aircrafts around the Mediterranean to prepare for the transfer of responsibility from the United States to the alliance, Germany removed its naval assets from NATO command. Both states later refused to participate in the NATO-led Operation Unified Protector (Gertler 2011).

Legitimacy and Multilateralism in Phase 2

Despite the objections of US Democratic legislators, as well as a handful of states, Operation Odyssey Dawn was largely perceived as legitimate. The two Security Council resolutions, UNSCR 1970 and UNSCR 1973, authorized the no-fly zone, sanctions, and the protection of civilians by individual states or regional organizations. Legitimacy was enhanced by the endorsement of non-NATO allies and regional organizations such as the Arab League. In addition to the UNSCR 1970 and UNSCR 1973, the endorsement of a number of non-NATO allies, and support from regional organizations, legitimacy for the American actions in Libya was enhanced by the United Nations' Responsibility to Protect (R2P) doctrine, as articulated by the 2005 World Summit participants and adopted by the United Nations (Weitsman 2014). As discussed in Chap. 3, the R2P doctrine established the conditions under which, in the event of a possible humanitarian crisis, states could supersede another state's sovereignty to protect civilian populations. The R2P doctrine was repeatedly cited in the case for intervention in Libya. As David Rieff explained, "Muammar el-Qaddafi's threat in March to unleash a bloodbath in rebel-held Benghazi was just the kind of extreme instance that R2P's framers had in mind. And the U.N.-sanctioned NATO intervention did forestall a massacre" (Rieff 2011).

Additionally, because France and Great Britain spearheaded the charge for international support for the Libyan campaign, the United States lacked the need to actively pursue multilateralism for its legitimation

effects. However, military planners agreed NATO would lend more legitimacy to the operation replacing OOD than if it were led by an individual
state or an ad hoc coalition (Michaels 2014). Thus, legitimacy enhancement became a factor in establishing OOD's successor, Operation Unified
Protector (OUP).

The Obama administration's multilateral push stemmed from its desire
to make the United States an equal partner, not a leader, in any engagement in Libya. President Obama, much like President Clinton during the
1990s Balkans engagements, felt those calling for intervention should
bear their fair share of the costs of war. Further, the administration strongly
believed multilateral intervention—both political and military—would
yield a more successful outcome for Libya, the United States, and the
international community as a whole. US military planners pursued allied
participation and NATO leadership to alleviate the United States' military
and economic burdens. President Obama repeatedly expressed his reluctance to engage US troops and resources for a prolonged campaign in
Libya. When the Security Council voted in favor of UNSCR 1973,
President Obama affirmed the United States' participation to enforce the
resolution in Qaddafi failed to immediately comply with the UN guidelines. However, in his March 18 address he also stated that the United
States would not lead a sustained coalition effort: "American leadership is
essential, but that does not mean acting alone. It means shaping the conditions for the international community to act together" (Obama 2011b).
The Obama administration also applauded the efforts of France and Great
Britain and continued to pressurize its NATO allies to support a NATO-
led operation to replace the coalition assembled under Operation Odyssey
Dawn. Secretary of State Hillary Clinton held conference calls with her
counterparts in France, Great Britain, and Turkey to settle the dispute
over command of NATO operations in Libya (Burns and Werner 2011).

Following NATO's announcement on March 24 that it would assume
responsibility for the NATO mission, President Obama addressed the
nation from the National Defense University in Washington, D.C. During
the speech, the president referred to his earlier promise to engage the military in a limited capacity, stating:

I said that America's role would be limited; that we would not put ground
troops into Libya; that we would focus our unique capabilities on the front
end of the operation and that we would transfer responsibility to our allies
and partners. Tonight, we are fulfilling that pledge. Our most effective alli-

ance, NATO, has taken command of the enforcement of the arms embargo and the no-fly zone. Last night, NATO decided to take on the additional responsibility of protecting Libyan civilians. This transfer from the United States to NATO will take place on Wednesday. Going forward, the lead in enforcing the no-fly zone and protecting civilians on the ground will transition to our allies and partners, and I am fully confident that our coalition will keep the pressure on Qaddafi's remaining forces. (Obama 2011c)

Additionally, Obama praised the alliance's capacity for conflict engagement, confirming the United States' support for the transition was rooted in beliefs about the military utility of the alliance.

In [the Operation Unified Protector] effort, the United States will play a supporting role – including intelligence, logistical support, search and rescue assistance, and capabilities to jam regime communications. Because of this transition to a broader, NATO-based coalition, the risk and cost of this operation – to our military and to American taxpayers – will be reduced significantly. (Ibid)

Although President Obama's push to engage the international community was born out of both domestic and international pressure, advocating for NATO's role stemmed from a belief in its ability to effectively coordinate between states, reduce redundancies, and execute the war.

Operation Unified Protector

As the United States ended Operation Odyssey Dawn on March 31, NATO commenced Operation Unified Protector (OUP). The three components of OUP—"enforcing an arms embargo in the Mediterranean Sea to prevent the transfer of arms, related materials and mercenaries to Libya; enforcing a no-fly zone to prevent planes from bombing civilian targets; and conducting air and naval strikes against military forces involved in attacks or threatening to attack Libyan civilians and civilian populated area"—mirrored those of Odyssey Dawn and were framed as part of a humanitarian mission to enforce UNSCR 1973. Command of OUP was given to Canadian Air Force Lieutenant General Charles Bouchard after Turkey blocked France and Great Britain's bid to take command of the operation. Although the United States refused leadership of OUP, several of its officers played an integral role in the decision-making process. NATO Joint Force Command (JFC) in Naples, led by US Navy Admiral

Samuel Locklear, was responsible for implementing the decisions of the NAC, and the Supreme Allied Headquarters Allied Power Europe (SHAPE). SHAPE was led by US Navy Admiral James Stavridis, who served in dual roles as commander of US European command (USEUCOM) and NATO Supreme Allied Commander Europe (SACEUR) (Weitsman 2014; Michaels 2014; United States Mission to NATO 2011).

In exchange for NATO leadership under the new operation, the United States agreed to continue participation in military operations, intelligence collection and analysis, refueling and support capabilities, and by a contribution of advanced military technology (Stavridis and Daalder 2012). During the operations, the US Navy deployed command and assault ships, cargo ships, transport docks, frigates, destroyers, and submarines. These deployments included the following assets: *USS Bataan*, *USS Halyburton*, *USNS Kanawha*, *USS Mahan*, *USS Mesa Verde*, *USS Mount Whitney*, *USS Ponce*, *USS Whidbey Island*, *USNS Lewis and Clark*, and *USNS Robert E. Peary* (McMichael 2011). The Air Force also contributed resources to the Operation Unified Protector efforts, including reconnaissance aircraft, ground surveillance aircraft, refueling tankers, psychological warfare aircraft, and electronic attack aircraft. These efforts were executed with the use of the U-2 high-altitude aircraft, E-8 Joint Surveillance Target Attack Radar System, EC-130J aircraft, KC-10 aircraft, KC-135 aircraft, and F-15 and F-16 aircrafts (Majumdar 2011).

During the first month of operations, Colonel Qaddafi made several appeals to the international community to end the NATO airstrikes. On April 6, he sent a letter to President Obama in which he claimed the opposition forces were terrorists affiliated with al Qaeda and asked the president to appeal to its allies to stop the bombing campaign. In the days that followed, Qaddafi also met with a delegation of African leaders, and on April 10 announced he would accept the proposed road map for ending the conflict. However, the rebels rejected plan, which did not include Qaddafi's removal from power, and the fighting continued. In late April, Qaddafi addressed the international community again in a speech wherein he accused the NATO coalition of killing civilians and destroying Libya's infrastructure. As fighting continued into May, Qaddafi stayed out of the public eye, but resurfaced later in the month for renewed discussions with African leaders for a ceasefire (Reuters 2011; CNN 2011).

In the first few months of OUP, several high-ranking members of the Qaddafi regime resigned to join the opposition fighters or seek asylum elsewhere. The National Transition Council (NTC) also gained more legitimacy as it continued to appeal to the international community. In early June, Germany and Spain joined France in recognizing the NTC, and on July 15, the United States and Great Britain followed. By late July, over 30 states recognized the NTC as the legitimate representative of the Libyan people. This allowed the states recognizing the authority of the NTC, including the NATO allies engaged in OUP, to begin unfreezing Libyan funds to support the rebel efforts against Qaddafi (CNN 2011; Champion and Parkinson 2011).

As Qaddafi refused to step down and the fighting continued, the rebels made a number of advances in capturing territory once controlled by the Qaddafi forces. On August 11, the rebels captured the eastern part of Brega, but Qaddafi forces maintained control of oil facilities in the west. On August 11, the rebels also captured Zawiyah, a strategically advantageous location because of a supply highway to Tunisia. The following day, rebels captured Garyan, another strategic highway city. On August 19, the rebels began their final siege into Tripoli, and after intense fighting, Colonel Qaddafi and his family were forced to flee to Algeria as opposition forces stormed his compound and took control of the capital city on August 22, 2011 (CNN 2011; Reuters 2011; BBC 2015).

After the rebels captured Tripoli on August 22, the international community reaffirmed its commitment to restoring peace and ensuring Qaddafi and members of his regime were brought to justice. On the same day the rebels captured Tripoli, NATO Secretary General Rasmussen confirmed NATO would continue its efforts to protect Libyan citizens. On September 16, the UN Security Council passed Resolution 2009 to establish the UN Support Mission to Libya (UNSMIL). By the end of September, more than 60 states and international organizations recognized the NTC's authority, including the African Union. In early October, the NATO defense ministers met in Brussels to discuss ending OUP. Though they agreed to continue the operation, both the ministers and the Secretary General insisted the alliance would work with the United Nations and the NTC to end the mission as soon as possible (BBC 2015).

On October 20, opposition forces took control of Sirte, the last Qaddafi regime stronghold, and captured and killed Colonel Qaddafi. On October 27, both the UN Security Council and NATO announced they would end operations in Libya (Gladstone 2011). On October 31 at midnight, NATO officially ended OUP. In the 222 days of engagement, the OUP coalition flew more than 26,000 sorties (120 sorties per day), of which almost 11,000 were strike sorties. NATO allies carried out 75 percent of the airstrikes and assumed full responsibility for maritime operations. At the peak of the operation, 8000 troops were engaged in OUP aerial and maritime operations, though no ground troops were deployed. The coalition partners deployed over 250 aircrafts and 21 NATO ships. According to the official reports, the airstrikes hit almost 6000 targets, including 600 battle tanks, 400 rocket launchers, and 300 ammunition dumps (Nygren 2014).

In the days leading up to the transition from the US-led Operation Odyssey Dawn to the NATO-led Operation Unified Protector, President Obama, Defense Secretary Gates, and other members of the administration pressed the allies to take a leading role in Libya, a sentiment that was repeated several times over the course of OUP. Still, the United States played an integral role despite its refusal to command the operation. The United States contributed the largest number of troops (8507 deployed), followed by Italy (4800 deployed), France (4200 deployed), and Great Britain (3500 deployed). The United States also executed the most sorties (25 percent), followed by France and Great Britain (33 percent combined). However, France and Great Britain flew more of the strike sorties (33 and 20 percent, respectively) than US aircraft (Weitsman 2014; NATO 2011b). The United States also spent more money than any other coalition partner. From the beginning of Operation Odyssey Dawn through the end of September 2011, the United States spent $1.1 billion in Libya, compared to an estimated $257–$482 million in spending by the United Kingdom and $415–$485 million by France. Only a small proportion of the OUP budget came from the NATO common fund. The alliance spent an estimated $52 million during the operation to deploy its Airborne Warning and Control System (AWACS) and another $8 million for structural and personnel costs (Rettig 2011).

American political elites and the public had mixed perceptions of the United States' participation in Operation Unified Protector. As responsibility for the Libya operation shifted from the US mission to the NATO-led OUP, Congress remained divided on whether the United States should participate in the ongoing operations. On April 1, the US Justice Department released a memorandum confirming the president was within his legal and constitutional authority to authorize the limited use of military power in Libya "because he could reasonably determine that such use of force was in the national interest" (United States Justice Department 2011). Senators John Kerry, John McCain, and Richard Lugar stood behind the Justice Department's finding, arguing the United States' deferral to NATO alleviated any immediate concerns of violations of the 1973 War Powers Resolution (Rogin 2011). Senators Kerry and McCain also pushed for a resolution in support of the United States' participation in OUP. However, as NATO operations continued, legislators again raised concerns over violations of the War Powers Resolution. In June, Democratic Representative Dennis Kucinich and Republican Representative Walter Jones, along with eight other representatives, filed a lawsuit against the president, but a US district court judge later dismissed the lawsuit (Bendery 2011).

Public support for the United States' engagement in Libya was also inconsistent. Prior to the commencement of Operation Odyssey Dawn, only 44 percent of those surveyed supported US enforcement of a no-fly zone, and even fewer (16 percent) supported a bombing campaign (Pew Research 2011). However, a Gallup poll conducted on March 22 (three days after the beginning of OOD) indicated 47 percent of those polled approved of the United States' participation in military action in Libya (Jones 2011). When the United States shifted leadership to NATO under Operation Unified Protector, American support for the intervention grew: a May 2011 poll conducted by the German Marshall Fund (GMF) indicated that 59 percent of those polled approved of the international intervention. Nearly 60 percent of US respondents also supported sending military advisors to Libya to support the rebels. Support for ground troops remained low, however, with only 31 percent in favor of a ground operation (The German Marshall Fund 2011). In a follow-up survey conducted by the German Marshall Fund in 2012, 49 percent of respondents believed the intervention in Libya was the right thing to do (The German Marshall Fund 2012).

International and NATO Support for Phase 3: Operation Unified Protector

As the proceeding section demonstrates, NATO played a significant leadership role in the execution of Operation Unified Protector—so much so, in fact, the United States and President Obama were forced to refute criticisms US foreign policy had shifted to a weaker, "lead from behind" strategy. Fifteen NATO and four non-NATO states participated in Operation Unified Protector: Belgium, Bulgaria, Canada, Croatia, Denmark, France, Greece, Italy, Jordan, the Netherlands, Norway, Qatar, Romania, Spain,

Sweden, Turkey, the United Arab Emirates, the United Kingdom, and the United States. Although Germany and Italy publicly objected to the operation, both agreed to provide logistical support for humanitarian assistance. The participating states collectively contributed 195 aircraft (including 64 strike aircraft) and nine states deployed ships for the operation.

Although the United States was the leading contributor of troops and executed the most sorties during OUP, the French and British allies were integral to OUP operations. Alison Pargeter writes, "Had NATO not entered the conflict when it did, it is likely that the rebel forces would not have been able to dislodge Qaddafi from the west of the country and would not have prevented him from re-taking the east" (Pargeter 2012). In addition to the roles of the United Nations and NATO, several regional organizations and non-NATO allies impacted the execution of Operation Unified Protector. On March 12, the Arab League formally requested the United Nations to establish a no-fly zone over Libya, setting the precedent for UNSCR 1973 (Bronner and Sanger 2011). Despite NATO's reputation in the region as an aggressive Western organization, both the United Arab Emirates and Qatar participated in its operation. Sweden, Morocco, and Jordan also contributed to OUP. The participation of these non-NATO allies enhanced the legitimacy of Operation Unified Protector, but support for the operation dwindled within the first few weeks. By mid-April, only 8 of the original 15 states (the United States, the United Kingdom, France, Canada, Belgium, Denmark, Italy, and Norway) were conducting airstrikes, though several other states provided maritime support and access to necessary resources (such as airfields) (Weitsman 2014; Michaels 2014; United States Mission to NATO 2011).

The African Union did not play a significant role in OUP, though several African leaders met with Qaddafi and the rebels in April to formulate a roadmap for ending the conflict. The African Union recognized the legitimacy of the NTC in August, further strengthening its ability to establish an interim government. Several AU states also worked with the UN, the European Union, the Arab League, the Organization of the Islamic Conference, and other states as part of the "Friends of Libya" group organized by the United Nations Secretary General (The Telegraph 2011; BBC 2015; Reuters 2011).

International public opinion on the NATO intervention in Libya was divided. According to the GMF poll conducted in May 2011, only 48 percent of European respondents approved of the intervention (compared to 47 percent of respondents who disapproved of OUP). Support was highest in Sweden and the Netherlands. Although France and Great Britain spearheaded the NATO operation, both publics were reluctant to endorse their states' participation—only 52 percent of French and 50 percent of British respondents approved of the intervention. Of the NATO allies and OUP participants, Germany and Turkey had the lowest approval rates. Although over half of the respondents from Turkey approved of removing Qaddafi from power, only 23 percent of Turkish respondents approved of the intervention (The German Marshall Fund 2011). In a second GMF poll conducted in June 2012, the collective European attitude remained unchanged regarding the appropriateness of the Libya intervention: 48 percent of EU respondents agreed with the decision to intervene. Despite Germany's nonparticipation in Operation Unified Protector, German attitudes about the intervention were much more positive than in 2011, with 53 percent of respondents approving the intervention (The German Marshall Fund 2012).

Legitimacy and Multilateralism in Operation Unified Protector

Operation Unified Protector was justified as fulfilling the international community's commitment to R2P as well as the mandate of UNSCR 1973, enhancing the legitimacy of the United States and NATO's actions. The International Criminal Court's acknowledgment of possible crimes against humanity bolstered the legitimacy of the UN and NATO's decision to intervene as well. UNSCR 1973 referred the case of Libya to the International Criminal Court, and in late June 2011 the ICC issued arrest warrants for Colonel Qaddafi, his son Saif al-Islam Qaddafi, and his brother-in-law, Abdullah al-Sanussi (CNN 2011).

Although Operation Unified Protector enjoyed a high degree of legitimacy, there were threats to maintaining it throughout the intervention. Regional support for enforcement of the no-fly zone over Libya was high, as evidenced by the Arab League's formal request to the United Nations on March 12. However, NATO's regional partners were less enthusiastic about the alliance's bombing campaign. Arab League Secretary General Amr Moussa publicly condemned the airstrikes, and South African President Jacob Zuma criticized NATO for using the UN resolution for "regime change" in Libya (CNN 2011; Cody 2011). As David Rieff noted, "The Security Council resolutions that authorized an R2P-based intervention to protect Benghazi did not authorize outside powers to provide air support for the subsequent rebellion against Qaddafi. And it is almost certain that without that support he would not have been over-thrown" (Rieff 2011). Of the three elements of Operation Unified Protector—enforcement of the arms embargo, enforcement of the no-fly zone, and the protection of civilians—the decision to employ targeted aerial campaign for civilian protection quickly became the most essential to the effort to overthrow Qaddafi. However, the bombing was also problematic for many states, and thus was the most controversial and least legitimate component of the operation.

The legitimacy of OUP, and in particular the airstrikes, was also threatened by several reports of civilian casualties. In August 2011, just before the fall of Tripoli, the Libyan government reported to Human Rights Watch (HRW) that NATO bombs killed 1108 civilians and wounded over 6000 more from March until August 2011. However, after the regime collapsed in late August, several former government officials indicated the casualty figures were fabricated to garner sympathy from the international community. The United States and NATO could not verify the total number of civilians killed by airstrikes either: although some states conducted covert operations and collected intelligence from assets located inside Libya, the alliance never deployed any personnel to monitor accidental deaths or friendly fire incidents. Human Rights Watch verified 9 incidents of civilian casualties in which 72 people were killed (Human Rights Watch 2012). There were also reports of several friendly fire incidents between NATO and the rebels, including incidents in Brega, Misrata, and Zawiyah (Weitsman 2014). Although NATO cited evidence of measures taken to minimize an accidental targeting of civilians—including "patterns of life" surveillance and a heavy reliance on precision munitions—the reports of civilian casualties and friendly fire incidents threatened the legitimacy of OUP (BBC 2011b).

The United States' role in Operation Unified Protector reflected the personal and political preferences of the Obama administration to avoid engaging American troops in another protracted conflict such as the Afghanistan and Iraq intervention. However, its continued participation in the NATO operation, and willingness to contribute significantly more resources and financial support than the other allies, indicated the administration's belief in the alliance's ability to enforce UNSCR 1973. The United States also maintained a significant influence over OUP operations through high-ranking officers serving in dual roles as US and NATO commanders, but the day-to-day command of OUP operations was relegated to Lieutenant General Bouchard (CAN). Thus, the US engagement of NATO was based in part on the utility of the alliance.

At the same time, Operation Unified Protector revealed both operational weaknesses and tensions between the United States and the alliance. In addition to providing fewer resources and financial support than the United States, the European allies did not have adequate stockpiles of laser-guided munitions or the necessary technological infrastructure for timely information exchanges. The United States also contributed more intelligence, surveillance, and reconnaissance (ISR) such as unmanned aerial vehicles, as well as air-to-air refueling resources (Weitsman 2014).

The inabilities of the European allies to provide the necessary resources caused tension between the United States and NATO. In some cases, such as the shortage of laser-guided munitions, the inability of the allies to maintain adequate stockpiles resulted from the significant decline in military spending since the end of the Cold War. In other cases, such as the provision of aircraft, the United States contributed more resources because although they had the necessary equipment, the allies refused to deploy them. Although the European allies affirmed the necessity of OUP, US officials argued that the inability to fulfill their commitment to the operation stemmed from a lack of political willpower. Secretary Gates deepened the tensions between the United States and NATO when he publicly chastised states such as Germany, Turkey, Poland, the Netherlands, and Spain for refusing to take part in the airstrikes while praising Denmark and Norway for their disproportionate contributions (Michaels 2014). NATO Secretary General Rasmussen agreed the European allies' weaknesses stemmed primarily from political, not military, constraints (Rasmussen 2011).

When the European allies appealed to the United States in mid-April for more participation, US officials refused to engage more personnel and resources. However, the United States did provide more precision munitions and continued leading surveillance and intelligence collection efforts. As the European weapons stockpiles were exhausted, the United States increased its weapons contributions as well. The United States' contributions, especially in the later months of OUP, were necessary for the success of NATO operations, but drove the cost of the American contribution higher while causing embarrassment for the European allies (Engelbrekt and Wagnsson 2014).

Still, despite these operational difficulties, the United States' pursuit of NATO leadership was driven in part by the utility of the alliance. Geographically, NATO participation gave the United States access to necessary logistical support, such as access to airfields, supply routes, regular maintenance, and the use of existing equipment and weapons stockpiles

(Ibid). NATO's well-established command and control systems facilitated the transition of operations from the United States (under Operation Odyssey Dawn) to NATO. NATO's integrated command structure also facilitated an easier integration of non-NATO allies into OUP. Unlike the previous engagements in Kosovo and Afghanistan, there were no reports of friendly fire incidents between NATO allies—all of the reported incidents occurred between the alliance and the Libyan rebels. Although this was due in part to the lack of ground troops, it also reflected the alliance's growth from previous engagements (Weitsman 2014).

CONCLUSION

Both the United States and NATO entered the Libyan conflict with the stated intent of protecting human rights and limiting civilian casualties during the Arab Spring uprising against Colonel Muammar Qaddafi. The Obama administration, as well as its allied counterparts, would likely agree in the success of the mission. The subsequent overthrow of Qaddafi—which was not the administration's official position—came at a cost to the Libyan people, region, and international peace and security as a whole. Libya continues to face instability, civil conflict, terrorism, displacement, and the consequences of a lack of adequate resources to support the civilian population. Many have argued against the United States and NATO's actions because of this, citing the deteriorating conditions as evidence of the multilateral operation's failure, as well as a failure of the UN and international community to prevent powerful states from conducting unlawful activities such as regime change under the guise of R2P or other humanitarian mandates. The Libyan intervention also did little to quell criticism of the alliance's ability to persist in the Cold War period or speculation it would soon meet its demise (O'Donnell and Vaisse 2011).

In evaluating the United States' multilateral and allied relationships more directly, the mission was successful in engaging resources the Obama administration saw as imperative to operations. In the leadup to the 2014 Chicago Summit, Deputy Assistant Secretary for European and NATO Policy for the Department of Defense James Townsend reflected on NATO's contributions to the Libyan campaign in testifying to Congress:

> NATO serves as the organizing framework to ensure that we have allies willing and able to fight alongside us in conflict, and provides an integrated military structure that puts the military teeth behind alliance political deci-

sions to take action. In addition to ensuring the interoperability of our allies, NATO serves as a hub and an integrator of a network of global security partners. The NATO air and maritime operation in Libya illustrates this point. The operation began as a coalition of the willing, involving the United States, the United Kingdom, and France. However, when NATO answered the U.N.'s call to protect the Libyan people, it was able to take on the mission and execute it successfully. Had NATO not been there, or had NATO been too weak an institution to take on such an operation, the coalition would have had to carry on alone. Keeping NATO strong both politically and militarily is critical to ensuring NATO is ready when it is needed. This has been true for the past 20 years, when the turbulence of the international system has demanded that NATO respond nearly continuously to crises throughout the globe. (United States. Congress, House. Subcommittee on Europe and Eurasia 2012)

When the UN Security Council authorized an intervention under UNSCR 1973, the United States moved quickly to mobilize its allies in a two-week coalition effort to begin enforcement of the no-fly zone and arms embargo, as well as the protection of the civilian population. The United States also pushed for a quick transition from US leadership. Despite the French-British coalition's willingness to lead, the United States argued NATO leadership would enhance the operation's legitimacy. The United States agreed to continue its participation in Libyan operations in exchange for a NATO-led operation, and its participation was seen as crucial in ensuring Operation Unified Protector's success. This confirms the hypothesis on the United States' pursuit of NATO for legitimacy enhancement. Furthermore, the United States' actions throughout the course of the operations in Libya indicate the importance of adhering to international norms regarding the use of force for the Obama administration, thus confirming the second hypothesis on US-NATO relations.

Although legitimacy enhancement was a factor in the United States' insistence on NATO leadership in Libyan operations, the principal reason the Obama administration pushed for the alliance's participation was its preference for multilateralism and its belief in the utility of NATO, confirming the trend seen in earlier cases. The integrated command and control systems, improved interoperability, and the information-sharing mechanisms of NATO facilitated the coordination of both allies and non-NATO participants. Additionally, the collective pool of NATO resources simplified important components of OUP, particularly the alliance's patrol of the Central Mediterranean.

Operation Unified Protector was not without operational flaws, however, which were revealed as further indications of US-NATO relations. While Secretary General Rasmussen repeatedly expressed NATO's commitment to OUP and the protection of Libyan civilians, both he and US officials struggled to convince many European allies to participate or contribute resources to OUP missions. In addition to lacking the necessary political willpower, OUP reminded the allies of the growing capabilities gap between the United States and Europe. This became especially evident in later months of the operation when the United States was forced to increase its financial and resource contributions to OUP because of dwindling European stockpiles. Ultimately, the United States contributed more money, aircraft, weapons, and intelligence, surveillance, and reconnaissance support than any other ally. As a result of the United States' longstanding leadership within the alliance, it was also able to exert a significant influence on NATO missions through several high-ranking military officers serving in dual US-NATO roles. Subsequently, the Obama administration enjoyed political and military benefits from NATO participation, as well as enhanced legitimacy for the operation, indicating the United States' likely engagement of NATO for future operations.

As with earlier cases, however, the case of Libya raises important questions about the nature of US-conflict engagement in the twenty-first century. While the American perspective of NATO is one of both utility and legitimization, the results of major engagements in the Balkans, Afghanistan, Iraq, and Libya have been mixed at best. Further, as the nature and goals of engagement have evolved, the effectiveness of US efforts has been challenged. Ideas regarding tactical and operational success have never been synonymous—and at times have contradicted—measures of success in ensuring international peace and security, or even more proximate state and regional peace and security, raising a litany of questions about US-NATO relations. Regarding long-term success, there is no evidence in any of these cases to suggest multilateral engagement sacrifices anything. It is true the track record for NATO's engagement leading to long-term stability in any given country is poor. But it is no worse than the United States' record.

In assessing the value of this relationship, then, one must go beyond the reasons for alliance engagement (legitimacy and utility) demonstrated in each of these chapters. Examination of the inter-conflict periods, detailed in the proceeding chapter, reveals the depth of US influence in the alliance's evolution, supplementing understandings of NATO's persistence in the post-Cold War era as well as its utility to the United States. Finally, Chap. 8 examines the value of the relationship in light of the contemporary international environment, as well as the United States' foreign policy objectives.

REFERENCES

BBC. Libya Protests: Defiant Gaddafi Refuses to Quit. Last Modified Feb 22, 2011a. http://www.bbc.com/news/world-middle-east-12544624. Accessed 1 Mar 2015.

———. Libya Protests: EU Condemns Violence and Fears Influx. Last Modified Feb 21, 2011b. http://www.bbc.co.uk/news/mobile/world-europe-12525155. Accessed 1 Mar 2015.

———. Libya Profile. Last Modified Feb 16, 2015. http://www.bbc.com/news/world-africa-13755445. Accessed 1 Mar 2015.

Bendery, Jennifer. Kucinich Sues Obama for Violating War Powers Act in Libya. Last Modified Jun 15, 2011. www.huffingtonpost.com/2011/06/15/Kucinich-obama-war-powers-act-libya_n_877396.html?view=print&comm_ref=false. Accessed 7 Nov 2013.

Blight, Garry, Sheila Pulham, and Paul Torpey. 2012. Arab Spring: An Interactive Timeline of Middle East Protests. *The Guar*, January 5. http://www.theguardian.com/world/interactive/2011/mar/22/middle-east-protest-interactive-timeline

Bronner, Ethan, and David E. Sanger. 2011. Arab League Endorses No-Fly Zone over Libya. *The New York Times*, March 12. http://www.nytimes.com/2011/03/13/world/middleeast/13libya.html?pagewanted=all

Burns, Robert, and Erica Werner. 2011. U.S. Pressures Allies to Command Libya Mission. *The Washington Post*, March 24. http://www.washingtonpost.com/wp-dyn/content/article/2011/03/24/AR2011032400506.html

Champion, Marc, and Joe Parkinson. 2011. U.S. Recognizes Libyan Rebel Group. *The Wall Street Journal*, July 16. http://www.wsj.com/articles/SB10001424052702304203304576447551762812720

Chivvis, Christopher S. 2014. *Toppling Qaddafi: Libya and the Limits of Liberal Intervention*. New York: Cambridge University Press.

CNN. A Timeline of the Conflict in Libya. Last Modified Aug 24, 2011. www.cnn.com/2011/WORLD/Africa/08/18/Libya.timeline/. Accessed 1 Mar 2015.

———. Pan Am Flight 103 Fast Facts. Last Modified Dec 19, 2014. http://www.cnn.com/2013/09/26/world/pan-am-flight-103-fast-facts. Accessed 1 Mar 2015.

Cody, Edward. 2011. Arab League Condemns Broad Bombing Campaign in Libya. *The Washington Post*, March 20. http://www.washingtonpost.com/world/arab-league-condemns-broad-bombing-campaign-in-libya/2011/03/20/AB1pSg1_story.html

Cooper, Helene, and Mark Landler. 2011. U.S. Imposes Sanctions on Libya in Wake of Crackdown. *The New York Times*, February 25. https://www.nytimes.com/2011/02/26/world/middleeast/26diplomacy.html

Cowell, Alan. 2001. Protests Take Aim at Leader of Libya. *The New York Times*, February 16. www.nytimes.com/2011/02/17/world/middleeast/17libya.html?ref=Libya&pagewanted=print

Cowell, Alan, and Steven Erlanger. 2011. France Becomes First Country to Recognize Libyan Rebels. *The New York Times*, March 20. http://www.nytimes.com/2011/03/11/world/europe/11france.html

Dagher, Sam, Yaroslav Trofimov, and Nathan Hodge. 2011. Allies Press Libya Attack. *The Wall Street Journal*, March 21. http://online.wsj.com/article/SB10001424052748704021504576211690643186556.html

Engelbrekt, Kjell, and Charlotte Wagnsson. 2014. Introduction. In *The NATO Intervention in Libya: Lessons Learned from the Campaign*, ed. Kjell Engelbrekt, Marcus Mohlin, and Charlotte Wagnsson. New York: Routledge.

Fahim, Kareen. 2011. Slap to a Man's Pride Set Off Tumult in Tunisia. *The New York Times*, January 21. www.nytimes.com/2011/01/22/world/Africa/22sidi.html?pagewanted=print

Gardner, Frank. 2011. Libya Protests: Defiant Gaddafi Refuses to Quit. *BBC*, February 22. http://www.bbc.com/news/world-middle-east-12544624. Accessed 1 Mar 2015.

Gertler, Jeremiah. 2011. *Operation Odyssey Dawn (Libya): Background and Issues for Congress*. Congressional Research Service.

Gladstone, Rick. 2011. U.N. Votes to End Foreign Intervention in Libya. *The New York Times*, October 27. http://www.nytimes.com/2011/10/28/world/middleeast/security-council-ends-libya-intervention-mandate.html?_r=0

Goldberg, Jeffrey. 2016. The Obama Doctrine. *The Atlantic*, April.

Human Rights Watch. 2012. Unacknowledged Deaths, Civilian Casualties in NATO's Air Campaign in Libya. Last Modified May 13, 2012, https://www.hrw.org/report/2012/05/13/unacknowledged-deaths/civilian-casualties-natos-air-campaign-libya

———. 2017. Libya Events of 2016. https://www.hrw.org/world-report/2017/country-chapters/libya. Accessed 21 Nov 2018.

Hunter, Robert E. NATO's Decline over Libya. Last Modified Apr 19, 2011. https://www.cfr.org/interview/natos-decline-over-libya. Accessed 22 Nov 2018.

Jones, Jeffrey M. Americans Approve of Military Action Against Libya, 47% to 37%. Last Modified Mar 22, 2011. http://www.gallup.com/poll/146738/americans-approve-military-action-against-libya.aspx. Accessed 1 Mar 2015.

Kuperman, Alan J. 2015. Obama's Libya Debacle. Foreign Affairs: March/April. https://www.foreignaffairs.com/articles/libya/2019-02-18/obamas-libya-debacle. Accessed 19 May 2019.

Majumdar, Dave. 2011. AFRICOM: AF, Navy Still Flying Libya Missions. *Air Force Times*, July 30. http://www.airforcetimes.com/news/2011/06/defense-africom-air-force-navy-flying-libya-missions-063011/

Malinarich, Nathalie. 2001. Flashback: The Berlin Disco Bombing. Last Modified Nov 13. http://news.bbc.co.uk/2/hi/europe/1653848.stm. Accessed 1 Mar 2015.

McMichael, William. 2011. Bataan ARG Heads to Libya Duty in Med. *Marine Corps Times*, March 23. http://www.marinecorpstimes.com/news/2011/03/navy-libya-bataan-arg-deploys-early-032311w

Michaels, Jeffrey H. 2014. Able but Not Willing. In *The NATO Intervention in Libya: Lessons Learned from the Campaign*, ed. Kjell Engelbrekt, Marcus Mohlin, and Charlotte Wagnsson. New York: Routledge.

NATO. NATO Defence Ministers Will Discuss Situation in Libya and Longer Term Prospects in Middle East. Last Modified Mar 7, 2011a. www.nato.int/cps/en/SID-B6E67EC7-D86A96C6/natolive/news_71277.htm?selectedLocale=en. Accessed 1 Mar 2015.

———. Operational Media Update: NATO and Libya. Last Modified Oct 31, 2011b. http://www.nato.int/cps/en/natohq/news_71994.htm. Accessed 9 Apr 2015.

———. NATO and Libya: Operation Unified Protector. Last Modified Mar 27, 2012. http://www.nato.int/cps/en/natolive/71679.htm. Accessed 6 Sept 2017.

Nygren, Anders. 2014. Executing Strategy from the Air. In *The NATO Intervention in Libya: Lessons Learned from the Campaign*, ed. Kjell Engelbrekt, Marcus Mohlin, and Charlotte Wagnsson. New York: Routledge.

Obama, Barack H. Address to the Nation on the Situation in Libya. Last Modified Mar 28, 2011a. http://www.presidency.ucsb.edu/ws/index.php?pid=90195

———. Remarks on the Death of Former Leader Muammar Abu Minyar Al-Qadhafi of Libya. Last Modified Oct 20, 2011b. https://www.presidency.ucsb.edu/documents/remarks-the-death-former-leader-muammar-abu-minyar-al-qadhafi-libya

———. Remarks on the Situation in Libya. Last Modified Feb 23, 2011c. http://www.presidency.ucsb.edu/ws/index.php?pid=89480. Accessed 1 Mar 2015.

———. Remarks on the Situation in Libya. Last Modified Mar 18, 2011d. http://www.presidency.ucsb.edu/ws/index.php?pid=90162. Accessed 1 Mar 2015.

———. 2015 National Security Strategy. http://nssarchive.us/wp-content/uploads/2015/02/2015.pdf

O'Donnell, Clara M., and Justin Vaisse. 2011. Is Libya NATO's Final Bow? *Brookings*, December 2. https://www.brookings.edu/opinions/is-libya-natos-final-bow/

Pargeter, Alison. 2012. *Libya: The Rise and Fall of Qaddafi*. New Haven: Yale University Press.

Pew Research Center. Public Wary of Military Intervention in Libya. Last Modified Mar 14, 2011. http://www.people-press.org/2011/03/14/public-wary-of-military-intervention-in-libya. Accessed 1 Mar 2015.

Rasmussen, Anders Fogh. 2011. NATO After Libya. *Foreign Affairs* 90 (4) (Jul/Aug). https://www.foreignaffairs.com/articles/libya/2011-07-01/nato-after-libya

Rettig, Jessica. End of NATO's Libya Intervention Means Financial Relief for Allies. Last Modified Oct 31, 2011. www.usnews.comnews/articles/2011/10/31/end-of-natos-libya-intervention-means-financial-relief-for-allies. Accessed 1 Mar 2015.

Reuters. Timeline: Libya's Uprising Against Muammar Gaddafi. Last Modified Aug 21, 2011. www.reuters.com/article/2011/08/21/us-libya-events-idUS-TRE77K2QH20110821. Accessed 1 Mar 2015.

Rice, Susan. 2011. Remarks by Ambassador Susan E. Rice, U.S. Permanent Representative to the United Nations, at the Security Council Stakeout, on Resolution 1970, Libya Sanctions. *States News Service*, February 26.

Rieff, David. 2011. R2P, R.I.P. *The New York Times*, November 8. http://www.nytimes.com/2011/11/08/opinion/r2p-rip.html?scp=1&sq=NATO%20intervention%20in%20libya%20&st=cse

Rogin, Josh. Senate Has No Plans to Invoke War Powers Act over Libya. *Foreign Policy: The Cable*. Last Modified May 10, 2011. thecable.foreignpolicy.com/posts/2011/05/10/senate_has_no_plans_to_invoke_war_powers_act_over_libya. Accessed 1 Mar 2015.

Salama, Hana. 2018. *Counting Casualties*. Small Arms Survey, February.

Shaughnessy, Larry. Wide Array of U.S. Warplanes Used in Libya Attacks. Last Modified Mar 21, 2011. http://edition.cnn.com/2011/WORLD/africa/03/20/libya.planes/. Accessed 5 Apr 2015.

Spencer, Richard. 2011. Libya: Col Gaddafi Damns the 'Rats' as He Clings to Power. *The Telegraph*, February 22. http://www.telegraph.co.uk/news/worldnews/africaandindianocean/libya/8341567/Libya-Col-Qaddafi-damns-the-rats-as-he-clings-to-power.html

Stavridis, James, and Daalder, Ivo. NATO's Victory in Libya. Last Modified Feb 2, 2012. http://nato.usmission.gov/foreign_affairs_02_02_13.html. Accessed 5 Apr 2015.

The German Marshall Fund of the United States. 2011. *Transatlantic Trends: Key Findings 2011*.

———. 2012. *Transatlantic Trends: Key Findings 2012*.

The Telegraph. 2011. World Powers Agree to Set Up Contact Group to Map Out Libya's Future. March 29. http://www.telegraph.co.uk/news/worldnews/africaandindianocean/libya/8414410/World-powers-agree-to-set-up-contact-group-to-map-out-Libyas-future.html

U.S. House of Representatives. Committee on Foreign Affairs. 2012. *NATO: The Chicago Summit and U.S. Policy.* 112th Congress Session.

U.S. Navy. U.S. Naval Forces Open Odyssey Dawn, Prepare No-Fly Zone. Last Modified Mar 19, 2011. http://www.navy.mil/submit/display.asp?story_id=59192. Accessed 5 Apr 2015.

UNHCR. 2018. Libya. Last Modified Aug. http://reporting.unhcr.org/sites/default/files/UNHCR%20Libya%20Fact%20Sheet%20-%20August%202018.pdf. Accessed 21 Nov 2018.

United Nations. Security Council Approves 'No-Fly Zone' over Libya, Authorizing 'All Necessary Measures' to Protect Civilians, by Vote of 10 in Favour with 5 Abstentions. Last Modified Mar 17, 2011. http://www.un.org/press/en/2011/sc10200.doc.htm. Accessed 9 Apr 2015.

United Nations Security Council. 2011a. *UNSCR 1970 Peace and Security in Africa.* February 26.

———. 2011b. *UNSCR 1973 Libya.* March 17.

United States Justice Department. 2011. Authority to Use Military Force in Libya. April 1. https://www.justice.gov/sites/default/files/olc/opinions/2011/04/31/authority-military-use-in-libya.pdf

United States Mission to NATO. Libya: Operation Unified Protector: Fact Sheet. Last Modified Apr 28, 2011. http://nato.unmission.gov/issues/our_issues/Libya/Libya-fact-sheet2/Libya-fact-sheet.html. Accessed 1 Mar 2015.

Weitsman, Patricia. 2014. *Waging War: Alliances, Coalitions, and Institutions of Interstate Violence.* Stanford: Stanford University Press.

CHAPTER 7

The Evolution and Persistence of NATO

NATO's participation in the four conflicts analyzed in the preceding chapters revealed the major strengths and weaknesses of the alliance in combat, as well as the advantages to the United States' efforts to engage NATO. Each episode was a watershed moment for the alliance, allowing the allies to regroup and reassess NATO's operational and political needs. In the two decades following the collapse of the Soviet Union, NATO faced declining troops (from 5 million to 3.8 million active military) and facilities (from 78 headquarters to just 11) (Gaub 2013). Still, the allies undertook several new initiatives in the inter-conflict periods to improve the alliance's political and military infrastructure. Some of the efforts to streamline NATO resources reflected the defense budget cuts of many of the European allies and changing domestic and international priorities. Other changes resulted from the recognition of a new security environment and the need for a modernization of capabilities. NATO's reforms of existing programs, establishment of new initiatives, expanding membership and non-NATO state partnerships, and summit declarations further reflected the alliance's attempts to evolve and persist in the post-Cold War environment.

Existing analyses on NATO after the Cold War, however, largely overlook the inter-conflict development, instead identifying decisions to engage in conflict as the primary critical juncture in alliance evolution (Johnston 2017). More importantly, the American role in facilitating many of these initiatives is diminished. The following chapter analyzes the

© The Author(s) 2020
J. Garey, *The US Role in NATO's Survival After the Cold War*,
Palgrave Studies in International Relations,
https://doi.org/10.1007/978-3-030-13675-8_7

ways in which the alliance responded to these watershed moments in the
inter-conflict periods. In addition to exercising a substantial influence during the four conflicts, the United States significantly impacted the inter-
conflict development of the alliance. This allows for a more complete
understanding of NATO's evolution and fills important gaps in the existing perspectives on alliance persistence.

NATO's Inter-conflict Evolution

NATO's intervention in the Balkans—including Operation Deliberate
Force in Bosnia in 1995 and Operation Allied Force in Kosovo in 1999—
was NATO's first real post-war engagement. These operations raised concerns about the alliance's unity, credibility, command and control
mechanisms, and the growing capabilities gaps among allies. Disagreement
between the United States, the United Kingdom, and France (as well as
Russia) in the UN Security Council and the North Atlantic Council signaled to Serbian President Slobodan Milosevic that the allies were not
united on the decision to intervene in the Balkans. After the 1995 operation in Bosnia, President Clinton and other allied leaders wrongly believed
the alliance could make a credible threat for the use of force in Kosovo and
Milosevic would end the violence between the Serbian forces and ethnic
Albanians. Milosevic, however, was emboldened by the disunity between
the allies and continued his campaign without concern of NATO intervention. When the violence in Kosovo escalated in 1998, the United States
cited Operation Deliberate Force as precedent for insisting on an air-only
campaign, much to the chagrin of other allies. The conflict in Kosovo
threatened European peacekeeping troops in surrounding areas and the
stability of the greater Yugoslav region. The continued humanitarian
abuses also threatened the values of Western nations. However, both
China and Russia's unwillingness to authorize an intervention through a
Security Council resolution exacerbated the discord between the allies,
furthering the perception of the alliance's disunity.

As Operation Allied Force commenced on March 24, 1999, NATO's
miscalculations about Milosevic's capitulation became clear. Additionally,
because the allies failed to plan for an extended campaign, it authorized
only a few bombing targets at the outset of operations. The process to
approve new targets through the alliance's consensus-based command
structure was slow and cumbersome, revealing evidence of NATO's operational weaknesses. The two Balkans operations highlighted the growing

capabilities gap between the United States, which maintained its defense spending in the post-Cold War period, and the European allies, many of whom shrank their defense budgets and resource stockpiles after the collapse of the Soviet Union. As a result, the United States carried significantly more of the burden than the European allies in many aspects of the aerial campaign, as demonstrated in Chap. 3. The Kosovo intervention also demonstrated the European allies' inability to act through other European organizations and without the leadership of the United States. The April 1999 Washington Summit provided an opportunity for the alliance to regroup and address the ongoing difficulties of the Kosovo operation. At the summit, the allies resolved to remain committed to the objectives of Operation Allied Force and strategized to intensify the airstrikes. This intensification caused substantial damage to Serbian infrastructure and military assets, which bolstered the negotiations between the G8, Russian President Boris Yeltsin, and Milosevic, and eventually led to the ceasefire.

For just the second time in alliance history, NATO declassified its new Strategic Concept following the 1999 Washington Summit. The Strategic Concept stressed the importance of the allies' solidarity and cohesion, stating, "The Alliance embodies the transatlantic link by which the security of North America is permanently tied to the security of Europe." The ambitious agenda also reflected the allies' experiences during the two Balkans operations, noting the necessity of increasing European contributions to alleviate burden-sharing issues and narrow the growing capabilities gap, improving communications technologies and interoperability, developing the European Security and Defense Identity (EDSI) to allow European allies to take more responsibility for their security and defense, and stressing the need to continue relations with international organizations such as the United Nations, the Organisation for Security and Cooperation in Europe (OSCE), the European Union, and the Western European Union, as well as non-NATO partnerships (NATO 1999a).

In the aftermath of Operation Allied Force, NATO attempted to overcome some of the political and military challenges during the Balkans operations. The allies recognized the necessity of change to its political and military infrastructure if the alliance was to persist in the contemporary environment. In addition to growing concerns about the proliferation of weapons of mass destruction, ongoing peacekeeping missions, and crisis prevention, the 1999 Washington Summit and Strategic Concept identified several immediate threats to the alliance's periphery, including ethnic and religious rivalries, failed political or economic reforms, territorial disputes, human rights abuses, and instability resulting from the dissolution or reorganization of states. For the first time, the Strategic Concept addressed the threat of international terrorism as well, though most states maintained the position that terrorism was primarily a domestic issue.

In addition to the Washington Summit discussions and the renewed Strategic Concept, the alliance established the Defense Capabilities Initiative (DCI) in December 1999. The purpose of the DCI was to "ensure the effectiveness of future multinational operations across the full spectrum of Alliance missions in the present and foreseeable security environment with a special focus on improving interoperability among Alliance forces" (NATO 1999b). The allies continued to expand their relationships with non-NATO members through the North Atlantic Cooperation Council (renamed Euro-Atlantic Partnership Council in 1997) and the Mediterranean Dialogue. In 1999, NATO extended membership to the Czech Republic and Hungary, and encouraged other Eastern European states to partner with the alliance (and possibly pursue NATO membership) through its Partnership for Peace (PfP) program. Although these programs were established prior to the Balkans interventions, after Operation Allied Force the allies recognized the need for these partnerships, particularly in the changing security environment.

These efforts were unexpectedly derailed by the terrorist attacks of September 11, 2001, and the US-led war in Afghanistan. The alliance invoked Article 5 of the Washington Treaty and quickly assembled multiple proposals in support of the United States. However, the legacy of the Kosovo operation weighed heavily on US policymakers' decision to engage the alliance. Because of the burdensome command and control structure of the alliance and the capabilities gap between the United States and many of the allies, the United States largely refrained from engaging the alliance at the outset of Operation Enduring Freedom, opting instead to engage individual allies based on their ability to contribute to the United States' operational needs. The alliance agreed to increase its intelligence-sharing capabilities and to provide support for Operation Enduring Freedom by conducting two parallel missions. The first, Operation Eagle Assist, highlighted the utility of the alliance's airborne early warning and control system (AWACS). The operation deployed the alliance's AWACS aircraft over the United States, allowing the United States to secure its domestic airspace while deploying its own resources elsewhere. NATO also deployed its naval resources to the Mediterranean for patrolling and tracking possible terrorist activities under a second mission, Operation Active Endeavour. The second operation is still active today.

Prior to assuming command of the International Security Assistance Force (ISAF), established in 2003 by the United Nations, the NATO allies continued to adopt new policies to improve the alliance's political resources and military capabilities. The alliance capitalized on improved relations with Russia and established the NATO-Russia Council (NRC) at the 2002 Prague Summit. The NRC enabled information sharing between the partners and allowed them to coordinate on shared security concerns. In 2004, the NRC released its first Action Plan on terrorism, reaffirming NATO and Russia's common goals of preventing terrorism, combatting terrorist activity, improving states' abilities to respond and manage terrorist attacks, and supplementing the counterterrorism and anti-terrorism efforts of other states and international organizations (NATO 2011). In addition to establishing the NATO-Russia Council, the summit declaration announced a new framework to engage its PfP partners, revealing the Partnership Action Plan against Terrorism (NATO 2015a). In 2004, NATO expanded its non-member state relationships in the Middle East by establishing the Istanbul Cooperation Initiative.

Reflecting on the Kosovo intervention and the alliance's inability to meet the United States' capabilities demands for Operation Enduring Freedom, the 2002 Prague Summit emphasized the need for alliance transformation (NATO 2002). The allies also agreed to establish the NATO Response Force (NRF), as imagined by US Secretary of Defense Donald Rumsfeld. The proposal for a response force called for a lightweight military force with roughly 20,000 ground soldiers, flexible communication and strikes capabilities, and the ability to combat nuclear, biological, and chemical threats (U.S. Department of Defense 2002). The force was modeled after the Fourth Marine Expeditionary Brigade (MEB), established by General James L. Jones (USMC) (Mihalka 2005). The United States intended for the NRF to complement both the NATO Allied Rapid Reaction Corps and the EU European Security and Defense Policy (ESDP), and to serve as a secondary force for short-notice operations lasting no longer than 30 days.

While NATO participation could increase the political legitimacy of intervention, there existed a large gap between the military needs of the United States and the alliance's military capabilities. For the United States, the NRF proposal was intended to augment its own fighting capabilities and reflected the lessons learned from Afghanistan. Writes Michael Mihalka, "A more plausible scenario (for the use of the NRF) would be one where the United States is tied down in a major conflict (such as Iraq) when a transnational terrorist group conducts a mass casualty attack…the NRF would be tasked to take out the training camps of the transnational terrorist group." When asked about the likelihood of the United States seeking NATO assistance in Iraq, Rumsfeld said "(the issue is) seeing if we can have more of our capabilities available in days or weeks rather than months or years. If we can have a larger fraction of our capabilities agile and able to get in and out of places and move around in places with a smaller footprint. This is something that NATO countries are perfectly capable of doing if they decided to do it" (Graham and Kaiser 2002). Rumsfeld hoped NATO would adopt the proposal, thus creating a rapidly deployable force embodying his domestic RMA campaign and creating a deployable unit to use in Iraq.

The United States' proposal was formally presented at the November 2002 Prague Summit, and approved by the Allied Ministers of Defense in June 2003. By June 2004, the NRF was operational, and US officials commented that the NRF could allow the alliance to overcome some of the operational challenges it faced in the contemporary threat environment (Miles 2004). At the Riga Summit in 2006, NATO leaders announced the NRF was fully operational, and has been adjusted in the time since to "provide a more flexible approach to force generation, thereby facilitating force contributions which were being hampered by the enduring high operational tempo arising from Iraq, Afghanistan and other missions" (NATO 2014). The formation and maintenance of the NRF, as well as the Mediterranean Dialogue, the Istanbul Cooperation Initiative, and other counterterrorism operations also led the Bush administration to voice its support for the alliance's evolution.

NATO's leadership of the ISAF mission revealed the strengths of the alliance in ground operations. As demonstrated in Chap. 4, a major component of the NATO mission was to build civil-military partnerships and strengthen the alliance's relationships with nongovernmental organizations to deploy into the Afghan communities. The United States lacked the necessary knowledge of the different cultures, ethnicities, religions, and languages of Afghanistan, and the allies brought these critically needed skills to the ISAF mission. The alliance also retrained the Afghan National Army (ANA) and the Afghan National Police (ANP) and re-established the justice system. Under the ISAF mission, NATO took the lead in stabilization and reconstruction efforts and eventually took responsibility for the Provincial Reconstruction Teams (PRTs) throughout Afghanistan.

However, the NATO-led ISAF mission also indicated the alliance's weaknesses. Because of the structure of the Washington Treaty, individual states were able to place caveats on how and where their troops deployed, as well as restrictions on combat activities. At times, the command and control system was arduous, just as in the 1999 Kosovo operation. The alliance also struggled with ensuring adequate burden-sharing between the participating allies and disparities in troop contributions. One of the most evident weaknesses was the allies' inability to conduct joint intelligence, surveillance, and reconnaissance (JISR) missions. The United States was forced to execute the majority of these efforts, as well as supply the necessary equipment, personnel, and communications networks (Martin 2014).

The NATO alliance's efforts to maintain its relevance was once again challenged in 2003 with the United States invasion of Iraq. After several refusals by the allies to assist the US efforts, NATO agreed to lead the multinational force established by the UN under UNSCR 1546. From the resolution, and as a result of the request from the Iraqi Interim Government, NATO prepared to launch NATO Training Mission-Iraq (NTM-I). The United States was willing to provide security and funding for the NATO effort in exchange for a training schedule coinciding with the United States' timetables, as well as command over the mission (Rupp 2006). However, because it was a noncombat mission, NATO maintained political control of its forces, which fell under the command of the US mission's Deputy Commanding General for Advising and Training (NATO 2015b). As previously demonstrated, many NATO members believed the United States' demands for leadership in NTM-I indicated its unwillingness to cede control to the alliance; thus, while all NATO member states contributed to the mission, several states (including France and Germany) refused to allow their troops in Iraq to prevent them from falling under US command (Weitsman 2014).

According to Lieutenant General Michael Barbero, the US Army officer who commanded the NTM-I from 2009 until 2011, the disagreement between the NATO allies over the NTM-I mission (and US leadership) did not necessarily inhibit the NATO operation's success. Several of the allies, including Turkey, Great Britain, and Italy, played an integral role in training the Iraqi leaders and police force. In addition to the symbolic value of a NATO presence, the allies contributed real capabilities to the NTM-I; General Barbero cited Turkey's acceptance of dozens of military leaders into slots in their schools and the Italian Carabinieri's (military police) establishment of a training school to teach tactical skills, professionalism, and investigative skills as examples of allied capabilities contributions that enhanced the United States' OIF and the NTM-I (Barbero 2015).

As the result of NATO's leadership in ISAF and its NTM-I mission in Iraq, the alliance continued to evolve to better fit the contemporary security environment. In 2004, the alliance welcomed seven new member states, many of who supported US and NATO operations in Afghanistan and Iraq. In 2006, the allies agreed to a memorandum of understanding (MOU) spearheaded by US Marine Corps General James Jones (who served as NATO SACEUR from 2003 to 2006) to establish the NATO Intelligence Fusion Centre (NIFC). The NIFC was intended to address the alliance's ISR shortcomings, particularly in out-of-area missions such as Afghanistan (and later Libya), as well as to support the NRF (NATO Intelligence Fusion Centre 2015; NATO 2015c). NATO's shortcomings in ISR also led to reforms to the Alliance Ground Surveillance (AGS) program. Although the AGS program was conceived in 1992 to "pursue work on a minimum essential NATO-owned and operated core capability supplemented by interoperable national assets," the allies struggled to reach a consensus regarding the necessary state contributions (largely due to the ongoing defense budget cuts in many European states) prior to the 9/11 attacks. However, operational difficulties in Afghanistan forced the allies to reorganize and reprioritize the program several times. At the 2010 NATO Summit in Lisbon, the AGS program was incorporated into the revised Strategic Concept, and in 2012 the North Atlantic Council settled the funding dispute to move new AGS acquisition forward.

The allies repeatedly reaffirmed their commitments to the ISAF mission in Afghanistan and the NTM-I mission in Iraq, as well as counterterrorism and efforts to prevent the proliferation of WMDs, at the 2006 Riga Summit, the 2008 Bucharest Summit, and the 2009 Strasbourg/Kehl Summit. Each summit produced an ambitious list of initiatives the Heads of States hoped the alliance would undertake, including more rapid deployment of troops during crises, better inter-theatre airlift, improved networked capabilities, better information sharing, and improvements in special operations forces training and deployability. In 2009, the alliance also extended membership to Albania and Croatia, and the alliance grew to 28 members. At the 2010 Lisbon Summit, the allies agreed on a new

Strategic Concept and a plan to restructure the NATO command structure. The 2010 Strategic Concept outlined an ambitious agenda reflecting the ongoing difficulties in Afghanistan and the political pressure to reduce defense spending and streamline the alliance's operations. Still, the allies remained committed to ensuring the alliance's ability to respond to emerging crises, as well as play an integral role in stabilization and reconstruction efforts around the world (NATO 2006, 2008, 2009, 2010a, b).

In 2011, NATO's evolution was again challenged by the Libyan intervention. The United States, France, and Britain pushed the alliance to assume responsibility for the no-fly zone, arms embargo, and protection of the civilian population, because it was one of the only organizations with the necessary capabilities to do so. Throughout the first 20 years of the post-Cold War period, NATO's conflict engagements and peacetime evolution equipped the alliance with the necessary political and military infrastructure to coordinate both NATO and non-NATO allies. This was especially important to the United States, which wanted to relinquish leadership of the Libya operations as quickly as possible.

NATO's air campaign was limited not only by the unwillingness or inability of some allies to commit ground troops, but also by the UN Security Council Resolution 1973, which prohibited a ground presence. Because of these limitations, it was difficult for the alliance to coordinate with the rebel fighters on the ground. The alliance's justification for intervention, the Responsibility to Protect (R2P) doctrine, led to disagreement over target selection (Woodward and Morrison 2013). Although the alliance had successfully provided a deep understanding of Afghanistan's culture, ethnicity, and religions during the ISAF mission, it failed to bring the same kind of resources for understanding to the Libyan conflict (Gaub 2013). Operation Unified Protector (OUP) also suffered as support for operations declined within the first few weeks of the airstrikes, and while half of the NATO allies participated in OUP activities, only eight states conducted airstrikes. Meanwhile, the other half of the alliance refrained completely from participation in OUP. Once again, the alliance's deficiency in ISR resources was highlighted and the United States was forced to increase its contributions in the later months of the operation to compensate for these shortcomings.

The strengths and weaknesses of the alliance during Operation Unified Protector led to another set of reforms to the alliance's political and military structures. In early October 2011—just a few weeks before the end of OUP—NATO Secretary General Anders Fogh Rasmussen introduced a new initiative, Smart Defense. The Smart Defense initiative was formally incorporated into the alliance's strategy at the 2012 Chicago Summit. The three components of the initiative—prioritization of capability adoption and advancement, specialization to capitalize on the strengths of each member, and cooperation between allies to share resources integral to common issues—reflected the alliance's evolution as well as the continued political and financial pressures on the alliance to become more efficient and cost effective (Rasmussen 2011; NATO 2015d). As demonstrated earlier, the Heads of State came together at the 2012 Chicago Summit to settle the funding dispute over the NATO Response Force, to enable the project's advancement. The allies also addressed the alliance's ongoing intelligence resource shortages and created the Joint Intelligence, surveillance, and reconnaissance (JISR) initiative to increase intelligence-sharing efficiency, conduct training for JISR staff and allied nations' military officers, and establish the necessary standardization agreements to improve ISR interoperability (Martin 2014). The Chicago Summit also allowed the allies to formulate its exit strategy for Afghanistan, while member states reaffirmed their commitments to NATO's ongoing counterterrorism efforts and recognized new security challenges facing the alliance such as cyberterrorism (NATO 2012).

As evidenced here, the NATO command structure and operational capacities have undergone several transformations, resulting in new initiatives and improvements to the alliance's ability to respond to crises in the contemporary threat environment. Many of the existing analyses of NATO overlook this evolution, thus leading scholars to faulty conclusions about the alliance's persistence as it is linked to bureaucratic momentum, normative expectations for conflict engagement, identity politics, or something else entirely. Inter-conflict evolution as well as the four major conflict engagements in the post-Cold War era reveal something else entirely: an alliance predicated on the needs of 29 states but shaped with particular regard to one: the United States. Despite its consensus decision-making mechanisms and its commitment to the collective defense of all of the allies, NATO has evolved to play a specific role in conflict engagement, one consistent with US interests of utility enhancement and legitimization. This role and the benefits derived are not limited to the United States, of course, but as its most militarily capable ally, it arguable reaps the rewards of multilateralism more frequently than its peers.

A word of caution, however: it is important to note the United States does not enjoy these benefits because it has superseded the aforementioned consensus framework, threatened its partners, devoted more money, time, and resources to the alliance, or successfully extolled its virtues to the rest of the international community. Rather, as a powerful ally who regularly engages in conflict, and who attempts to frame its conflict engagement as adhering to international norms and shared liberal democratic values, the United States has deliberately sought an alliance that would do the same, and devoted its resources to those missions which enhance its military and political pursuits.

AN AMERICAN ALLY

Analysis of each of the four cases—the 1999 Kosovo intervention, the 2001 war in Afghanistan, the 2003 Iraq War, and the 2011 intervention in Libya—elucidates the evolution of NATO and the United States' role in NATO development during these engagements, as well as US-NATO relations more broadly. During combat operations, the alliance remained heavily reliant on US contributions. Subsequently, the United States used each of these engagements as opportunities to press the European allies for increased defense spending and a greater contribution to NATO. Many of the European allies maintained divergent philosophies about the most imminent threats to European security; however, American interests took priority on the alliance's political and military agendas during and in between conflicts. Although NATO represents the collective interests of each of the 29 member states, its post-Cold War evolution was largely dominated by one.

The two Balkans operations resulted from European security concerns, and the United States was unmatched in its military contributions to the alliance's efforts. The United States' refusal to intervene in the first years of the Bosnian War, despite having established a precedent for intervention in both the Persian Gulf War and in Panama, was frequently cited as the reason for NATO's delayed response to the ongoing violence. Additionally, the decision to only intervene in Kosovo with aerial strikes reflected the Clinton administration's refusal to commit ground troops. President Clinton and others believed the Bosnian operation, Operation Deliberate Force, projected a high likelihood of success with a second air-only campaign in Kosovo. Due to both its political power and unparalleled capabilities, the United States exerted significant influence on the execution of Operation Allied Force. Two US proposals—codenamed Operation Flexible Anvil and Operation Sky Anvil—and one of the United States' concepts of operations plan (CONOPLAN 10601) provided the framework for the NATO operation.

During Operation Allied Force, the United States elected to maintain a parallel command structure to the NATO command structure. This decision was based on concerns about the United States' aerial capacities being restrained by the alliance and the need to protect its most sensitive intelligence assets, but proved to be problematic for several reasons. The two command structures were slow to provide information to one another, and the United States sometimes withheld information about its operations from NATO to prevent leaks (Weitsman 2014). There was also tension between the officers serving the United States' efforts and the US officers assigned to the NATO mission. The United States maintained its influence over the NATO operation through NATO SACEUR General Wesley Clark and Admiral James Ellis, who had operational and tactical control of the NATO forces. However, General Clark and Admiral Ellis regularly clashed with the United States' counterparts General John Jumper, who maintained operational control over the United States' ISR resources, and General Michael Short, who maintained operation control over the United States' other resources (Nardulli et al. 2002). Compounding the difficulties of maintaining two separate command structures was the NATO alliance's slowness to approve targets and disagreements over the rules of engagement between all of the participating allies (Lambeth 2001). These difficulties led the United States to spearhead efforts to reform the alliance's command and control systems at the 1999 Washington Summit and following the end of Operation Allied Force. Although the Clinton administration encouraged the European allies to develop the European Defense and Security Initiative, it also recognized the importance of continued US participation in the alliance and strongly advocated for the 1999 Defense Capabilities Initiative (Douglas 2007).

The United States also led the diplomatic efforts of NATO and the European allies during the Kosovo operation as the founding member of the Contact Group and party to the 1995 Dayton Peace Accords that effectively ended the war in Bosnia. Although it was ultimately the efforts of Russian President Boris Yeltsin that resulted in Milosevic's capitulation, the United States' political efforts—led by Ambassador Christopher Hill and Special Envoy Richard Holbrooke—set a precedent for US diplomatic efforts in future NATO operations.

The United States declined many of the offers for assistance from NATO during the initial stages of the 2001 war in Afghanistan; however, the alliance's evolution after 9/11 and its leadership of the ISAF mission directly reflected the United States' influence on the alliance. The World

Trade Center and Pentagon attacks shifted the paradigm for the European allies—al Qaeda's attacks on the most powerful ally prompted NATO to recognize the international threat of terrorism instead of recognizing it as a largely domestic issue. Prior to 9/11, there was very little momentum for changes to the alliance's anti-terrorism measures. At the 2002 Prague Summit, the allies set about ambitious counterterrorism and anti-terrorism initiatives that reflected the alliance's shortcomings, particularly in intelligence sharing. Many of these new measures also reflected the United States' interests in combating international terrorism.

US Secretary of Defense Donald Rumsfeld and other Bush administration officials publicly cited the alliance's command and control difficulties in Kosovo as one of the deciding factors in the Bush administration's decision to prefer limited contributions from NATO during the Afghanistan war. This public acknowledgment of one of the alliance's greatest weaknesses was frequently cited as evidence of declining US-NATO relations. However, the allies used this information to make reforms to the alliance through new programs such as the Allied Command Transformation. Additionally, the NATO Response Force was inspired by and modeled after Secretary Rumsfeld's Revolution in Military Affairs (RMA) initiative and the United States' special forces-led teams in Afghanistan. The NRF was intended to be "able to execute the full range of missions…from Peace to high intensity war-fighting." The NRF brought together land, air, maritime, and special operations forces to facilitate a rapid (and temporary) response to emerging threats and disaster relief (NATO Response Force 2014). Bush administration officials hoped that the NRF could be used to provide assistance when US forces were engaged elsewhere.

The ISAF mission in Afghanistan and the training mission in Iraq reflected the NATO alliance's attempts to remain relevant and fulfill important gaps in the United States' efforts. NATO's leadership of ISAF reflected the interests of the European allies, who agreed to execute the UN-mandated mission but struggled to maintain unit cohesion and assemble the necessary resources and leadership prior to the alliance's participation in 2003. NATO's leadership also reflected the interests of the United States, who needed the support for stabilization and reconstruction efforts. Despite the reluctance to participate in the United States' Iraq operation, the NATO Training Mission-Iraq (NTM-I) provided invaluable enhancements to the United States' efforts to rebuild the justice and police systems and train Iraqi officers. As noted in Chap. 4, the ISAF mission facilitated a coalition culture and allowed the United States and the NATO allies to improve interoperability. The United States provided resources for the allies, while improving the standardization of tactics, techniques, and procedures (TTPs) (Barry 2012). The alliance's efforts to engage with the local communities, as well as its coordination of civil and military actors in the provincial reconstruction teams (PRTs), also reflected the needs and interests of the United States while highlighting the strengths of the European allies. The PRTs played an integral role in the stabilization and reconstruction phase in Afghanistan while allowing the United States to run its Afghanistan operation in parallel and divert some resources to the Iraq mission.

Improvements to the alliance's command and control system, as well as its aerial capabilities, were highlighted in the 2011 Libya operation. The alliance's integrated command structure allowed the United States, France, and Great Britain to transfer leadership of their operations to NATO quickly and with far fewer operational difficulties than those experienced during Operation Allied Force. However, the alliance's shortcomings—particularly in its intelligence, surveillance, and reconnaissance capabilities—led the United States to once again push for reform within the alliance. Because the United States was forced to increase its contributions of ISR resources over the eight-month Operation Unified Protector, the Obama administration pressured the alliance to again reprioritize ISR capabilities acquisition. The establishment of the Joint ISR initiative and the re-engagement of the Allied Ground Surveillance initiative at the 2012 Chicago Summit reflected the allies' experiences during both Afghanistan and Libya.

CONCLUSION

The NATO alliance faced significant challenges in each of the aforementioned conflicts, and struggled to overcome political, military, and operational difficulties during and after each conflict. From each of these conflicts and inter-conflict periods, the alliance has evolved to be more responsive to the contemporary security environment and the United States' interests. NATO has become better equipped to respond to out-of-area missions, improved interoperability during both aerial and ground campaigns, and developed a capacity to engage civil and military leaders in the local communities. It adopted new programs to address some of the most pressing security threats to the United States and its allies, such as terrorism, human rights abuses and ethnic conflict, and cyber warfare. Because of the United States' leadership, the alliance's ability to conduct airstrikes with a high success rate improved dramatically from Kosovo to Libya.

The gap between NATO's proposals and the execution of many of these initiatives remains a concern, as does whether the American foreign policy paradigm regarding multilateralism's value will shift in subsequent decades. The alliance continues to face declining contributions from almost all of the 29 member states and uneven burden-sharing in combat. The United States remains the largest contributor to the alliance. Although the non-US allies collectively have a higher GDP than the United States, their defense spending is less than half of the American defense budget. US defense expenditures account for 71 percent of the alliance's total defense spending. Furthermore, the United States contributes more than 20 percent of the direct funding for NATO, which is twice the amount of the alliance's second highest contributor, the United Kingdom (NATO 2017). The alliance also maintains a growing capabilities gap. Despite having undertaken a variety of missions with different levels of authorization from the United Nations, the allies have not agreed on the necessity of UN authorization for NATO missions, leading to disagreements among member states over the appropriateness of intervention in places like Syria, Yemen, and Ukraine. According to some American officials, NATO is still perceived as a useful tool for longer-term operations (such as stabilization and reconstruction efforts), but unequipped to provide a rapid response to immediate threats (Ham 2015; Stavridis 2015). Though these shortcomings pose a threat to the alliance's future prosperity, earlier analyses of NATO's persistence after the Cold War overstated the likelihood of the alliance's demise because of these issues. Instead, as this research demonstrates, beyond occasional expressions of disapproval by American policymakers at its allies' reluctance to increase its defense spending or adopt radical change to their militaries, there is no evidence to suggest a departure from NATO is imminent—or in the United States' best interests.

Throughout the first 25 years of the post-Cold War period, the United States remained the top contributor to the NATO alliance, used its contributions and hegemonic status to influence the alliance agenda, pushed for an expanded membership, exercised influence over the military operations of the alliance by retaining key leadership positions such as the Supreme Allied Commander, Europe (SACEUR), and fostered its relationships with the individual allies. Conversely, the United States also demonstrated its willingness to act unilaterally or outside of the alliance if it deemed necessary, and regularly downplayed the importance of a UN Security Council authorization when it interfered with US objectives. Still, as US Navy Admiral and NATO SACEUR James Stavridis characterized, NATO remains the United States' "partner of first refusal" (Stavridis 2015).

European allies also played a significant role during each conflict and during the inter-conflict periods. Some of the initiatives undertaken by the alliance reflected European interests—strengthening the ISR capabilities of the alliance, streamlining the alliance's resources in light of shrinking defense spending, and improving NATO's ability to respond rapidly to emerging crisis was beneficial to all of the allies. However, as demonstrated here, the United States played a key role in advocating for many of these changes despite the European allies' inability or unwillingness to increase its own contributions. Although some of the allies, such as France, called for an independent European defense organization following the Cold War, the alliance did not implement measures in order to lessen the United States' role in European security and defense. Rather, the European allies remained just as reliant on the United States' role in NATO and NATO's role in international conflict as it was during the Cold War, despite divergent attitudes about the alliance's shared interests.

Thus, NATO's evolution and persistence is largely the result of the United States' continued hegemonic status and leadership within the alliance, confirming hypotheses concerning the reasons for NATO persistence and the American role in ensuring the alliance's survival. As revealed by the Balkans, Afghanistan, Iraq, and Libya, the United States was able, willing, and sometimes willing and able to engage in military operations across the globe without the support of its European allies. However, the value of NATO—utility enhancement, legitimacy enhancement, and the ability to reshape the alliance as needed to make it more capable—played a prominent role in US decisions to engage multilaterally.

References

Barbero, Michael (USA-Ret., Former Commander NTM-I). Interview with Author, Jan 15, 2015.

Barry, Charles. 2012. Building Future Transatlantic Interoperability Around a Robust NATO Response Force. *Transatlantic Current* 7: 1–14.

Douglas, Frank. 2007. *The United States, NATO, and a New Multilateral Relationship*. Westport, PSI Reports.

Gaub, Florence. 2013. *The North Atlantic Treaty Organization and Libya: Reviewing Operation Unified Protector*. Carlisle: U.S. Army War College Press.

Graham, Bradley, and Robert G. Kaiser. 2002. On Iraq Action, US Is Keeping NATO Sidelined. *The Washington Post*, September 24.

Ham, Carter (USA-Ret., Commander, USAFRICOM). Interview with Author. *Carter Ham*, Jan 19, 2015.

Johnston, Seth Allen. 2017. *How NATO Adapts: Strategy and Organization in the Atlantic Alliance Since 1950*. Baltimore: Johns Hopkins University Press.

Lambeth, Benjamin S. 2001. *NATO's Air War for Kosovo: A Strategic and Operational Assessment*. Santa Monica: Rand.

Martin, Matthew J. 2014. *Unifying Our Vision: Joint ISR Coordination and the NATO Joint ISR Initiative*. Washington, DC: National Defense University.

Mihalka, Michael. 2005. NATO Response Force: Rapid? Responsive? A Force? *Connect* 4 (2): 67–80.

Miles, Donna. 2004. NATO Response Force Ready for Duty, Rumsfeld Says. June 27. http://www.defense.gov/News/NewsArticle.aspx?ID=26194. Accessed 6 Apr 2015.

Nardulli, Bruce R., Walter L. Perry, Bruce R. Pirnie, John Gordon IV, and John G. McGinn. 2002. *Disjointed War: Military Operations in Kosovo, 1999*. Santa Monica: Rand.

NATO. The Alliance's Strategic Concept. Last Modified Apr 24, 1999a. https://www.nato.int/cps/en/natolive/official_texts_27433.htm. Accessed 6 Feb 2014.

———. Defence Capabilities Initiative (DCI). Last Modified Dec 2, 1999b. www.nato.int/docu/comm/1999/9912-hq/fs-dci99.htm. Accessed 11 Nov 2014.

———. Prague Summit Declaration. Last Modified Nov 21, 2002. www.nato.int/cps/en/natolive/official_texts_19552.htm?selectedLocale=eng. Accessed 3 Feb 2014.

———. Riga Summit Declaration. Last Modified Nov 29, 2006. https://www.nato.int/docu/pr/2006/p06-150e.htm. Accessed 9 Apr 2015.

———. Bucharest Summit Declaration. Last Modified Apr 3, 2008. http://www.nato.int/cps/en/natolive/official_texts_8443.htm. Accessed 9 Apr 2015.

———. Strasbourg/Kehl Declaration. Last Modified Apr 4, 2009. http://www.nato.int/cps/en/natolive/news_52837.htm

———. Lisbon Summit Declaration. Last Modified Nov 20, 2010a. http://www.nato.int/cps/en/natolive/official_texts_68828.htm. Accessed 9 Apr 2015.

———. Strategic Concept 2010. Last Modified Nov 19, 2010b. http://www.nato.int/cps/nl/natohq/topics_82705.htm. Accessed 9 Apr 2015.

———. NATO-Russia Council Action Plan on Terrorism: Executive Summary. Last Modified Apr 15, 2011. http://www.nato.int/cps/en/natolive/official_texts_72737.htm. Accessed 9 Apr 2015.

———. Chicago Summit Declaration. Last Modified May 20, 2012. http://www.nato.int/cps/en/natolive/official_texts_87593.htm. Accessed 9 Apr 2015.

———. Countering Terrorism. Last Modified Apr 8, 2015a. http://nato.int/cps/en/natohq/topics_77646.htm? Accessed 9 Apr 2015.

———. NATO Assistance to Iraq. Last Modified Sept 1, 2015b. https://www. nato.int/cps/en/natohq/topics_51978.htm

———. The Partnership Action Plan Against Terrorism. Last Modified Mar 11, 2015c. http://www.nato.int/cps/en/natohq/topics_50084.htm. Accessed 9 Apr 2015.

———. Smart Defence. Last Modified Feb 4, 2015d. http://www.nato.int/cps/en/natohq/topics_84268.htm? Accessed 21 Mar 2015.

———. 2017. *The Secretary General's Annual Report.* https://www.nato.int/nato_static_fl2014/assets/pdf/pdf_2018_03/20180315_SG_AnnualReport_en.pdf

———. NATO Intelligence Fusion Centre – NIFC History. http://web.ifc.bices.org/about.htm. Accessed 15 Mar 2015.

———. NATO Response Force. http://www.nato.int/cps/en/natolive/topics_49755.htm. Accessed 24 July 2014.

Rasmussen, Anders F. Keynote Speech by NATO Secretary General Anders Fogh Rasmussen at the NATO Parliamentary Assembly in Bucharest, Romania. Last Modified Oct 10, 2011. www.nato.int/cps/en.natolive/opinions_79064. Accessed 6 Mar 2015.

Rupp, Richard E. 2006. *NATO After 9/11: An Alliance in Continuing Decline.* New York: Palgrave Macmillan.

Stavridis, James (USN-Ret., Former Commander, USEUCOM, NATO SACEUR). Interview with Author, 2015.

U.S. Department of Defense. U.S. Will Propose a New, Agile Military Response Force for NATO. Last Modified Sept 24, 2002. http://iipdigital.usembassy.gov/st/english/article/2002/09/20020920183018porth@pd.state.gov0.751034.html#axzz3EozjCWk2. Accessed 14 July 2014.

Weitsman, Patricia. 2014. *Waging War: Alliances, Coalitions, and Institutions of Interstate Violence.* Stanford: Stanford University Press.

Woodward, Margaret H., and Philip G. Morrison. 2013. The Responsibility to Protect: The Libya Test Case. *Joint Forces Quarterly* 71: 20–24.

CHAPTER 8

The United States and Multilateralism

The North Atlantic Treaty Organization's (NATO's) evolution and persistence in the post-Cold War period is demonstrated by the four cases presented in this volume. Whereas previous analyses tend to treat these cases as separate watershed moments, I also posit the importance of examining the inter-conflict periods. A more complete understanding of NATO's evolution reveals an understated element in the existing explanations of the alliance's persistence: the role of the United States. Because the United States believed the alliance was valuable to its security and defense interests, it continued to invest in NATO, despite declining investments from the European allies and divergent attitudes regarding collective security and defense. Thus, the NATO alliance persists in part because the United States is a hegemonic power with a vested interest in the continuation of the alliance and subsequently exerted its political influence, asserted its military supremacy, and contributed the necessary economic resources to ensure the alliance's survival, thus confirming each of the book's hypotheses.

The expansion and adaptation of NATO challenged structural realist assertions that in the absence of a clearly identifiable threat, member states would abandon the alliance (Waltz 1993). The hegemonic status of the United States was underestimated as a driving factor to unite the allies in peacetime. The traditional structural realist frameworks for understanding states' behavior as balancing or bandwagoning were insufficient to explain why the European allies sometimes refused to comply with the United States' requests, yet remained committed to the alliance. Although liberal

© The Author(s) 2020
J. Garey, *The US Role in NATO's Survival After the Cold War*,
Palgrave Studies in International Relations,
https://doi.org/10.1007/978-3-030-13675-8_8

institutionalist explanations posited the changing nature of the international system and the transnational nature of emerging threats as explanations for NATO's evolution, these explanations also failed to fully realize the reasons for its persistence. Liberal institutionalist scholars asserted the importance of the allies' shared democratic values as the likely cause of continued participation in the alliance. However, as demonstrated in the preceding chapters, many of the allies repeatedly argued the importance of establishing European security mechanisms independent of the United States.

NATO's persistence is better understood by the analysis of US-NATO relations. However, the question of why the allies have remained committed to NATO remains largely unanswered in the existing theoretical traditions. This analysis provides insight into the incentives for the United States to remain an active member of the alliance. While some of these incentives reflect the military or political utility of NATO participation, the United States is also driven by value-based incentives—namely, the alliance's effect on the perception of moral and legal legitimacy, as well as American policymakers' desire to appear to adhere to international norms regarding the use of force.

This analysis provides a more comprehensive explanation of the incentives for the United States' continued participation in NATO, as demonstrated in the four cases: the 1999 Kosovo intervention, the 2001 war in Afghanistan, the 2003 Iraq War, and the 2009 Libya operation. The United States pursued NATO for legitimacy enhancement and to project an image of adherence to international norms regarding international intervention. Despite its military dominance, the United States also benefitted from the military contributions of the allies.

US Incentives for NATO Persistence

Each of the four cases presented in the preceding chapters demonstrates a variety of incentives for the United States to continue its membership in NATO. Collectively, these cases illustrate four dimensions of legitimacy: the legal and moral legitimacy of the actions of the United States, the legal and moral legitimacy of the actions of NATO, the effects of NATO participation on the United States' legitimacy, and the effects of NATO participation on perceptions of legitimacy among local indigenous personnel in the conflict zones. Each case also highlights operational and military advantages that encouraged the United States to engage the NATO alliance. The alliance provided a unique interoperability advantage—particularly in later conflicts—because of its highly institutionalized command and control systems. The alliance also enhanced US operations by providing the necessary access to airfields and overflight privileges, as well as resources that bolstered reconstruction and stabilization efforts.

Legitimacy Enhancement and Adherence to Norms

In the 1999 Kosovo operation, the decision to engage NATO was based in part on the need to enhance the legitimacy of the intervention. Despite the objections of Russia and China, two of the five permanent members of the UN Security Council, the Western powers commenced an aerial bombing campaign to stop the ongoing human rights abuses and ethnic cleansing campaign by Serbian President Slobodan Milosevic. Without an explicit authorization for intervention by the Security Council, France, Great Britain, and the United States believed NATO's leadership would provide a higher degree of legitimacy than an ad hoc coalition. The allies also hoped NATO's Kosovo operation would be a precedent for future humanitarian inventions, particularly if the Security Council was unable to reach a consensus. For the European allies, NATO engagement would enhance the legitimacy of its actions by committing the most powerful state in the international system, the United States, to the operation. The decision to engage the alliance was successful in conferring legitimacy on the intervention—in retroactive evaluations of Operation Allied Force, the alliance's actions were deemed to be "illegal but legitimate" by the UN Secretary General and many members of the international community.

The United States also used NATO's participation in Kosovo to enhance the legitimacy of its actions with the domestic population. As demonstrated in Chap. 3, the majority of Americans supported the NATO airstrikes at the beginning of the operation. However, after a month of bombing with only limited success, the United States and the other allies began considering the deployment of ground troops. While a Program on International Policy Attitudes (PIPA) poll indicated a majority of Americans disapproved of the United States committing a ground force, support for US ground operations was considerably higher if it was conducted through the NATO alliance (Program on International Policy Attitudes 1999).

The legitimizing effects of NATO participation were much different in the 2001 war in Afghanistan. As demonstrated in Chap. 4, the United States enjoyed an unprecedented degree of legitimacy for its actions because of the September 11, 2001, attacks, including both domestic and international authorization for the use of force. This was a significant factor in the Bush administration's decision to decline many of the alliance's offers of support in the beginning phases of the war. However, the December 2001 Bonn Conference revealed a legitimacy "gap" for the United States among the various ethnic groups and local communities within Afghanistan. Thus, the United States recognized the need for a greater international presence and encouraged the United Nations to establish the International Security Assistance Force (ISAF). Although the ISAF force was not well-received by some of the local tribes and communities, many were receptive to the allies' efforts to rebuild schools and hospitals, provide literacy classes and basic healthcare, and rebuild Afghanistan's infrastructure.

In Iraq, the legitimacy of American actions was damaged by the absence of a Security Council resolution and poor intelligence about Saddam Hussein's weapons of mass destruction (WMD) program. Legitimacy was also lessened by the vociferous disagreement between the United States, France, and Germany. The absence of NATO in the Bush administration's ad hoc coalition of the willing further hindered attempts to legitimize its actions. As demonstrated in Chap. 5, domestic support was much higher than international support for the war in Iraq, and some of the United States' closest allies refused to support Operation Iraqi Freedom.

However, in 2004, NATO agreed to take command of the training mission for Iraqi forces, as established by UNSCR 1546. According to Lieutenant General Michael Barbero, commander of the NATO Training Mission-Iraq (NTM-I) from 2009 to 2011, the allies brought real capabilities to the training mission's efforts, but the NATO presence was also "important symbolically, and also for the future of Iraq, to try and pull it into the right spheres of influence and have some sort of lasting relationship" (Barbero 2015). Thus, although the NTM-I mission consisted of only a few hundred personnel and participating states placed significant caveats on the use of troops, Iraqi leaders accepted the mission as a legitimate international presence because of NATO's leadership. As General Barbero notes, US officials hoped NATO's leadership of the training mission would also build better relationships with Iraqi leaders and confer legitimacy on the new Iraqi forces.

The 2011 operation in Libya enjoyed a higher level of legitimacy than the United States' efforts in Iraq due to both the United Nations and NATO's participation. While the UN Security Council refused to authorize the intervention, many allies believed the Responsibility to Protect (R2P) doctrine justified the US, UK, and France's parallel operations. As demonstrated in Chap. 6, the United States repeatedly expressed its desire to transfer responsibility for Libya operations to NATO because the alliance was the most capable, coordinated, and legitimate option for enforcing UNSCR 1973. US officials did not believe a coalition would have the same capabilities or political strength as the alliance, and pushed the allies to accept the leadership of the operation. Although Russia and China argued that Operation Unified Protector violated international law and was illegitimate, the Western allies assert the authority of the two Security Council resolutions, the precedent of Kosovo and R2P, and NATO's leadership as evidence of the operation's legitimacy.

The presence or absence of NATO in each of the conflicts affected the perception of legitimacy by both domestic and international audiences. At times, the United States pursued NATO participation to legitimize its actions and adhere to norms governing the use of force and conflict engagement. As demonstrated in Chap. 5, most states agreed that the United Nations is the most appropriate mechanism for legitimizing the use of force. However, to a lesser extent, NATO enhances the legitimacy of states' actions in the absence of a UN endorsement. NATO is considered to be a more legitimate mechanism for the use of force than coalition or unilateral engagement, due to a high degree of institutionalization for decision-making and its consensus-based command and control systems.

The Utility of Multilateralism Through NATO and American Primacy

NATO's contributions to each of the four conflicts enhanced US efforts and demonstrated the utility of multilateralism. Despite the alliance's shortcomings—particularly in intelligence, surveillance, and reconnaissance resources—NATO contributions were key to the Kosovo operation, and more importantly, allowed the alliance to identify crucial areas of improvement. While the United States' participation was an integral part of the success of Operation Allied Force, the Clinton administration was extremely reluctant to act without the contributions of the alliance. Operation Allied Force was an air-only campaign, but some of the allies' most important contributions were on the ground, as access to bases, airfields, and overflight rights were paramount to conducting strike and non-strike sorties.

The 2001 war in Afghanistan required a more substantial contribution from NATO and further demonstrated the utility of multilateralism to US interests. The European allies brought invaluable skills for the stabilization and reconstruction efforts of the ISAF operation. The ISAF mission filled important gaps in access to healthcare and education. The allies were adept at engaging governmental and nongovernmental organizations, humanitarian organizations, and agencies such as USAID. The alliance's deployment of its Airborne Warning and Control Systems (AWACS) aircraft under Operation Eagle Assist freed up a number of US planes and manpower to be diverted to Afghanistan. The alliance also contributed the same types of ground resources as in Kosovo, allowing the United States to utilize military installations and airfields. NATO reassigned resources from the Kosovo mission, and when the United States sent more troops to Afghanistan during the 2009 surge, the allies contributed an additional 10,000 troops to the ISAF mission (Stavridis 2015). NATO's anti-terrorism operation in the Mediterranean, Operation Active Endeavor, enhanced anti- and counterterrorism efforts as well.

As demonstrated in Chap. 5, the utility of engaging NATO in Iraq was evident in the small NATO Training Mission-Iraq (NTM-I) contingent. The contributions of the allies—particularly the Italian Carabinieri (military police) and the Turkish military—were invaluable to training new military and police officers, as well as establishing the justice system and other infrastructure to ensure the stability of Iraq.

The Libyan operation benefitted from the allies' contributions of aircraft, overflight rights, access to airfields and aircraft carriers, and the contributions of non-US allies to both strike and nonstrike sorties. Moreover, according to the commander of Operation Odyssey Dawn, General Carter Ham, the decision to transition responsibility from the United States to NATO enhanced the alliance's reputation: the alliance had "proven its competency as a standing organization, so the transition would not be particularly difficult from a US-led coalition effort to a NATO-led effort [and] it could be done quickly, with minimal destruction. Trust was probably the most important ingredient – trust that this mission would be handled properly, would be effective, and it would be well led if it was done within the NATO construct" (Ham 2015).

The alliance also demonstrated its capacity to execute several operations simultaneously. During Operation Unified Protector, the NATO alliance was engaged in ongoing missions in both Kosovo (the KFOR operation) and Afghanistan (ISAF), as well as continued patrols of the Mediterranean under Operation Active Endeavor. However, former NATO SACEUR Admiral James Stavridis said the Libya operation was not hindered by a shortage of military capabilities: "I never felt resource-constrained in either Afghanistan or Libya. We were maxed out, but I did not feel resource-constrained. I think probably the tightest resources were lawyers, international legal advice, public affairs, and planners [as well as] people who were doing the very detailed planning of the logistics movement. But again, we were able. We had capacity in the system to do that" (Stavridis 2015). Thus, despite shortages in precision munitions and intelligence, reconnaissance, and surveillance (ISR) capabilities, the Libya operation and the United States' pursuit of multilateralism proved to be beneficial.

As demonstrated in the previous chapter, the inter-conflict periods allowed the United States to exert its influence over the alliance to encourage improvements to the allies' ability to formulate rapid responses to immediate crises, become more effective in combat, and develop necessary intelligence, reconnaissance, and surveillance (ISR) capabilities to lessen its reliance on the US. Policymakers continually pushed the European allies to contribute more resources to NATO and increase their defense budgets.

At times, the disparities between the United States' contributions and European contributions caused tension between the allies. Still, many policymakers accepted the United States' role as the largest contributor in the alliance. According to Admiral Stavridis,

> We always felt like the rules of the game were such that the U.S. would provide two and the Europeans would provide one. In terms of dollars, in terms of troops, in terms of aircraft. The U.S. was always ready, willing, able with its two. It was hard work to get the Europeans to provide their one, and that's unfortunate…by any rational measure, we ought to see a NATO alliance that is about half U.S., half NATO. That's just not the reality of the world. The Europeans are not as prolific in their defense spending. The Europeans' DNA is much less one of using hard power and much more of using soft power. So the reality is, the best deal you're going to get is two and one. (Ibid)

Policymakers acknowledge the political, military, and economic benefits of NATO engagement for ensuring US interests, despite disparities in alliance contributions. According to Lieutenant General Barbero, commander of the NATO Training Mission in Iraq from 2009 to 2011, "If the U.S. is planning a mission somewhere in the world and doesn't make a stop in Brussels to try and consult with and enlist NATO's support and make that a prime objective, then we're missing the boat...NATO brings unique capabilities that bring credibility and they do produce real effects" (Barbero 2015).

CONCLUSION: THE UNITED STATES, NATO, AND THE FUTURE OF US MULTILATERALISM

The impending change to the bipolar balance of power system experienced at the end of the Cold War resulted in a rift among scholars about the future of the United States. They compared the United States to the many hegemonic and even imperial powers of centuries' past, and many acknowledged that the malleability of the post-World War II environment led to decades of US dominance and the creation of an international system predicated on US interests (Ikenberry 2001b; Snyder 2003; Zakaria 2008). Many pointed to the institutions established by the United States in the aftermath of World War II as a source of both continuity and change in the new environment (Keohane 1984; Haass 1997; Ikenberry 2001a, 2008; Nye 2002; Walt 2005). There was little consensus in both the scholarly and policy communities about what the new distribution of power would be, how states would organize around it, and whether it would bring about peace and stability. Structural realists debated over the balance of power while liberal theorists urged policymakers to abandon this conceptualization of the international system in favor of one that emphasized institutional cooperation. Both realist and liberal scholars warned policymakers about the sustainability of US primacy, and many affirmed the importance of continued participation in international institutions (Drozdiak 2005; Glennon 1999).

Additionally, many scholars and policymakers argued that US foreign policy could have a significant impact on regional stability, particularly in regard to Western Europe, China, and Russia (Mearsheimer 2001). They sought to prevent the United States from expanding its power too much, out of fears that rising states would be incentivized to build their capabilities and threaten the United States. Samuel Huntington asserted the United States should stop referring to its interests as congruent with the rest of the world's interests and abandon its "unipolar world" rhetoric, urging policymakers to instead consider how the United States could best employ its superpower status and strengthen its most worthwhile relationships to obtain a favorable position in the emerging multipolar system (Huntington 1999). Christopher Layne (2012) advocated a similar position, arguing that the United States should take advantage of the institutions it created in the wake of World War II to maintain the international conditions favorable to it under an emerging multipolar system. Additionally, Layne argued, the United States should abandon its strategy of preponderance and look to alternative grand strategies to preserve its powerful status (Layne 1997). Richard Haass (1997) urged the United States to actively engage with other states, build relationships that could be employed in times of crisis (thus preventing the United States from having to act unilaterally as much as possible), and establish and maintain institutional arrangements (including alliances) that would mitigate conflict whenever possible.

Concerns over US imperialism also abounded. Paul Kennedy warned against "imperial overstretch," writing, "decision-makers in Washington must face the awkward and enduring fact that the sum total of the United States' global interests and obligations is nowadays far larger than the country's power to defend them all simultaneously" (Kennedy 1987). Jack Snyder argued against an expansionist, offensive advantage-based agenda by US policymakers in an attempt to quell terrorism and preserve its power (Snyder 2003). John Ikenberry posited the United States had a responsibility to both itself and the international community to mitigate the threat posed by its predominance: "A global backlash to U.S. power is not inevitable…particularly if the United States remembers its own political history. Our leaders have the ideas, means and political institutions that can allow for stable and cooperative order even in the midst of sharp and shifting asymmetries of power" (Ikenberry 2001b).

Ideas about the ability of the United States to maintain its hegemony subsequently resulted in debates over the United States' grand strategy and the importance of multilateralism. As Timothy Crawford writes, "When the Eastern Bloc dissolved and the Soviet Union broke up, the United States became a unipolar power…The resulting power vacuum, predictably, invited greater U.S. activism. The United States found new freedom of action, and more reasons to use it" (Crawford 2003). The George H.W. Bush administration struggled with its temporarily unrivaled leadership, encouraging other states to pursue their interests with the inherent acceptance of US hegemony under the "New World Order" (Joffe 1995; Hook 2014). The Clinton administration's strategy of engagement and enlargement met with several difficulties. Contentious disagreement between Clinton and Congress—particularly after the 1994 elections, in which Republicans regained a majority in the House—centered on the United States' participation in the United Nations and NATO. Crises in Somalia, Lebanon, the former Yugoslavia, Haiti, and elsewhere immediately challenged the United States' resolve as a global leader (Joffe 1995). As the Clinton administration shifted foreign policy concerns away from the politics of the Cold War and toward transnational issues of globalization, human rights, and the environment, new nonstate actors created another level to the already complex defense puzzle (McCormick 1998).

US hegemony remained relatively unrivaled at the end of the century. However, US-NATO involvement in the former Yugoslavia (first in Bosnia and later in Kosovo) raised new questions concerning the ability of both NATO and the United States to effectively engage in "out-of-area" missions. Subsequently, the attacks of 9/11, the decisions of the Bush administration to engage in warfare in both Afghanistan and Iraq, the economic prosperity of China, and the Obama administration's decision to engage US forces in Libya again reignited the debate over the sustainability over US hegemony (Weitsman 2014).

The unexpectedly sudden and peaceful end of the Cold War caused temporary uncertainty for the United States. As the lone superpower, each of the aforementioned conflicts demonstrated to policymakers that the United States had much to gain and much more to lose from the new balance of power, leading to a ferocious debate about whether its hegemonic status was worth more to the United States' interests than the costs of fulfilling the responsibilities and obligations of its unipolar position. Earlier debates over whether the United States could achieve a more advantageous global position without overextending itself and whether the obligations as a "world police" force would tax US resources were reignited. Additionally, policymakers wondered whether US power would be the source of future tension among partner states and whether it would be able to adapt to the new type of threat its status posed.

The utility of NATO to US efforts was an issue that was frequently revisited by policymakers. Some policymakers argued that in the case of future conflict, the United States had an unquestionable responsibility to act multilaterally—that is, through institutions like NATO—to protect and foster a more cooperative, transparent international system (Fukuyama 2006; Haass 2005, 2013; Kaplan 2013; Leffler 2013; Mearsheimer 2001; Walt 2004, 2005). Writes Joseph Nye, "The element of the American order that reduces worry about power asymmetries is our membership in institutions ranging from the UN to NATO...the multilateralism of

American preeminence is a key to its longevity, because it reduces the incentives for constructing alliances against us" (Nye 2002). Others argued that the nature of conflict, combined with the preponderance of American military strength, meant that the United States could—and should—act unilaterally when it deemed appropriate (Davidson 2011; Kagan 2002; Krauthammer 2001; Kreps 2011; Sterling-Folker 1999; Weitsman 2010).

As demonstrated by this analysis of US-NATO relations, the United States has continued to value multilateralism for conflict engagement. Despite its hegemonic status, which has remained relatively unchallenged in the post-Cold War era, it regularly engages its allies. Although the United States maintains the military capacity to act unilaterally, it continues to sustain its contributions to NATO to enhance the alliance's capabilities. The United States recognizes the advantages of its relationship with the alliance, and has acted to ensure the alliance's persistence in the post-Soviet era. Politically, NATO allows the United States to maintain political relations with some of its closest European partners, many of whom share the same values of freedom and democracy as the United States. Its relationship with NATO projects unity among the Western powers and demonstrably impacts international perceptions of legal and moral legitimacy in conflict engagement. Militarily, US-NATO relations provide US policymakers with a shared pool of resources and the command and control systems necessary to coordinate multilateral aerial, maritime, and ground exercises. The European allies benefit from NATO persistence and US leadership of NATO as well. The political and military incentives identified in this study may explain why, despite some discontent with NATO, the European allies remain committed to the alliance.

Although the threat of major power war between the United States and NATO and the Soviet Union and the Warsaw Pact is gone, Russia remains a threat to the allies, and in recent years has flexed its muscles along multiple fronts: the 2014 invasion of Ukraine and annexation of Crimea, occupation of territory in both Georgia and Moldova, extensive use of force in Syria, deployment of prohibited chemical weapons against a NATO ally, and disinformation campaigns in Montenegro and the United States, to name a few. While this places Russia at the top of the agenda, it is not the only state threat. Should NATO's nonmember partners, such as Japan and South Korea, face threats from a hostile China or North Korea, the alliance would likely be called to once again engage in out-of-area conflicts. Further, the alliance maintains a presence in both Kosovo and Afghanistan in addition to crisis response resources, while also looking to develop innovative solutions to nontraditional threats such as terrorism and cyberthreats. At a time when American commitment to the alliance is in question, overextension or perceived ineffectiveness in addressing one or more of these threats congruent with domestic political conditions may be enough to push the allies away from each other and toward unilateral action.

However, the politics of the day may be the greatest threat to NATO. As this research demonstrates, American policymakers would be remiss in seizing the opportunity of episodic transatlantic riffs to dissociate from its European allies. Not only would the alliance suffer military, political, and economic losses—perhaps to a severe enough degree to strip its ability to persevere, or force it to be rebuilt without American participation—but the United States itself would likely lose important advantages. Replacing or forgoing the alliance could hinder transparency and unity between the United States and its Western European counterparts, threaten pursuit of values important to American policymakers including norm proliferation and legitimation, and hamper the ability to most effectively engage militarily.

REFERENCES

Barbero, Michael (USA-Ret., Former Commander NTM-I). Interview with Author, Jan 15, 2015.

Crawford, Timothy W. 2003. *Pivotal Deterrence: Third-Party Statecraft and the Pursuit of Peace.* Ithaca: Cornell University Press.

Davidson, Jason. 2011. *America's Allies and War.* New York: Palgrave Macmillan.

Drozdiak, William. 2005. The North Atlantic Drift. *Foreign Affairs* 84 (1): 88–98.

Fukuyama, Francis. 2006. *America at the Crossroads: Democracy, Power, and the Neoconservative Legacy.* New Haven: Yale University Press.

Glennon, Michael J. 1999. The New Interventionism: The Search for a Just International Law. *Foreign Affairs* 78 (3): 2–7.

Haass, Richard. 1997. *The Reluctant Sheriff: The United States After the Cold War.* New York: Council on Foreign Relations.

———. 2005. *The Opportunity.* New York: Public Affairs.

———. 2013. *Foreign Policy Begins at Home: The Case for Putting America's House in Order.* New York: Basic Books.

Ham, Carter (USA-Ret., Commander, USAFRICOM). Interview with Author. *Carter Ham,* Jan 19, 2015.

Hook, Steven W. 2014. *U.S. Foreign Policy: The Paradox of World Power.* 4th ed. Washington, DC: Sage/CQ Press.

Huntington, Samuel P. 1999. The Lonely Superpower. *Foreign Affairs* 78 (2): 35–49.

Ikenberry, G. John. 2001a. *After Victory: Institutions, Strategic Restraint, and the Rebuilding of Order After Major Wars.* Princeton: Princeton University Press.

———. 2001b. Getting Hegemony Right. *The National Interest*, 63: 17–24.

———. 2008. State Power and International Institutions: America and the Logic of Economic and Security Multilateralism. In *Multilateralism and Security Institutions in an Era of Globalization*, ed. Dimitris Bourantonis, Kostas Ifantis, and Panayotis Tsakonas. New York: Routledge.

Joffe, Josef. 1995. 'Bismark' Or 'Britain'? Toward and American Grand Strategy After Bipolarity. *International Security* 19 (4): 94–117.

Kagan, Robert. 2002. Power and Weakness: Why the United States and Europe See the World Differently. *Policy Review* 113: 3–28.

Kaplan, Robert D. 2013. *The Coming Anarchy.* New York: Random House.

Kennedy, Paul. 1987. *The Rise and Fall of the Great Powers.* New York: Random House.

Keohane, Robert. 1984. *After Hegemony: Cooperation and Discourse in the World Political Economy.* Princeton: Princeton University Press.

Krauthammer, Charles. 2001. The New Unilateralism (Editorial). *Washington Post*, June 8.

Kreps, Sarah E. 2011. *Coalitions of Convenience: United States Military Interventions After the Cold War.* New York: Oxford University Press.

Layne, Christopher. 1997. From Preponderance to Offshore Balancing: America's Future Grand Strategy. *International Security* 22 (1): 86–124.

———. 2012. This Time It's Real: The End of Unipolarity and the Pax Americana. *International Studies Quarterly* 56: 203–213.

Leffler, Melvyn P. 2013. Defense on a Diet: How Budget Crises Have Improved U.S. Strategy. *Foreign Affairs* 92 (6): 65–76.

McCormick, James M. 1998. Interest Groups and the Media. In *After the End: Making U.S. Foreign Policy in the Post-Cold War World*, ed. James M. Scott. Durham: Duke University Press.

Mearsheimer, John J. 2001. The Future of the American Pacifier. *Foreign Affairs* 80 (5): 46–61.

Nye, Joseph S. 2002. *The Paradox of American Power.* New York: Oxford University Press.

Program on International Policy Attitudes. Americans on Kosovo: A Study of US Public Attitudes. Last Modified May 27, 1999. http://www.pipa.org/OnlineReports/Kosovo/Kosovo_May99/Kosovo_May99_rpt.pdf. Accessed 5 Apr 2015.

Snyder, Jack. 2003. Imperial Temptations. *The National Interest* 78, Spring.

Stavridis, James (USN-Ret., Former Commander, USEUCOM, NATO SACEUR). Interview with Author, Jan 5, 2015.

Sterling-Folker, Jennifer. 1999. Between a Rock and Hard Place: Assertive Multilateralism and Post-Cold War U.S. Foreign Policymaking. In *After the End: Making U.S. Foreign Policy in the Post-Cold War World*, ed. James M. Scott, 277–304. Durham: Duke University Press.

Walt, Stephen M. 2004. The Imbalance of Power. *Harvard Magazine* 106 (4): 32–35.

———. 2005. *Taming American Power: The Global Response to U.S. Primacy*. New York: Norton.

Waltz, Kenneth N. 1993. The Emerging Structure of International Politics. *International Security* 18 (2): 44–79.

Weitsman, Patricia. 2010. Wartime Alliances Versus Coalition Warfare. *Strategic Studies Quarterly* 4 (2): 113–138.

———. 2014. *Waging War: Alliances, Coalitions, and Institutions of Interstate Violence*. Stanford: Stanford University Press.

Zakaria, Fareed. 2008. The Future of American Power. *Foreign Affairs* 87 (3): 111–124.

BIBLIOGRAPHY

Abyat, Gulnar, and Rebecca R. Moore. 2010. *NATO in Search of a Vision.* Washington, DC: Georgetown University Press.

Allen, Mike, and Robin Wright. 2004. Bush Seeks NATO Help on Iraq. *The Washington Post,* June 25.

Allin, Dana H. 2002. *NATO's Balkan Interventions.* London: Routledge.

Armstrong, David, and Theo Farrell. 2005. Force and Legitimacy in World Politics: Introduction. *Review of International Studies* 31 (S1): 3–13. https://www.jstor.org/stable/40072145

Asmus, Ronald D., Richard L. Kluger, and F. Stephen Larrabee. 1993. Building a New NATO. *Foreign Affairs* 72 (4): 28–40.

Attanasio, J.B., and J.J. Norton. 2004. *Multilateralism V Unilateralism: Policy Choices in a Global Society.* London: The British Institute of International and Comparative Law.

Auerswald, David P., and Stephen Saideman. 2014. *NATO in Afghanistan: Fighting Together, Fighting Alone.* Princeton: Princeton University Press.

Balz, Dan. 2001. Bush Warns of Casualties of War. *The Washington Post,* September 18.

Barbero, Michael (USA-Ret., Former Commander NTM-I). Interview with Author, Jan 15, 2015.

Barry, Charles. 2012. Building Future Transatlantic Interoperability Around a Robust NATO Response Force. *Transatlantic Current* 7: 1–14.

BBC. Libya Protests: Defiant Gaddafi Refuses to Quit. Last Modified Feb 22, 2011a. http://www.bbc.com/news/world-middle-east-12544624. Accessed 1 Mar 2015.

© The Author(s) 2020   223
J. Garey, *The US Role in NATO's Survival After the Cold War,*
Palgrave Studies in International Relations,
https://doi.org/10.1007/978-3-030-13675-8

————. Libya Protests: EU Condemns Violence and Fears Influx. Last Modified Feb 21, 2011b. http://www.bbc.co.uk/news/mobile/world-europe-12525155. Accessed 1 Mar 2015.

————. Libya Profile. Last Modified Feb 16, 2015. http://www.bbc.com/news/world-africa-13755445. Accessed 1 Mar 2015.

BBC News. Timeline: Breakup of Yugoslavia. Last Modified May 22, 2006. http://news.bbc.co.uk/2/hi/europe/4997380.stm. Accessed 1 Mar 2015.

Bendery, Jennifer. Kucinich Sues Obama for Violating War Powers Act in Libya. Last Modified June 15, 2011. www.huffingtonpost.com/2011/06/15/Kucinich-obama-war-powers-act-libya_n_877396.html?view=print&comm_ref=false. Accessed 7 Nov 2013.

Bereuter, Doug. *Grace Shortfalls in NATO's International Security Assistance Force in Afghanistan.* U.S. House of Representatives, June 3, 2004.

Biddle, Stephen D. 2005. Allies, Airpower, and Modern Warfare: The Afghan Model in Afghanistan and Iraq. *International Security* 30 (3): 161–176.

Bjola, Corneliu. 2009. *Legitimising the Use of Force in International Politics,* Contemporary Security Studies. London: Routledge.

Black, Ian, and Michael White. 2003. Chirac Pledges to Veto New Resolution. *The Guardian,* February 17. http://www.theguardian.com/world/2003/feb/18/iraq.france/print

Blight, Garry, Sheila Pulham, and Paul Torpey. 2012. Arab Spring: An Interactive Timeline of Middle East Protests. *The Guardian,* January 5. http://www.theguardian.com/world/interactive/2011/mar/22/middle-east-protest-interactive-timeline

Borger, Julian. 2002. Straw Threat to Bypass UN over Attack on Iraq. *The Guardian,* October 18. http://www.theguardian.com/world/2002/oct/19/iraq.foreignpolicy

Braun, Aurel. 2008. *NATO-Russia Relations in the Twenty-First Century.* New York: Routledge.

Bronner, Ethan, and David E. Sanger. 2011. Arab League Endorses No-Fly Zone over Libya. *The New York Times,* March 12. http://www.nytimes.com/2011/03/13/world/middleeast/13libya.html?pagewanted=all

Brown, Michael E. 1999. Minimalist NATO: A Wise Alliance Knows When to Retrench. *Foreign Affairs* 78 (3): 204–218.

Brown, Seyom. 2015. The Just War Tradition. In *The Use of Force: Military Power and International Politics,* ed. Robert J. Art and Kelly M. Greenhill, 8th ed. Lanham: Rowman & Littlefield Publishing Group, Inc.

Buchanan, Allen. 2010. *Human Rights, Legitimacy, and the Use of Force.* New York: Oxford University Press.

Burns, Robert, and Erica Werner. 2011. U.S. Pressures Allies to Command Libya Mission. *The Washington Post,* March 24. http://www.washingtonpost.com/wp-dyn/content/article/2011/03/24/AR2011032400506.html

Bush, George W. Remarks Following a Meeting with Secretary of State Colin L. Powell and an Exchange with Reporters. Last Modified Sept 19, 2002. www. presidency.ucsb.edu/ws/print.php?pid=73123. Accessed 8 Apr 2015.

———. Address Before a Joint Session of the Congress on the United States Response to the Terrorist Attacks of September 11. Last Modified Sept 20, 2001. http://www.presidency.ucsb.edu/ws/index.php?pid=64731. Accessed 30 Nov 2017.

———. Address to the Nation on Iraq from Cincinnati, Ohio. Last Modified Oct 7. http://www.presidency.ucsb.edu/ws/print.php?pid=73139. Accessed 8 Apr 2015.

Cahen, Alfred. 1989. *The Western European Union and NATO*. McLean: Brassey's Ltd.

Champion, Marc, and Joe Parkinson. 2011. U.S. Recognizes Libyan Rebel Group. *The Wall Street Journal*, July 16. http://www.wsj.com/articles/SB10001424 052702304203304576447551762812720

Chan, Sewell. 2016. Donald Trump's Remarks Rattle NATO Allies and Stoke Debate on Cost Sharing. *The New York Times*, July 21. https://www.nytimes. com/2016/07/22/world/europe/donald-trumps-remarks-rattlenato-allies-and-stoke-debate-on-cost-sharing.html

Cheney, Richard B., and Elizabeth Perry Cheney. 2012. *In My Time*. New York: Threshold Ed.

Chivvis, Christopher S. 2014. *Toppling Qaddafi: Libya and the Limits of Liberal Intervention*. New York: Cambridge University Press.

Cimbala, Stephen J., and Peter Forster. 2005. *The US, NATO and Military Burden-Sharing*, Cass Contemporary Security Studies Series. London: Routledge.

Civic, Melanne A., and Michael Miklaucic. 2011. *Monopoly of Force: The Nexus of DDR and SSR*. Washington, DC: National Defense University Press.

Clinton, William J. Message to the Congress Transmitting Proposed Legislation to Combat Terrorism. Last Modified May 3, 1995. www.presidency.ucsb.edu/ ws/print.php?pid=51310. Accessed 15 Nov 2017.

———. Remarks with President Jacques Chirac of France on the G-7 Response to Terrorism and an Exchange with Reporters in Lyons. Last Modified June 27, 1996. www.presidency.ucsb.edu/ws/print.php?pid=53001. Accessed Nov 15 2017.

———. European Union/United States Joint Statement on Shared Objectives and Close Cooperation on Counterterrorism. Last Modified May 18, 1998. www.presidency.ucsb.edu/ws/print.php?pid=55984. Accessed 15 Nov 2017.

———. Address to the Nation on Airstrikes Against Serbian Targets in the Federal Republic of Yugoslavia (Serbia and Montenegro). Last Modified Mar 24, 1999. http://www.presidency.ucsb.edu/ws/?pid=57305. Accessed 1 Mar 2015.

CNN. G-8 Ministers Draft Kosovo Peace Formula. Last Modified May 6, 1999. http://www.cnn.com/WORLD/europe/9905/06/kosovo.03/. Accessed 1 Mar 2015.

———. Bin Laden Says He Wasn't Behind Attacks. Last Modified Sept 17, 2001. http://edition.cnn.com/2001/US/09/16/inv.binladen.denial/index. html?iref=storysearch. Accessed 8 Dec 2017.

———. A Timeline of the Conflict in Libya. Last Modified Aug 24, 2011. www.cnn. com/2011/WORLD/Africa/08/18/Libya.timeline/. Accessed 1 Mar 2015.

———. Pan Am Flight 103 Fast Facts. Last Modified Dec 19, 2014. http://www. cnn.com/2013/09/26/world/pan-am-flight-103-fast-facts. Accessed 1 Mar 2015.

Cody, Edward. 2011. Arab League Condemns Broad Bombing Campaign in Libya. *The Washington Post*, March 20. http://www.washingtonpost.com/ world/arab-league-condemns-broad-bombing-campaign-in-libya/2011/03/20/AB1pSgl_story.html

Cohen, Roger. 1994. U.S. Clashes with Russia over Bosnia. *The New York Times*, May 18. http://www.nytimes.com/1994/05/18/world/us-clashes-with-russia-over-bosnia.html

Cohen, William S., and Shelton, Henry H. Joint Statement on the Kosovo After Action Review. Last Modified Oct 14, 1999. www.au.af.mil/au/awc/aecgate/ kosovoaa/jointstmt.htm. Accessed 7 Feb 2015.

Coicaud, Jean-Marc, and Veijo Heiskanen. 2001. *The Legitimacy of International Organizations*. New York: The United Nations University Press.

Coll, Steve. 2004. *Ghost Wars: The Secret History of the CIA, Afghanistan, and Bin Laden, from the Soviet Invasion to September 10, 2001*. New York: Penguin Books.

Cooper, Helene. 2017. U.S. Says It Has 11,000 Troops in Afghanistan, More than Formerly Disclosed. *The New York Times*, August 30. https://www. nytimes.com/2017/08/30/world/asia/afghanistan-troop-totals.html

Cooper, Helene, and Mark Landler. 2011. U.S. Imposes Sanctions on Libya in Wake of Crackdown. *The New York Times*, February 25. https://www.nytimes. com/2011/02/26/world/middleeast/26diplomacy.html

Cowell, Alan. 2001. Protests Take Aim at Leader of Libya. *The New York Times*, February 16. www.nytimes.com/2011/02/17/world/middleeast/17libya. html?ref=Libya&pagewanted=print

Cowell, Alan, and Steven Erlanger. 2011. France Becomes First Country to Recognize Libyan Rebels. *The New York Times*, March 20. http://www. nytimes.com/2011/03/11/world/europe/11france.html

Crawford, Timothy W. 2003. *Pivotal Deterrence: Third Party Statecraft and the Pursuit of Peace*. Ithaca: Cornell University Press.

Crawford, Neta C. Human Cost of the Post-9/11 Wars: Lethality and the Need for Transparency. Last Modified Nov 2018. https://watson.brown.edu/cost-sofwar/files/cow/imce/papers/2018/Human%20Costs%2C%20Nov%20 8%202018%20CoW.pdf. Accessed 22 Nov 2018.

Crotty, William J. 1995. *Post-Cold War Policy*. Chicago: Nelson-Hall.

Daalder, Ivo H. 1998. Decision to Intervene: How the War in Bosnia Ended. *Foreign Service Journal* 73 (12): 24–31.

———. 2007. *Beyond Preemption*. Washington, DC: Brookings Institution Press.

Daalder, Ivo H., and James Goldgeier. 2006. Global NATO. *Foreign Affairs* 85 (5): 105–113.

Daalder, Ivo H., and Michael E. O'Hanlon. 2000. *Winning Ugly: NATO's War to Save Kosovo*. Washington, DC: Brookings Institution Press.

Dagher, Sam, Yaroslav Trofimov, and Nathan Hodge. 2011. Allies Press Libya Attack. *The Wall Street Journal*, March 21. http://online.wsj.com/article/SB10001424052748704021504576211690643186556.html

Davidson, Jason. 2011. *America's Allies and War*. New York: Palgrave Macmillan.

Deighton, Anne. 2000. The European Union and NATO's War over Kosovo: Toward the Glass Ceiling? In *Alliance Politics, Kosovo, and NATO's War: Allied Force or Forced Allies?* ed. Pierre Martin and Mark R. Brawley. New York: Palgrave.

Dempsey, Judy. 2011. Beginning of the End for NATO. *The New York Times*, June 14. http://www.nytimes.com/2011/06/14/world/europe/14iht-letter14.html?ref=libya

Deudney, Daniel, and G. John Ikenberry. 1999. The Nature and Sources of Liberal International Order. *Review of International Studies* 25 (2): 179–196.

Dobbs, Michael. 2001. Bin Laden: A 'Master Impresario'. *The Washington Post*, September 13. http://www.washingtonpost.com/wp-dyn/content/article/2010/03/12/AR2010031201552.html

Donfried, Karen. 1999. *Kosovo: International Reactions to NATO Air Strikes*. CRS Report for Congress, April 21. Washington, DC: Congressional Research Service.

Douglas, Frank. 2007. *The United States, NATO, and a New Multilateral Relationship*. Westport: PSI Reports.

Drozdiak, William. 2005. The North Atlantic Drift. *Foreign Affairs* 84 (1): 88–98.

Duffield, John S. 1994. NATO's Functions After the Cold War. *Political Science Quarterly* 109 (5): 763–787.

———. 2001. Transatlantic Relations After the Cold War: Theory, Evidence, and the Future. *International Studies Perspectives* 2 (1): 93–115.

Dunn, David. 2009. Innovation and Precedent in the Kosovo War: The Impact of Operation Allied Force on US Foreign Policy. *International Affairs (Royal Institute of International Affairs 1944–)* 85 (3): 531–546.

Ek, Carl. 2007. *NATO's Prague Capabilities Commitment*. Washington, DC: Congressional Research Service.

Engelbrekt, Kjell, and Charlotte Wagnsson. 2014. Introduction. In *The NATO Intervention in Libya: Lessons Learned from the Campaign*, ed. Kjell Engelbrekt, Marcus Mohlin, and Charlotte Wagnsson. New York: Routledge.

Executive Order 13129, 64 Fed. Reg. 36759 (July 4, 1999). https://fas.org/irp/offdocs/eo/eo-13129.htm

Fahim, Kareen. 2011. Slap to a Man's Pride Set Off Tumult in Tunisia. *The New York Times*, January 21. www.nytimes.com/2011/01/22/world/Africa/22sidi.html?pagewanted=print

Fair, C. 2004. *Christine. The Counterterror Coalitions.* Santa Monica: RAND.

Federal Bureau of Investigation. 2007. Terror Hits Home: The Oklahoma City Bombing. November 15. http://www.fbi.gov/about-us/history/famous-cases/oklahoma-city-bombing

———. 2008. First Strike: Global Terror in America. February 26. https://archives.fbi.gov/archives/news/stories/2008/february/tradebom_022608

Flenley, Paul. 2009. Russia and NATO: The Need for a New Security Relationship. *The Magazine of International Affairs Forum: NATO at Sixty*, Spring.

Freisleben, Shanya. A Guide to Trump's Past Comments About NATO. *CBS News*, Last Modified April 12. http://www.cbsnews.com/news/trump-nato-past-comments/. Accessed 30 Aug 2017.

Fukuyama, Francis. 2006. *America at the Crossroads: Democracy, Power, and the Neoconservative Legacy.* New Haven: Yale University Press.

Gallup. Presidential Approval Ratings – George W. Bush. Last Modified July 14. http://www.gallup.com/poll/116500/presidential-approval-ratings-george-bush.aspx

Garden, Timothy. 2002. NATO in Trouble. *The World Today* 58 (11): 17–18.

Gardner, Frank. 2011. Libya Protests: Defiant Gaddafi Refuses to Quit. *BBC*, February 22. http://www.bbc.com/news/world-middle-east-12544624. Accessed 1 Mar 2015.

Gaub, Florence. 2013. *The North Atlantic Treaty Organization and Libya: Reviewing Operation Unified Protector.* Carlisle: U.S. Army War College Press.

Gelpi, Christopher. 1999. Alliances as Instruments of Intra-Allied Control. In *Imperfect Unions: Security Institutions over Time and Space*, ed. Helga Haftendorn, Robert Keohane, and Celeste Wallander. Oxford: Oxford University Press.

Gerleman, David J., Jennifer E. Stevens, and Steven A. Hildreth. 2001. Operation Enduring Freedom: Foreign Pledges of Military and Intelligence Support. CRS Report for Congress. October 17.

Gertler, Jeremiah. 2011. *Operation Odyssey Dawn (Libya): Background and Issues for Congress.* Washington, DC: Congressional Research Service.

Gladstone, Rick. 2011. U.N. Votes to End Foreign Intervention in Libya. *The New York Times*, October 27. http://www.nytimes.com/2011/10/28/world/middleeast/security-council-ends-libya-intervention-mandate.html?_r=0

Glennon, Michael J. 1999. The New Interventionism: The Search for a Just International Law. *Foreign Affairs* 78 (3): 2–7.

Global Terrorism Database. 2018. *National Consortium for the Study of Terrorism and Responses to Terrorism (START).*

Goldberg, Jeffrey. 2016. The Obama Doctrine. *The Atlantic*, April.

Goldgeier, James. 2009a. NATO Enlargement and Russia. *The Magazine of International Affairs Forum: NATO at Sixty*, Spring.

———. 2009b. NATO's Future: Facing Old Divisions and New Threats. *Harvard International Review* 31 (1): 48–51.

Gordon, Philip H. 1997. *NATO's Transformation: The Changing Shape of the Alliance*. Lanham: Rowman & Littlefield Publishers.

Gordon, Phillip H. 2002. NATO and the War on Terrorism a Changing Alliance. *The Brookings Review* 20 (3): 36–38.

Gordon, Philip, and Jeremy Shapiro. 2004. *Allies at War: America, Europe, and the Crisis over Iraq*. New York: McGraw Hill.

Graham, Bradley, and Robert G. Kaiser. 2002. On Iraq Action, US Is Keeping NATO Sidelined. *The Washington Post*, September 24.

Haass, Richard. 1997. *The Reluctant Sheriff: The United States After the Cold War*. New York: Council on Foreign Relations.

———. 2005. *The Opportunity*. New York: Public Affairs.

———. 2013. *Foreign Policy Begins at Home: The Case for Putting America's House in Order*. New York: Basic Books.

Hallams, Ellen. 2009. The Transatlantic Alliance Renewed: The United States and NATO Since 9/11. *Journal of Transatlantic Studies* 7 (1): 38–60.

Ham, Carter (USA-Ret., Commander, USAFRICOM). Interview with Author. *Carter Ham*, Jan 19, 2015.

Hancock, Jan. 2007. *Human Rights and US Foreign Policy*. New York: Routledge.

Hendrickson, Ryan C. 2000. The Constraint of Legitimacy: The Legal and Institutional Framework of Euro-Atlantic Security. In *Alliance Politics, Kosovo, and NATO's War: Allied Force or Forced Allies?* ed. Pierre Martin and Mark R. Brawley. New York: Palgrave.

———. 2005. Crossing the Rubicon. *NATO Review*, Autumn. http://www.nato.int/docu/review/2005/issue3/english/history_pr.html

Hendrickson, David C., and Robert W. Tucker. 2004. The Sources of American Legitimacy. *Foreign Affairs* 83: 18–32.

Holsti, Ole R. 2011. *American Public Opinion on the Iraq War*. Ann Arbor: University of Michigan Press.

Holsti, Ole R., Philip Terrence Hopmann, and John D. Sullivan. 1973. *Unity and Disintegration in International Alliances*. New York: Wiley.

Hook, Steven W. 2014. *U.S. Foreign Policy: The Paradox of World Power*. 4th ed. Washington, DC: Sage/CQ Press.

Howard, Michael. 1999. An Unhappy Successful Marriage: Security Means Knowing What to Expect. *Foreign Affairs* 78 (3): 164–175.

Huddy, Leonie, Nadia Khatib, and Theresa Capelos. 2002. The Polls – Trends: Reactions to the Terrorist Attacks of September 11, 2001. *Public Opinion Quarterly* 66 (3): 418–450.

Human Rights Watch. Afghanistan: U.S. Military Should Investigate Civilian Deaths. Last Modified Dec 14, 2003. http://www.hrw.org/news/2003/12/12/afghanistan-us-military-should-investigate-civilian-deaths. Accessed 8 Dec 2017.

———. 2012. Unacknowledged Deaths, Civilian Casualties in NATO's Air Campaign in Libya. Last Modified May 13, 2012. https://www.hrw.org/report/2012/05/13/unacknowledged-deaths/civilian-casualties-natos-air-campaign-libya

———. 2014. The Crisis in Kosovo. http://www.hrw.org/reports/2000/nato/Natbm200-01.htm. Accessed 7 Sept 2014.

———. 2017. Libya Events of 2016. https://www.hrw.org/world-report/2017/country-chapters/libya. Accessed 21 Nov 2018.

Hunter, Robert E. NATO's Decline over Libya. Last Modified Apr 19, 2011. https://www.cfr.org/interview/natos-decline-over-libya. Accessed 22 Nov 2018.

Huntington, Samuel P. 1999. The Lonely Superpower. *Foreign Affairs* 78 (2): 35–49.

Hurd, Ian. 1999. Legitimacy and Authority in International Politics. *International Organization* 53 (2): 379–408.

Ikenberry, G. John. 2001a. *After Victory: Institutions, Strategic Restraint, and the Rebuilding of Order After Major Wars*. Princeton: Princeton University Press.

———. 2001b. Getting Hegemony Right. *The National Interest* 63: 17–24.

———. 2008. State Power and International Institutions: America and the Logic of Economic and Security Multilateralism. In *Multilateralism and Security Institutions in an Era of Globalization*, ed. Dimitris Bourantonis, Kostas Ifantis, and Panayotis Tsakonas. New York: Routledge.

Independent International Commission on Kosovo. 2000. *The Kosovo Report: Conflict, International Response, Lessons Learned*. New York: Palgrave.

Jehl, Douglas. 2003. U.S. Bars Iraq Contracts for Nations that Opposed War. *The New York Times*, December 9. http://www.nytimes.com/2003/12/09/international/middleeast/09CND-DIPL.html

Jervis, Robert. 2002. Theories of War in an Era of Leading-Power Peace Presidential Address, American Political Science Association, 2001. *American Political Science Review* 96 (1): 1–14.

Joffe, Josef. 1995. 'Bismark' or 'Britain'? Toward and American Grand Strategy After Bipolarity. *International Security* 19 (4): 94–117.

Johnson, Jenna. 2017. Trump on NATO: 'I Said It Was Obsolete. It's No Longer Obsolete. *The Washington Post*, April 12. https://www.washingtonpost.com/news/post-politics/wp/2017/04/12/trump-on-nato-i-said-itwas-obsolete-its-no-longer-obsolete/?utm_term=.f16650f98609

Johnston, Seth Allen. 2017. *How NATO Adapts: Strategy and Organization in the Atlantic Alliance Since 1950*. Baltimore: Johns Hopkins University Press.

Jones, Philip. 2007. Colluding Victims: A Public Choice Analysis of International Alliances. *Public Choice* 132 (3/4): 319–332.

Jones, Jeffrey M. Americans Approve of Military Action Against Libya, 47% to 37%. Last Modified Mar 22, 2011. http://www.gallup.com/poll/146738/americans-approve-military-action-against-libya.aspx. Accessed 1 Mar 2015.

Kagan, Robert. 2002. Power and Weakness: Why the United States and Europe See the World Differently. *Policy Review* 113: 3–28.

Kaplan, Lawrence S. 2004. *NATO Divided, NATO United*. Westport: Praeger.

Kaplan, Robert D. 2013. *The Coming Anarchy*. New York: Random House.

Karadis, Mike. 2000. *Bosnia, Kosova, and the West*. Sydney: Resistance Books.

Kelly, Terrence K., Nora Bensahel, and Olga Oliker. 2011. *Security Force Assistance in Afghanistan*. Santa Monica: RAND.

Kennedy, Paul. 1987. *The Rise and Fall of the Great Powers*. New York: Random House.

Keohane, Robert. 1984. *After Hegemony: Cooperation and Discourse in the World Political Economy*. Princeton: Princeton University Press.

Keohane, Robert O. 1989. *International Institutions and State Power*. Boulder: Westview Press.

———. 1990. Multilateralism: An Agenda for Research. *International Journal* 45 (4): 731–764.

———. 2002. Institutional Theory in International Relations. In *Realism and Institutionalism in International Studies*, ed. Michael Brecher and Frank P. Harvey. Ann Arbor: University of Michigan Press.

Kitchen, Veronica M. 2010. *The Globalization of NATO: Intervention, Security and Identity*. New York: Routledge.

Klass, Roseanne. 1988. Afghanistan: The Accords. *Foreign Affairs* 66 (5): 922–945.

Klein, Bradley S. 1990. How the West Was One: Representational Politics of NATO. *International Studies Quarterly* 34 (3): 311–325.

Kornblut, Anne E., and Susan Milligan. 2002. President Seeking Free Hand on Iraq Congress Asked to Endorse Unilateral Action in Region. *Boston Globe*, September 20.

Kramer, Anne. 2007. What the World Thinks. In *Beyond Preemption: Force and Legitimacy in a Changing World*, ed. Daalder. Washington, DC: Brookings Institution Press.

Krauthammer, Charles. 2001. The New Unilateralism (Editorial). *Washington Post*, June 8.

Kreps, Sarah E. 2011. *Coalitions of Convenience: United States Military Interventions After the Cold War*. New York: Oxford University Press.

Ku, Charlotte, and Harold K. Jacobsen. 2002. *Democratic Accountability and the Use of Force in International Law*. New York: Cambridge University Press.

Kupchan, Charles A. 2000. Kosovo and the Future of U.S. Engagement in Europe: Continued Hegemony or Impending Retrenchement? In *Alliance Politics, Kosovo, and NATO's War: Allied Force or Forced Allies?* ed. Pierre Martin and Mark R. Brawley. Basingstoke: Palgrave.

Kuperman, Alan J. 2015. Obama's Libya Debacle. Foreign Affairs: March/April. https://www.foreignaffairs.com/articles/libya/2019-02-18/obamas-libya-debacle. Accessed 19 May 2019.

Laird, Robbin F. 1991. *The Europeanization of the Alliance*. Boulder: Westview Press.

Lambeth, Benjamin S. 2001. *NATO's Air War for Kosovo: A Strategic and Operational Assessment*. Santa Monica: Rand.

———. 2005. *Air Power Against Terror*. Santa Monica: Rand.

Lansford, Tom. 2012. *9/11 and the Wars in Afghanistan and Iraq*. Santa Barbara: ABC-CLIO.

Larson, Eric V., and Bogdan Savych. 2005. *American Public Support for US Military Operations from Mogadishu to Baghdad*. Santa Monica: RAND.

Latawski, Paul C., and Martin A. Smith. 2003. *The Kosovo Crisis and the Evolution of Post-Cold War European Security*. Manchester: Manchester University Press.

Layne, Christopher. 1997. From Preponderance to Offshore Balancing: America's Future Grand Strategy. *International Security* 22 (1): 86–124.

———. 2012. This Time It's Real: The End of Unipolarity and the Pax Americana. *International Studies Quarterly* 56: 203–213.

Leeds, B.A. 2003. Do Alliances Deter Aggression? The Influence of Military Alliances on the Initiation of Militarized Interstate Disputes. *American Journal of Political Science* 47 (3): 427–439.

Leffler, Melvyn P. 2013. Defense on a Diet: How Budget Crises Have Improved U.S. Strategy. *Foreign Affairs* 92 (6): 65–76.

Leigh, David. 2010. Afghanistan War Logs: Friendly Fire Deaths Plagued Invasion from the Start. *The Guardian*, July 10. http://www.theguardian.com/world/2010/jul/25/friendly-fire-deaths-toll-afghanistan

Levi, Margaret. 1997. A Model, a Method, and a Map: Rational Choice in Comparative and Historical Analysis. In *Comparative Politics: Rationality, Culture, and Structure*, ed. Mark Lichbach and Alan Zuckerman. Cambridge: Cambridge University Press.

Londoño, Ernesto. 2014. The U.S. Wants Its Allies to Spend More on Defense. *The Washington Post*, March 26. www.washingtonpost.com/blogs/worldviews/wp/2014/03/26/the-u-s-wants-its-allies-to-spend-more-on-defense-heres-how-much-theyre-shelling-out/?print=1

Lugar, Richard. 2002. NATO's Role in the War on Terrorism. January 18. http://avalon.law.yale.edu/sept11/lugar_001.asp

Macleod, Alex. 2000. France: Kosovo and the Emergence of a New European Security. In *Alliance Politics, Kosovo, and NATO's War: Allied Force or Forced Allies?* ed. Pierre Martin and Mark R. Brawley. New York: Palgrave.

Majumdar, Dave. 2011. AFRICOM: AF, Navy Still Flying Libya Missions. *Air Force Times*, July 30. http://www.airforcetimes.com/news/2011/06/defense-africom-air-force-navy-flying-libya-missions-063011/

Malinarich, Nathalie. 2001. Flashback: The Berlin Disco Bombing. Last Modified Nov 13. http://news.bbc.co.uk/2/hi/europe/1653848.stm. Accessed 1 Mar 2015.

Martin, Matthew J. 2014. *Unifying Our Vision: Joint ISR Coordination and the NATO Joint ISR Initiative*. Washington: National Defense University.

Mattox, Gale. 1999. NATO Enlargement and the United States: A Deliberate and Necessary Division? In *The Future of NATO: Enlargement, Russia, and European Security*, ed. Charles-Philippe David and Jack Lévesque. Ithaca: McGill-Queen's University Press.

McCalla, Robert B. 1996. NATO's Persistence After the Cold War. *International Organization* 50 (3): 445–475.

McCormick, James M. 1998. Interest Groups and the Media. In *After the End: Making U.S. Foreign Policy in the Post-Cold War World*, ed. James M. Scott. Durham: Duke University Press.

McMichael, William. 2011. Bataan ARG Heads to Libya Duty in Med. *Marine Corps Times*, March 23. http://www.marinecorpstimes.com/news/2011/03/navy-libya-bataan-arg-deploys-early-032311w

Mearsheimer, John J. 2001. The Future of the American Pacifier. *Foreign Affairs* 80 (5): 46–61.

Menon, Andrew. 2006. From Out of Adversity: Kosovo, Iraq, and EDSP. In *The Transatlantic Divide: Foreign and Security Policies in the Atlantic Alliance from Kosovo to Iraq*, ed. Osvaldo Croci and Amy Verdun. New York: Manchester University Press.

Michaels, Jeffrey H. 2014. Able but Not Willing. In *The NATO Intervention in Libya: Lessons Learned from the Campaign*, ed. Kjell Engelbrekt, Marcus Mohlin, and Charlotte Wagnsson. New York: Routledge.

Mihalka, Michael. 2005. NATO Response Force: Rapid? Responsive? A Force? *Connections* 4 (2): 67–80. https://www.jstor.org/stable/26323172

Miles, Donna. 2004. NATO Response Force Ready for Duty, Rumsfeld Says. June 27. http://www.defense.gov/News/NewsArticle.aspx?ID=26194. Accessed 6 Apr 2015.

Morelli, Vincent, and Paul Belkin. 2009. *NATO in Afghanistan: A Test of the Transatlantic Alliance*. Washington, DC: BiblioGov.

Morgenthau, Hans J. 1954. *Politics Among Nations: The Struggle for Power and Peace*. New York: Knopf.

Morrow, James D. 1991. Alliances and Asymmetry: An Alternative to the Capability Aggregation Model of Alliances. *American Journal of Political Science* 35 (4): 285–306.

Mowle, Thomas S., and David H. Sacko. 2007. Global NATO: Bandwagoning in a Unipolar World. *Contemporary Security Policy* 28 (3): 597–618.

Mueller, John. 2005. Force, Legitimacy, Success, and Iraq. *Review of International Studies* 31: 109–125.

Nardulli, Bruce R., Walter L. Perry, Bruce R. Pirnie, I.V. John Gordon, and John G. McGinn. 2002. *Disjointed War: Military Operations in Kosovo, 1999*. Santa Monica: Rand.

NATO. Statement by the Secretary General Following the ACTWARN Decision. Last Modified Sept 24, 1998. www.nato.int/docu/pr/1998/p980924e.htm

————. The Alliance's Strategic Concept. Last Modified Apr 24, 1999a. https://www.nato.int/cps/en/natolive/official_texts_27433.htm. Accessed 6 Feb 2014.

————. Defence Capabilities Initiative (DCI). Last Modified Dec 2, 1999b. www.nato.int/docu/comm/1999/9912-hq/fs-dci99.htm. Accessed 11 Nov2014.

————. Prague Summit Declaration. Last Modified Nov 21, 2002. www.nato.int/cps/en/natolive/official_texts_19552.htm?selectedLocale=eng.   Accessed 3 Feb 2014.

————. Riga Summit Declaration. Last Modified Nov 29, 2006. https://www.nato.int/docu/pr/2006/p06-150e.htm. Accessed 9 Apr 2015.

————. Bucharest Summit Declaration. Last Modified Apr 3, 2008. http://www.nato.int/cps/en/natolive/official_texts_8443.htm. Accessed 9 Apr 2015.

————. Strasbourg/Kehl Declaration. Last Modified Apr 4, 2009. http://www.nato.int/cps/en/natolive/news_52837.htm. Accessed 9 Apr 2015.

————. Lisbon Summit Declaration. Last Modified Nov 20, 2010a. http://www.nato.int/cps/en/natolive/official_texts_68828.htm. Accessed 9 Apr 2015.

————. Strategic Concept 2010. Last Modified Nov 19, 2010b. http://www.nato.int/cps/nl/natohq/topics_82705.htm. Accessed 9 Apr 2015.

————. The Alliance's New Strategic Concept. Last Modified Aug 26, 2010c. https://www.nato.int/cps/en/natohq/official_texts_23847.htm

————. NATO Defence Ministers Will Discuss Situation in Libya and Longer Term Prospects in Middle East. Last Modified Mar 7, 2011a. www.nato.int/cps/en/SID-B6E67EC7-D86A96C6/natolive/news_71277.htm?selectedLocale=en. Accessed 1 Mar 2015.

————. NATO-Russia Council Action Plan on Terrorism: Executive Summary. Last Modified Apr 15, 2011b. http://www.nato.int/cps/en/natolive/official_texts_72737.htm. Accessed 9 Apr 2015.

————. Operational Media Update: NATO and Libya. Last Modified Oct 31, 2011c. http://www.nato.int/cps/en/natohq/news_71994.htm. Accessed 9 Apr 2015.

————. Chicago Summit Declaration. Last Modified May 20, 2012a. http://www.nato.int/cps/en/natolive/official_texts_87593.htm.   Accessed 9 Apr 2015.

————. NATO and Libya: Operation Unified Protector. Last Modified Mar 27, 2012b. http://www.nato.int/cps/en/natolive/71679.htm.   Accessed 6 Sept 2017.

————. The Defence Planning Committee (Archived). Last Modified Mar 28, 2012c. http://www.nato.int/cps/en/natolive/topics_49201.htm. Accessed 20 June 2014.

————. Peace Support Operations in Bosnia and Herzegovina. Last Modified Nov 11, 2014. http://nato.int/cps/en/natohq/topics_52122.htm?selectedLocale=en. Accessed 1 Mar 2015.

————. Countering Terrorism. Last Modified Apr 8, 2015a. http://nato.int/cps/en/natohq/topics_77646.htm? Accessed 9 Apr 2015.

————. Kosovo Force: Key Facts and Figures. Last Modified Feb 1, 2015b. http://www.nato.int/nato_static/assets/pdf/pdf_2013_12/131201-kfor-placemat-final.pdf. Accessed 5 Apr 2015.

————. NATO Assistance to Iraq. Last Modified Sept 1, 2015c. https://www.nato.int/cps/en/natohq/topics_51978.htm

————. NATO's Role in Kosovo. Last Modified Jan 6, 2015d. http://www.nato.int/cps/en/natolive/topics_48818.htm#. Accessed 1 Mar 2015.

————. Smart Defence. Last Modified Feb 4, 2015e. http://www.nato.int/cps/en/natohq/topics_84268.htm? Accessed 21 Mar 2015.

————. The Partnership Action Plan Against Terrorism. Last Modified Mar 11, 2015f. http://www.nato.int/cps/en/natohq/topics_50084.htm. Accessed 9 Apr 2015.

————. 2017. The Secretary General's Annual Report. https://www.nato.int/nato_static_fl2014/assets/pdf/pdf_2018_03/20180315_SG_AnnualReport_en.pdf

————. Brussels Summit Declaration. Last Modified Aug 30, 2018a. https://www.nato.int/cps/en/natohq/official_texts_156624.htm.   Accessed 9 Mar 2019.

————. Resolute Support Mission (RSM): Key Facts and Figures. Last Modified Sept   2018b.   https://www.nato.int/nato_static_fl2014/assets/pdf/pdf_2018_09/20180903_2018-09-RSM-Placemat.pdf. Accessed 30 Oct 2018.

————. ISAF's Mission in Afghanistan. http://www.nato.int/cps/en/natohq/topics_69366.htm. Accessed 15 Dec 2014.

————. NATO Airborne Warning and Control System (AWACS). https://shape.nato.int/about/aco-capabilities2/nato-awacs. Accessed 8 Mar 2019.

————. NATO Intelligence Fusion Centre – NIFC History. http://web.ifc.bices.org/about.htm. Accessed 15 Mar 2015.

————. NATO Response Force. http://www.nato.int/cps/en/natolive/topics_49755.htm. Accessed 24 July 2014.

————. NATO's Operations: 1949 – Present. http://www.aco.nato.int/resources/21/NATO%20Operations,%201949-Present.pdf.   Accessed 8 Dec 2017.

————. Operation Active Endeavour. http://www.nato.int/cps/en/natolive/topics_7932.htm. Accessed 9 Dec 2017.

————. Resolute Support Mission in Afghanistan. https://www.nato.int/cps/en/natohq/topics_113694.htm. Accessed 22 Nov 2018.

————. The North Atlantic Treaty. http://www.nato.int/cps/en/natolive/official_texts_17120.htm. Accessed 15 Oct 2014.

————. Defence Committee Fonds, 1990–2001. NATO Online Archives, Brussels, Belgium.

———. NATO International Secretariat/International Staff Fonds, 1990–2001. NATO Online Archives, Brussels, Belgium.

———. NATO Military Committee Fonds, 1990–2001. NATO Online Archives, Brussels, Belgium.

———. NATO Secretary-General Fonds, 1990–2001. NATO Online Archives, Brussels, Belgium.

———. North Atlantic Council Fonds, 1990–2001. NATO Online Archives, Brussels, Belgium.

NATO Parliamentary Assembly. 2015. Policy Recommendations Adopted by the NATO Parliamentary Assembly in 2015. October. https://www.nato-pa.int/document/2015-236-sesa-15-e-nato-pa-policy-recommendations. Accessed 8 Mar 2019.

Nau, Henry. 2009. Whither NATO: Alliance, Democracy, or U.N.? *The Magazine of International Affairs Forum: NATO at Sixty*, Spring.

Nordland, Ron. 2018. The Death Toll for Afghan Forces Is Secret. Here's Why. *The New*, September 21. https://www.nytimes.com/2018/09/21/world/asia/afghanistan-security-casualties-taliban.html

Norris, John. 2005. *Collision Course: NATO, Russia and Kosovo*. Westport: Praeger.

Nuccitelli, Dana. 2017. NATO Joins the Pentagon in Deeming Climate Change a Threat Multiplier. *Bulletin of the Atomic Scientists*, May 25. https://thebulletin.org/2017/05/nato-joins-the-pentagon-in-deeming-climate-change-a-threat-multiplier/

Nye, Joseph S. 2002. *The Paradox of American Power*. New York: Oxford University Press.

Nygren, Anders. 2014. Executing Strategy from the Air. In *The NATO Intervention in Libya: Lessons Learned from the Campaign*, ed. Kjell Engelbrekt, Marcus Mohlin, and Charlotte Wagnsson. New York: Routledge.

O'Donnell, Clara M., and Justin Vaisse. 2011. Is Libya NATO's Final Bow? *Brookings*, December 2. https://www.brookings.edu/opinions/is-libya-natos-final-bow/

Obama, Barack H. 2011a. Address to the Nation on the Situation in Libya. Last Modified Mar 28. http://www.presidency.ucsb.edu/ws/index.php?pid=90195

———. Remarks on the Situation in Libya. Last Modified Mar 18, 2011b. http://www.presidency.ucsb.edu/ws/index.php?pid=90162. Accessed 1 Mar 2015.

———. 2011c. Remarks on the Death of Former Leader Muammar Abu Minyar Al-Qadhafi of Libya. Last Modified Oct 20. https://www.presidency.ucsb.edu/documents/remarks-the-death-former-leader-muammar-abu-minyar-al-qadhafi-libya

Owen, Robert C. 2001. *Operation Deliberate Force: A Case Study on Humanitarian Constraints in Aerospace Warfare*. Paper Presented at Humanitarian Challenges in Military Intervention Workshop, November 29–30.

Panetta, Leon. 2014. *Worthy Fights*. New York: Penguin Group (USA) LLC.

Pargeter, Alison. 2012. *Libya: The Rise and Fall of Qaddafi.* New Haven: Yale University Press.

PBS. A Kosovo Chronology. http://www.pbs.org/wgbh/pages/frontline/shows/kosovo/etc/cron.html. Accessed 26 Aug 2018.

PBS Frontline. 2014. A Biography of Osama Bin Laden. http://www.pbs.org/wgbh/pages/frontline/shows/binladen/who/bio.html. Accessed 22 Oct 2014.

———. 2015. War in Europe: Facts and Figures. http://www.pbs.org/wgbh/pages/frontline/shows/kosovo/etc/facts.html. Accessed 1 Mar 2015.

———. 2017a. Campaign Against Terror March 2002: Operation Anaconda. http://www.pbs.org/wgbh/pages/frontline/shows/campaign/etc/epilogue.html. Accessed 8 Dec 2017.

———. 2017b. Campaign Against Terror Filling the Vacuum: The Bonn Conference. Last Modified Dec 8, 2017. http://www.pbs.org/wgbh/pages/frontline/shows/campaign/withus/cbonn.html

Perl, Raphael, and Ronald O'Rourke. 2001. *Terrorist Attack on USS Cole: Background and Issues for Congress.* Washington, DC: Congressional Research Service.

Peterson, James W. 2011. *NATO and Terrorism: Organizational Expansion and Mission Transformation.* New York: Continuum.

Pew Global Attitudes Project. What the World Thinks in 2002. Last Modified Dec 4, 2002. http://www.pewglobal.org/files/2002/12/2002-Report-Final-Updated.pdf. Accessed 8 Apr 2015.

Pew Research Center. Continued Public Support for Kosovo, but Worries Grow. Last Modified Apr 21, 1999a. http://www.people-press.org/1999/04/21/continued-public-support-for-kosovo-but-worries-grow/. Accessed 5 Apr 2015.

———. Support for NATO Air Strikes with Plenty of Buts. Last Modified Mar 29, 1999b. http://www.people-press.org/1999/03/29/support-for-nato-air-strikes-with-plenty-of-buts/

———. Public Wary of Military Intervention in Libya. Last Modified Mar 14, 2011. http://www.people-press.org/2011/03/14/public-wary-of-military-intervention-in-libya. Accessed 1 Mar 2015.

Pierson, Paul. 2000. Increasing Returns, Path Dependence, and the Study of Politics. *The American Political Science Review* 94 (2): 251–267.

Pourchot, Georgeta. 2009. Collision Course: NATO, Russian, and the Former Communist Block in the 21st Century. *The Magazine of International Affairs Forum: NATO at Sixty*, Spring.

Powell, Colin. 2003. *An Enlarged NATO: Mending Fences and Moving Forward on Iraq, Hearing Before the Comm. on Foreign Relations.* 108th Cong. United States Senate.

Program on International Policy Attitudes. Americans on Kosovo: A Study of US Public Attitudes. Last Modified May 27, 1999. http://www.pipa.org/OnlineReports/Kosovo/Kosovo_May99/Kosovo_May99_rpt.pdf. Accessed 5 Apr 2015.

Rafferty, Kirsten. 2003. An Institutionalist Reinterpretation of Cold War Alliance Systems: Insights for Alliance Theory. *Canadian Journal of Political Science* 36 (2): 341–362.

Rasmussen, Anders F. Keynote Speech by NATO Secretary General Anders Fogh Rasmussen at the NATO Parliamentary Assembly in Bucharest, Romania. Last Modified Oct 10, 2011a. www.nato.int/cps/en.natolive/opinions_79064. Accessed 6 Mar 2015.

Rasmussen, Anders Fogh. 2011b. NATO After Libya. *Foreign Affairs* 90 (4). https://www.foreignaffairs.com/articles/libya/2011-07-01/nato-after-libya

Reisman, W. Michael, and Scott Shuchart. 2004. Unilateral Action in an Imperfect World Order. In *Multilateralism V Unilateralism: Policy Choices in a Global Society*, ed. J.B. Attanasio and J.J. Norton. London: The British Institute of International and Comparative Law.

Rettig, Jessica. End of NATO's Libya Intervention Means Financial Relief for Allies. Last Modified Oct 31, 2011. www.usnews.comnews/articles/2011/10/31/end-of-natos-libya-intervention-means-financial-relief-for-allies. Accessed 1 Mar 2015.

Reuters. What Happened During the War in Bosnia? Last Modified July 21, 2008. http://www.reuters.com/article/2008/07/21/idUSL21644464

———. Timeline: Libya's Uprising Against Muammar Gaddafi. Last Modified Aug 21, 2011. www.reuters.com/article/2011/08/21/us-libya-events-idUS-TRE77K2QH20110821. Accessed 1 Mar 2015.

Rhodes, Matthew. 2012. US Perspectives on NATO. In *Understanding NATO in the 21st Century*, ed. Graeme P. Herd and John Kriendler. New York: Routledge.

Rice, Condoleezza. 2011a. *No Higher Honor*. New York: Crown.

Rice, Susan. 2011b. Remarks by Ambassador Susan E. Rice, U.S. Permanent Representative to the United Nations, at the Security Council Stakeout, on Resolution 1970, Libya Sanctions. *States News Service*, February 26.

Rice, Susan E., and Andrew Loomis. 2007. Evolution of Humanitarian Intervention. In *Beyond Preemption: Force and Legitimacy in a Changing World*, ed. Ivo Daalder. Washington, DC: Brookings Institution Press.

Richburg, Keith B. 2003. NATO Blocked on Iraq Decision: France, Germany Lead Opposition to War. *The Washington Post*, January 23.

Ricks, Thomas E. 2003. NATO Allies Trade Barbs over Iraq. *The Washington Post*, February 9.

Riding, Alan. Conflict in the Balkans; Mitterand Will Send Troops Only to Protect Bosnia Relief. Last Modified Aug 14, 1992. https://www.nytimes.com/1992/08/14/world/conflict-balkans-mitterrand-will-send-troops-only-protect-bosnia-relief.html. Accessed 1 Mar 2015.

Rieff, David. 2011. R2P, R.I.P. *The New York Times*, November 8. http://www.nytimes.com/2011/11/08/opinion/r2p-rip.html?scp=1&sq=NATO%20intervention%20in%20libya%20&st=cse

Risse-Kappen, Thomas. 1995. *Cooperation Among Democracies: The European Influence on US Foreign Policy*. Princeton: Princeton University Press.

Rogin, Josh. Senate Has No Plans to Invoke War Powers Act over Libya. *Foreign Policy: The Cable*. Last Modified May 10, 2011. thecable.foreignpolicy.com/posts/2011/05/10/senate_has_no_plans_to_invoke_war_powers_act_over_libya. Accessed 1 Mar 2015.

Rupp, Richard E. 2006. *NATO After 9/11: An Alliance in Continuing Decline*. New York: Palgrave Macmillan.

Saideman, Stephen M., and David P. Auerswald. 2012. Comparing Caveats: Understanding the Sources of National Restrictions upon NATO's Mission in Afghanistan. *International Studies Quarterly* 56 (1): 67–84.

Salama, Hana. 2018. *Counting Casualties*. Small Arms Survey, February.

Scheurer, Michael. 2011. *Osama Bin Laden*. New York: Oxford University Press.

Schmidt, Brian C., and Michael C. Williams. 2008. The Bush Doctrine and the Iraq War: Neoconservatives Versus Realists. *Security Studies* 17 (2): 191–220.

Sciolino, Elaine. 2004. NATO Chief Says Iraq and Afghanistan Are Doomed Without World Cooperation. *The New York Times*, July 2.

Shanker, Thom. 2003. Rumsfeld Rebukes the UN and NATO on Iraq Approach. *The New York Times*, February 9.

Shaughnessy, Larry. Wide Array of U.S. Warplanes Used in Libya Attacks. Last Modified Mar 21, 2011. http://edition.cnn.com/2011/WORLD/africa/03/20/libya.planes/. Accessed 5 Apr 2015.

Shea, Neil. 2018. Scenes from the New Cold War Unfolding at the Top of the World. *National Geographic*, October 25. https://www.nationalgeographic.com/environment/2018/10/new-cold-war-brews-as-arctic-ice-melts/

Shimko, Keith L. 2006. *The Iraq Wars and America's Military Revolution*. Cambridge: Cambridge University Press.

Shribman, David M. 2002. President Gambles, with Odds in His Favor. *Boston Globe*, September 5.

Simon, Jeffrey. 2008. NATO's Uncertain Future: Is Demography Destiny? *Strategic Forum* 236, October.

Sjursen, Helene. 2004. On the Identity of NATO. *International Affairs (Royal Institute of International Affairs)* 80 (4): 687–703.

Sloan, Stanley R. 1985. Managing the NATO Alliance: Congress and Burdensharing. *Journal of Policy Analysis and Management* 4 (3): 396–406.

———. 2005. *NATO, the European Union, and the Atlantic Community*. Lanham: Rowman & Littlefield.

———. 2006. Transatlantic Security Relations. In *The Transatlantic Divide: Foreign and Security Policies in the Atlantic Alliance from Kosovo to Iraq*, ed. Osvalso Croci and Amy Verdun. New York: Manchester University Press.

Smale, Alison, and Steven Erlanger. 2017. Merkel, After Discordant G7 Meeting, Is Looking Past Trump. *The New York Times*, May 28. https://www.nytimes.

com/2017/05/28/world/europe/angela-merkel-trumpalliances-g7-leaders.html

Smith, Edward M. 2003. Collective Security, Peacekeeping, and Ad Hoc Multilateralism. In *Democratic Accountability and the Use of Force in International Law*, ed. Charlotte Ku and Harold K. Jacobson. New York: Cambridge University Press.

Smith, Mark. 2009. *The Kosovo Conflict: U.S. Diplomacy and Western Public Opinion*. Los Angeles: Figueroa Press.

Snyder, Jack. 2003. Imperial Temptations. *The National Interest* 78, Spring.

Spencer, Richard. 2011. Libya: Col Gaddafi Damns the 'Rats' as He Clings to Power. *The Telegraph*, February 22. http://www.telegraph.co.uk/news/worldnews/africaandindianocean/libya/8341567/Libya-Col-Qaddafi-damns-the-rats-as-he-clings-to-power.html

Sprecher, Christopher, and Volker Krause. 2006. Alliances, Armed Conflict, and Cooperation: Theoretical Approaches and Empirical Evidence. *Journal of Peace Research* 43 (4): 363–369.

Stavridis, James (USN-Ret., Former Commander, USEUCOM, NATO SACEUR). Interview with Author, Jan 5, 2015.

Stavridis, James, and Daalder, Ivo. NATO's Victory in Libya. Last Modified Feb 2, 2012. http://nato.usmission.gov/foreign_affairs_02_02_13.html. Accessed 5 Apr 2015.

Sterling-Folker, Jennifer. 1999. Between a Rock and Hard Place: Assertive Multilateralism and Post-Cold War U.S. Foreign Policymaking. In *After the End: Making U.S. Foreign Policy in the Post-Cold War World*, ed. James M. Scott, 277–304. Durham: Duke University Press.

Stoltenberg, Jens. Keynote Address by NATO Secretary General Jens Stoltenberg. Last Modified Nov 24, 2014. http://www.nato.int/cps/en/natohq/opinions_115098.htm. Accessed 5 July 2017.

Strategic Airlift Capability Program. The Strategic Airlift Capability (SAC). https://www.sacprogram.org/en/Pages/The%20Strategic%20Airlift%20Capability.aspx. Accessed 9 Mar 2019.

Talbott, Strobe. 2002. From Prague to Baghdad: NATO at Risk. *Foreign Affairs* 81 (6): 46–57.

The Economist. 2017. Military Spending by NATO Members. February 16. https://www.economist.com/blogs/graphicdetail/2017/02/daily-chart-11

The German Marshall Fund of the United States. 2011. *Transatlantic Trends: Key Findings 2011.*

———. 2012. *Transatlantic Trends: Key Findings 2012.*

The International Coalition for the Responsibility to Protect. Paragraphs 138–139 of the World Summit Outcome Document. Last Modified Mar 1, 2015. http://responsibilitytoprotect.org/index.php/component/content/article/35-r2pcs-topics/398-general-assembly-r2p-excerpt-from-outcome-document

The New York Times. 1999. Crisis in the Balkans: Statements on the United States' Policy on Kosovo. *The New York Times*, April 18.

The Telegraph. 2011. World Powers Agree to Set Up Contact Group to Map Out Libya's Future. March 29. http://www.telegraph.co.uk/news/worldnews/africaandindianocean/libya/8414410/World-powers-agree-to-set-up-contact-group-to-map-out-Libyas-future.html

Thies, Wallace J. 2009. *Why NATO Endures.* New York: Cambridge University Press.

Todd, Sandler, and C. Murdoch James. 2000. On Sharing NATO Defence Burdens in the 1990s and Beyond. *Fiscal Studies* 21 (3): 297–327.

U.S. Department of Defense. U.S. Will Propose a New, Agile Military Response Force for NATO. Last Modified Sept 24, 2002. http://iipdigital.usembassy.gov/st/english/article/2002/09/20020920183018porth@pd.state.gov0.751034.html#axzz3EozjCWk2. Accessed 14 July 2014.

———. 2018. *Enhancing Security and Stability in Afghanistan.*

———. Casualty Status. https://dod.defense.gov/News/Casualty-Status/. Accessed 22 Nov 2018.

U.S. Department of Homeland Security. History. https://www.dhs.gov/history. Accessed 30 Nov 2017.

U.S. Department of State Office of the Historian. The War in Bosnia, 1992–1995. Last Modified Oct 21, 2013. https://history.state.gov/milestones/1993-2000/bosnia. Accessed 1 Mar 2015.

———. The Breakup of Yugoslavia. https://history.state.gov/milestones/1989-1992/breakup-yugoslavia. Accessed 1 Mar 2015.

———. United States Relations with Russia: After the Cold War. http://2001-2009.state.gov/r/pa/ho/pubs/fs/85962.htm. Accessed 1 Mar 2015.

———. Bill Clinton, Boris Yeltsin, and U.S.-Russian Relations. https://history.state.gov/milestones/1993-2000/clinton-yeltsin. Accessed 1 Mar 2015.

U.S. Department of the Treasury. USA PATRIOT Act. https://www.fincen.gov/resources/statutes-regulations/usa-patriot-act. Accessed 8 Dec 2017.

U.S. House of Representatives. 1999. *A Concurrent Resolution Authorizing the President of the United States to Conduct Military Air Operations and Missile Strikes Against the Federal Republic of Yugoslavia (Serbia and Montenegro).* 106th Congress Session.

———. 2002. H.J. Res. 114 *Authorization for Use of Military Force Against Iraq Resolution of 2002.* 107th Congress Session.

U.S. House of Representatives. Committee on Foreign Affairs. 2012. *NATO: The Chicago Summit and U.S. Policy.* 112th Congress Session.

U.S. Navy. U.S. Naval Forces Open Odyssey Dawn, Prepare No-Fly Zone. Last Modified Mar 19, 2011. http://www.navy.mil/submit/display.asp?story_id=59192. Accessed 5 Apr 2015.

UNHCR. 2018. Libya. Last Modified Aug. http://reporting.unhcr.org/sites/default/files/UNHCR%20Libya%20Fact%20Sheet%20-%20August%202018.pdf. Accessed 21 Nov 2018.

United Nations. 2001. Agreement on Provisional Arrangements in Afghanistan Pending the Re-Establishment of Permanent Government Institutions (the Bonn Agreement). May 12. https://peacemaker.un.org/afghanistan-bonnagreement2001

———. Security Council Approves 'No-Fly Zone' over Libya, Authorizing 'All Necessary Measures' to Protect Civilians, by Vote of 10 in Favour with 5 Abstentions. Last Modified Mar 17, 2011. http://www.un.org/press/en/2011/sc10200.doc.htm. Accessed 9 Apr 2015.

———. 2017. Afghanistan and the United Nations. http://www.un.org/News/dh/latest/afghan/un-afghan-history.shtml. Accessed 8 Dec 2017.

———. Security Council Committee Pursuant to Resolutions 1267 (1999) and 1989 (2011) Concerning Al-Qaida and Associated Individuals and Entities. https://www.un.org/sc/suborg/en/sanctions/1267. Accessed 8 Dec 2017.

United Nations Department of Public Information. United Nations Protection Force. Last Modified Sept 1, 1996. http://www.un.org/en/peacekeeping/missions/past/unprof_b.htm. Accessed 1 Mar 2015.

United Nations Security Council. *UNSCR 753 Admission of a New Member: Croatia*, May 18, 1992.

———. *UNSCR 1160 on the Letters from the United Kingdom (S/1998/223) and the United States (S/1998/272)*, Mar 31, 1998a.

———. *UNSCR 1199 Kosovo (FRY)*, Sept 23, 1998b.

———. *UNSCR 1244 On the Situation Relating Kosovo*, June 10, 1999a.

———. *UNSCR 1267 On the Situation in Afghanistan*, Oct 15, 1999b.

———. *UNSCR 1368 Threats to International Peace and Security Caused by Terrorist Acts*, Sept 12, 2001.

———. Security Council Endorses Formation of Sovereign Interim Government in Iraq (Resolution 1546) [Press Release]. Last Modified Aug 6, 2004. https://www.un.org/press/en/2004/sc8117.doc.htm

———. *UNSCR 1970 Peace and Security in Africa*, Feb 26, 2011a.

———. *UNSCR 1973 Libya*, Mar 17, 2011b.

United States. Barack Obama. 2015. *The National Security Strategy*. Washington, DC: White House.

United States. Congress. House. Committee on Foreign Affairs. *The Future of NATO: How Valuable an Asset? Hearing Before the Committee on Foreign Affairs, House of Representatives, One Hundred Tenth Congress, First Session*, 2007.

United States. 2002. Congress. Senate. Committee on Foreign Relations. *The Future of NATO. Hearing Before the Committee on Foreign Relations United States Senate, One Hundred Seventh Congress Second Session*.

United States Congress. S.J. Res. 23 *Joint Authorization for the Use of Military Force, Pub. L. No. 107-40, 115 Stat. 224*, 107th Congress Session, 2001. https://www.govtrack.us/congress/bills/107/sjres23

United States. Donald Trump. 2017. *The National Security Strategy of the United States of America*. Washington, DC: White House.

United States Justice Department. 2011. *Authority to Use Military Force in Libya*. April 1. https://www.justice.gov/sites/default/files/olc/opinions/2011/04/31/authority-military-use-in-libya.pdf

United States Mission to NATO. Libya: Operation Unified Protector: Fact Sheet. Last Modified Apr 28, 2011. http://nato.unmission.gov/issues/our_issues/Libya/Libya-fact-sheet2/Libya-fact-sheet.html. Accessed 1 Mar 2015.

Van Heuven, Marten. 2001. *NATO and Europe: Equality or a More Balanced Partnership?* Arlington: RAND Corporation.

Vershbow, Alexander. Deputy Secretary General: Russia's Aggression Is a Game-Changer in European Security. http://www.nato.int/cps/en/natohq/news_117068.htm. Accessed 5 July 2017.

Vincent, Jack E., Ira L. Straus, and Richard R. Biondi. 2001. Capability Theory and the Future of NATO's Decisionmaking Rules. *Journal of Peace Research* 38 (1): 67–86.

Wallack, Michael. 2006. From Compellence to Pre-Emption: Kosovo and Iraq as Responses to Contested Hegemony. In *The Transatlantic Divide: Foreign and Security Policies in the Atlantic Alliance from Kosovo to Iraq*, ed. Osvaldo Croci and Amy Verdun. New York: Manchester University Press.

Wallander, Celeste A. 2000. Institutional Assets and Adaptability: NATO After the Cold War. *International Organization* 54 (4): 705–735.

Walt, Stephen. 1987. *The Origins of Alliances*. Ithaca: Cornell University Press.

Walt, Stephen M. 2004. The Imbalance of Power. *Harvard Magazine* 106 (4): 32–35.

———. 2005. *Taming American Power: The Global Response to U.S. Primacy*. New York: Norton.

Waltz, Kenneth N. 1986. Anarchic Orders and the Balances of Power. In *Neorealism and Its Critics*, ed. Robert Keohane, 98–130. New York: Columbia University Press.

———. 1993. The Emerging Structure of International Politics. *International Security* 18 (2): 44–79.

Warren, Tarn D. 2010. *ISAF and Afghanistan: The Impact of Failure on NATO's Future*. Washington, DC: National Defense University.

Watson Institute for International and Public Affairs "Costs of War – Afghan Civilians". https://watson.brown.edu/costsofwar/costs/human/civilians/afghan. Accessed 22 Nov 2018.

Weisman, Steven R. 2003. Fallout from Iraq Rift: NATO May Feel a Strain. *The New York Times*, February 11. http://www.nytimes.com/2003/02/11/international/middleeast/11ASSE.html

Weitsman, Patricia A. 2004. *Dangerous Alliances: Proponents of Peace, Weapons of War*. Stanford: Stanford University Press.

Weitsman, Patricia. 2010. Wartime Alliances Versus Coalition Warfare. *Strategic Studies Quarterly* 4 (2): 113–136.

———. 2014. *Waging War: Alliances, Coalitions, and Institutions of Interstate Violence*. Stanford: Stanford University Press.

Weller, Marc. 1999. The Rambouillet Conference on Kosovo. *International Affairs* 75 (2): 211–252.

Williams, Ellen. 2008a. Out of Area and Very Much in Business? NATO, the U.S., and the Post-9/11 International Security Environment. *Comparative Strategy* 27 (1): 65–78.

Williams, Michael J. 2008b. *NATO, Security, and Risk Management*. Milton Park: Routledge.

Wintz, Mark. 2010. *Transatlantic Diplomacy and the Use of Military Force in the Post-Cold War Era*. New York: Palgrave Macmillan.

Woodward, Margaret H., and Philip G. Morrison. 2013. The Responsibility to Protect: The Libya Test Case. *Joint Forces Quarterly* 71: 20–24.

Zakaria, Fareed. 2008. The Future of American Power. *Foreign Affairs* 87 (3): 21–22.

Index[1]

[1] Note: Page numbers followed by 'n' refer to notes.

© The Author(s) 2020
J. Garey, *The US Role in NATO's Survival After the Cold War*,
Palgrave Studies in International Relations,
https://doi.org/10.1007/978-3-030-13675-8

245

CPSIA information can be obtained
at www.ICGtesting.com
Printed in the USA
LVHW081739010719
622886LV00002B/3/P